blue
rider
press

GHOSTBUSTER'S DAUGHTER

GHOSTBUSTER'S DAUGHTER

Life with My Dad, Harold Ramis

VIOLET RAMIS STIEL

BLUE RIDER PRESS

New York

blue
rider
press

An imprint of Penguin Random House LLC
375 Hudson Street
New York, New York 10014

Page 367 constitutes an extension of this page.

Library of Congress Cataloging-in-Publication Data
Names: Ramis Stiel, Violet, author.
Title: Ghostbuster's daughter : life with my dad, Harold Ramis / Violet Ramis Stiel.
Description: New York : Blue Rider Press, 2018.
Identifiers: LCCN 2017052504 | ISBN 9780735217874 (hardback) |
ISBN 9780735217898 (epub)
Subjects: LCSH: Ramis, Harold—Family. | Ramis Stiel, Violet. | Children of
celebrities—Biography. | Motion picture actors and actresses—United
States—Biography. | BISAC: BIOGRAPHY & AUTOBIOGRAPHY / Entertainment &
Performing Arts. | BIOGRAPHY & AUTOBIOGRAPHY / Personal Memoirs.
Classification: LCC PN2287.R2425 R36 2018 | DDC 791.4302/8092 [B]—dc23
LC record available at https://lccn.loc.gov/2017052504
p.   cm.

Printed in the United States of America
1   3   5   7   9   10   8   6   4   2

BOOK DESIGN BY MEIGHAN CAVANAUGH

*Penguin is committed to publishing works of quality and integrity.
In that spirit, we are proud to offer this book to our readers;
however, the story, the experiences, and the words
are the author's alone.*

CONTENTS

FOREWORD

I first met Harold Ramis at the Deauville Film Festival in 2005, when I was twenty-three. Before you start thinking I'm fancy, just know that it's kind of a bullshit film festival that's mostly like an overblown press event where they get Americans to come to the beach in France to show and promote their movies.

By then, I had been working as an actor and writer for a while, and had met a lot of famous people and entertainers I grew up loving, but Harold was the first person I met who'd made the movies and TV that my parents also loved. I knew they were the funniest movies, even though I didn't get all the jokes, because we were all laughing together, because they were the first movies I remember people quoting and making themselves laugh to hysterics at the mere thought of the scenes they hadn't actually seen in ages.

Basically, the movies that made me want to make movies.

Also, as an unconventional-looking, deep-voiced comedian, with aspirations of writing, directing, producing, and acting, I couldn't always find a lot of people to look up to—people who let you know that there's actually a chance you can succeed. To me, Harold was that guy. He was the first person I knew who actually gave me hope. I'm Canadian, so SCTV was a fixture in my life since I can remember, and so was Harold. I remember as a kid being like, "Egon ALSO wrote *Ghostbusters* AND *Meatballs* AND *Animal House* AND directed *Caddyshack* AND *Groundhog Day*?" It both blew my mind and made me think that maybe someone like me could find a way to make a living doing the same things.

So I'm in France with Judd Apatow, and he has this thing where he shamelessly gloms on to people he's a fan of. I kind of have a "Never meet your heroes" thing. I still cringe at some of the interactions I've had with some of my favorite filmmakers, and I'm pretty sure George Lucas would avoid me if he saw me, to this day. But Judd has the exact opposite instinct. He seeks out his heroes and barnacles himself until forcibly removed.

So Judd knocks on the door of my hotel room and is like, "Harold Ramis is here, I met him once or twice, let's find him."

We had heard he was at the other hotel, the one that was much nicer than ours. We went over to the restaurant in the lobby, and there he was, with a huge smile on his face, prayer beads hanging off his wrist, giving interviews to promote his new film, *The Ice Harvest*. We waited until his interview was over and basically sat ourselves down beside him as though we were the next scheduled journalists. He remembered Judd (thank God) and talked to us for like an hour, telling stories and being cool.

He invited us out to the fanciest restaurant I'd ever been to in my life, and that night, he not only showed me what a "tasting menu" was, he showed me that I *can* meet my heroes and not have it be a total disaster. They can be nice and gracious and everything I'd hope they'd be. It should probably be said that pretty much every other hero I've met since then has totally sucked.

About a year later, Judd and I were filming *Knocked Up* and needed someone to play my dad. Harold was our first choice, and I was amazed when he agreed to do it. It was a dream. Working together validated all the kinship I had felt with him as a kid. I always wanted to be a young Harold Ramis and I literally got to be. (Well, not literally, but in like a familial-but-also-in-a-movie sense).

Filming our father-son scene was one of the great joys of my life. Harold exuded such love and joy both onscreen and off. His (largely improvised) wisdom was so nurturing and kind, I honestly think it's one of the reasons the movie functions. You see he's my father and you think, "This guy can't be *that* bad if that's who raised him. Maybe he *can* raise a baby."

After we wrapped for the day, Harold came up to me and told me that when he wasn't in the same city as his kids, he gave himself permission to smoke weed, and he was wondering if I had any on me that I could give him. I weirdly didn't, but told him if he wanted to stop by my shitty West Hollywood apartment, I'd be more than happy to give him some. Shockingly, he said he would like that. He followed me home in his car, and I remember waiting nervously as he parked. I thought he'd come and just grab the tiny bag of weed I had prepared for him and bolt, presumably to go smoke it with someone way more cool than me.

But when he got there, he just stood in my doorway and leaned against the wall, talking to me. For a while. Like, a half hour or forty-five minutes, just talking. In no hurry, just happy to stand and smoke and shoot the shit.

This might seem like a small thing, but to me it was amazing and wonderful and something I still think about all the time.

And everyone I know who knew Harold has a similar story.

One of my good friends worked for Harold's agent for years, and eventually left to get a better job (with me). When he found out, Harold sent him a deep-dish pizza from Chicago to congratulate him. I mean, I think of myself as a pretty nice guy, but I've never sent anyone food to celebrate a new job.

But Harold would. And did.

The world is better for having had him, and I'm honored to have existed at the same time as him. And I'm glad Violet asked me to write this foreword. I hope it's good. Thanks. Enjoy the rest of the book.

—Seth Rogen

INTRODUCTION:
LIFE IS MESSY

I learned a thing or two about life from my dad, the late, great Harold Ramis. For those of you who knew him personally, I don't have to tell you what a sweet, generous, loyal, wise, supportive, and joyful person he was. For people familiar with him as a writer, director, and actor, his intelligence, humor, creativity, and subtly subversive worldview need no elaboration. For those of you who have no idea who he was or what he meant to the world of comedy filmmaking, I don't even know what to say—congrats on escaping from the fallout shelter after all these years?

Perhaps the simplest and most useful thing my father ever taught me was this: life is messy. His life was surprisingly messy, which you wouldn't necessarily believe, considering what a neatnik he was (I mean, truly, not a goddamn thing out of place). But, as with everything else in his life, he rolled with the chaos and ultimately embraced it, and, following his lead, so have I.

One night, when I was about twenty-three, I asked him what he thought signified adulthood. He took a thoughtful puff off the joint we were sharing and said, "Well, it's not having a job or a family, because you can have those things and still be emotionally and intellectually a child. I think, really, being an adult is about acknowledging ambiguity in all areas of life and finding a way to be okay with that." I guess I wasn't an adult yet, because even though I nodded sagely, I didn't have a clue what he was talking about. Now, fifteen years (three kids, three stepkids, one baby daddy, and one husband) later, I get it. Nobody really knows what they're doing. Bad things happen to good people. Great things happen to horrible people. Those horrible people were probably abused and neglected as children, so they're not really horrible anyway. Life is full of pain and suffering. Life is full of joy and wonder. There will be no final exam at the end of your life to tell you if you passed or failed. It's all a mess! Thanks, Dad!

Cue grainy, sepia-toned nostalgia filter in three, two, one . . . Harold Allen Ramis (a.k.a. Herschel, Hershey, Hersch) was born in Chicago on November 21, 1944, to Ruth (née Cokee) and Nathan "Nate" Ramis, who ran a family grocery store on the West Side. They lived with Ruth's mother, father, sister, and brother in a two-bedroom apartment. Little Harold and his older brother, Steven, started working—bagging and delivering groceries—when they were about eight years old and, famously in our family folklore, used their bar mitzvah money to buy their mother new wall-to-wall carpeting. My dad, nice Jewish boy that he was, wanted to be a neurosurgeon throughout high school and took German because it was the language of doctors. He started a little folk band, the Wanderers, with some friends when he was fourteen, so he wasn't shy about putting himself out there, but it wasn't until he went to Washington University in St. Louis, in 1962, that his life started to deviate from the straight and narrow. In a talk my dad gave at the Chicago Humanities Festival in 2009, he said, "I started college looking like John Kennedy and finished college looking like John Lennon . . . with the politics of Nikolai [sic] Lenin." At Wash U, he joined a fraternity (ZBT), got more seriously into writing and acting (and drugs), and married my mom, Anne, soon after graduation.

Over the years, he evolved through many phases. There was the acid-dropping, pot-smoking, world-traveling draft dodger who worked, in turn, as an adult psychiatric worker in a mental hospital, migrant farmworker (for a week), taxi driver, and guitar-strumming idealistic inner-city substitute teacher. There was the ambitious young journalist by day, improv theater nerd by night who became a Hollywood wunderkind and, ultimately, "a founding father of modern comedy" (*GQ*). There was the eager young husband and doting father who stuck it out for almost twenty years but who eventually realized he wanted a different life, and so, at forty-five, married his former assistant and started a new family. There was the rabbi, the Buddhist, the philosopher, the philanthropist, the snob, the everyman, the heartthrob, the glutton, the grandfather, and on and on. The range of experiences he lived through informed his unique mix of mischief-maker and mensch and made him complex without being complicated. Clearly, my father was not a purist in any sense of the word. If Carl Sagan, Pema Chödrön, Groucho Marx, and John Lennon had a baby, it might get close to the core elements of who he was. My dad was full of contradictions that he somehow managed to synthesize into a glorious whole person whom everyone admired, respected, and loved.

I loved my dad more than anything in this world (sorry, kids!) and I believe he felt the same way about me. In 2007, we started talking about writing a book together on parenting—existential parenting, to be exact. Our working title was *We're All Going to Die, Now Go to Sleep*, which should give you an idea of the tone we were going for. In spite of my bizarre Hollywood childhood, I turned out to be a generally well-adjusted, productive person, and I wanted to know what the secret to that was. Did the parenting even matter, or are we just born who we are? While starting to brainstorm on this project, my dad and I talked about how different my childhood was from his sons' and how he thought that might play out. We talked about my kids and what core values I wanted to impart to them. We mused on questions like "How do you teach your children to be engaged, optimistic, and hopeful when the world sucks and we all die alone in the end?" I wish so much that we had written that book.

I wish so many things.

But he got sick, and died, and here I am with all of these memories and stories and lessons that need to be shared. And since one lesson he taught me was to live without regrets, I don't want to waste another minute pining for what might have been. This is the way life went and I (am trying to) accept it.

"If you had done things differently," he would say, "you wouldn't be who you are today. So if you're relatively happy with where you are, congratulations! Enjoy it. You're one of the fortunate ones. Whatever mistakes you think you made are what brought you to this point, and it seems like a pretty sweet spot."

So, lucky me for having him as my dad, and lucky you for reading this and getting to know him through my eyes.

GHOSTBUSTER'S
DAUGHTER

All smiles. Santa Monica, 1985.

Dear Dad,

SO YOU'RE DEAD . . . NOW WHAT? I don't think I'd seen that SCTV sketch before, but during the Harold Ramis lovefest right after you died, people were posting it all over the place.

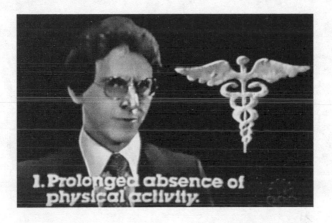

Now what, indeed.

I read somewhere that letter writing is a good way to help with the grieving process, so I'm going to try to write to you instead of just wallowing in my sadness. We'll see. It's been almost six months since you've been gone and I think about you all the time, Daddy. In some ways it's like you're with me now more than you were before. I am flooded with memories and stories and images and questions. It's like, everywhere I look, there you are. Walking through a bookstore, I see a table of books that I know you read and I want to talk to you about all of them. Your movies have been on TV a lot, and I remember how when TiVo came out, you were so excited to be able to see any time one of them was on ("Hey! This gives the search for self a whole new meaning!"). The world is seeming crazier and crazier and I want to talk to you about politics and police brutality and Robin Williams and the Middle East and gun control and being Jewish. Where are you? I need you.

Mural and photo by Jaber and Jonas Never

Some guys painted a great mural of you as Egon in downtown LA and somebody in Brooklyn is spray-painting your name all over the city. So many people have made amazing little tributes to you online and when I can't sleep at two a.m., I am obsessively combing through Instagram and Twitter for new posts. I don't know if you have social media where you are, but if you do, #haroldramis is the most obvious tag; however, you can also find yourself under #supersexyjewhunk. How funny is that? If you were still here, I would have made you a T-shirt. Julian also found a website called F Yeah, Harold Ramis!,

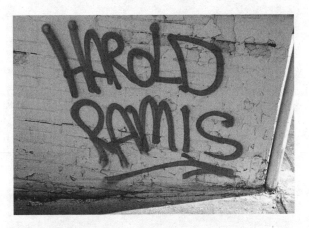

Brooklyn graffiti

which is pretty sweet. I know it seems silly that I take so much comfort and enjoyment from these little things, but if people who didn't even really know you are heartbroken and mourning, then it's okay that I am, too, right?

*Egon embroidery by
Mackenzie Mollo*

On top of missing you like crazy, I'm also feeling a lot of anxiety about loss. I already lost you and now I'm afraid I'm going to lose all of the "you" that's such a huge part of me. I mean, if you're not here, then who am I? How can I preserve what we had when I'm alone? I don't want to forget a single thing about you . . . it's all I have now.

I love you so much.
—V

Dad looking adorable, 1966

Mom with white pumpkin, 1966

YOUNG LOVE

Let's start at the beginning—*my* beginning—with the story of Harold and Anne. My parents first officially met in San Francisco during the summer of 1966. They both attended Washington University, and my dad knew my mom peripherally, as the beautiful girl who had briefly dated two of his roommates. After one of them came home from a hayride with my mom, my dad asked, "How was it?"

"Weird," the friend said.

"Weird? Really? How?" He was intrigued.

"Well," the guy said, "she only spoke in quotes from *Billy Budd* the whole time."

Oddly, my dad thought, *I gotta meet this girl.*

My mom was vaguely aware of my dad from his college theater work—most notably his role as the priest of Zeus in *Oedipus Rex*, and writing and performing in several fraternity-related shows.

The summer after he graduated, in 1966, my dad headed west with his brother, Steven, and college friend David. Soon after arriving in San

Francisco, they ended up at the apartment where my mom was staying with two of her girlfriends. He described first seeing her intently watching *The Dybbuk* (a 1937 Yiddish-language Polish fantasy film drama) on a TV so staticky, you could barely make out the picture. He tried casually chatting with her but she shushed him, leaning closer to the TV. Despite this, he thought she was interesting and beautiful and decided to ask her out for Friday night.

"I can't," she told him, "I'm seeing the Bolshoi Ballet."

"Okay, then how about Saturday?"

"I can't, I'm seeing the Bolshoi Ballet."

She had bought tickets for the whole run but agreed to go out with him the following week. He knew she was different from other girls he'd dated, but I don't think he realized just quite how different she was until they started spending more time together.

One day, after my mom and dad had gone out a few times, they were listening to music in her room when, out of nowhere, she slapped him hard across the face. He dramatized this encounter in an autobiographical script he wrote called *2b or Not 2b*, about his early twenties. As of now, this screenplay remains unproduced.

INT. JANE'S HOUSE—LATER It's a rambling Victorian with high ceilings, lots of woodwork, reasonably well-maintained. Her roommates, Haze and Ginger, are watching TV and reading in the living room, which is nicely decorated with inexpensive thrift shop furniture, colorful French posters, and cheap Asian folk art. Jane leads Julian into her bedroom.

CUT TO: INT. JANE'S ROOM—CONTINUOUS   Julian has
never seen anything like it. The decor is a cross
between an Edwardian boudoir and a harem, a mad mix
of Indian cloth, lace, floral prints, an oriental
rug, Moroccan leather ottoman, colorfully painted
camel-skin lamps with beautiful fringed silk scarves
artfully draped over them, ostrich feathers, an art
nouveau writing desk, and in the center of the room
a graceful, turn-of-the-century chaise longue.

                    JULIAN
        Wow. Incredible.

                    JANE
                (lighting candles)
        Do you want to sit down?

                    JULIAN
        Sure.

He looks around and sits on the chaise. The room
smells like it looks—like an exotic potpourri. Jane
puts on a record—a beautiful aria.

                    JULIAN
        Opera—cool.

                    JANE
        You like it?

                    JULIAN
        I don't know. I haven't heard that
        much.

                    JANE
        Well, give it a try. I'm just going
        to change. One second.

She disappears behind a lacquered three-panel
Chinese screen.

                    JULIAN
                (looking around)
        Where's your bed?

                    JANE
            (from behind the screen)
        You're sitting on it.

                    JULIAN
        This sofa? Chaise?

She emerges from behind the screen wearing an
exotic, floor-length, flowing white robe embroidered
with red roses.

                    JANE
        It's not really a chaise. It's
        called a "fainting couch."

                    JULIAN
                (regarding her robe)
        That's incredible.

                    JANE
        I just got it. It's from India.
                (She sits next to him.)
        Look at this needlework.

She gathers the skirt and lays the silken folds in
his hands for him to see.

                    JANE
        It's done by children in villages
        so poor they never know if they'll

even have anything to eat, but
somehow they manage to do this
beautiful work. I think that's
so . . . tragic.

Her eyes fill with tears. Julian doesn't know what
to say.

> JULIAN
> Are you okay?

> JANE
> Yes, I'm just sad. How can life be
> so cruel?
> *(really weeping now)*

Julian tentatively puts his arm around her
shoulders, trying to be comforting but feeling
helpless.

> JULIAN
> Can I get you anything?

> JANE
> *(stops crying)*
> No, thank you. I don't want you
> to think that you have to fix
> everything for me. It's okay to
> be sad sometimes. There are real
> things in life to be sad about.

> JULIAN
> I know.

They look into each other's eyes, then Julian slowly
leans in and kisses her tenderly. After a moment
their lips part and he sits back, still gazing into

her eyes. Suddenly, she slaps him surprisingly hard
across the face.

                    JULIAN
                (shocked and angry)
          What was that for?

                    JANE
          I don't know.

                    JULIAN
                 (baffled)
          You don't know? Was it because I
          kissed you?

                    JANE
          I don't think so. I liked it.

                    JULIAN
          Did I do something wrong?

                    JANE
          I don't know. Did you?

Julian stares at her, really indignant but not even
sure why.

                    JULIAN
          That was very weird.

                    JANE
          Don't you think you're making an
          awfully big deal about a little slap?

                    JULIAN
          It hurt.

                    JANE
That bad?

                    JULIAN
No, it was just—surprising, that's all.

                    JANE
Maybe that's a good thing.

                    JULIAN
Yeah, well, hitting me with a
chair would be surprising, too,
but I don't think it would be
a good thing. What were you
thinking?

                    JANE
I don't know—that I wanted to
slap you. I'm not angry. I'm not
offended or insulted. Does there
have to be a reason?

He looks at her for a moment.

                    JULIAN
Just tell me—are you going to be
doing that again?

                    JANE
Do you want me to?

                    JULIAN
No.

                    JANE
Then I won't.

She looks deep in his eyes, then he leans forward
and kisses her again, embracing her as they sink
down on the fainting couch.

How cute were they? Harold and Anne in 1967.
(St. Louis Post-Dispatch, *1984*)

IN CASE YOU HAVEN'T picked up on it yet, I'll just say that my mother,
Anne, is a very unusual person. She grew up in a suburb of St. Louis
with her parents, Rose and Harry, and her sister, Natalie, who was one
year younger. Harry was a hard man who owned a few women's clothing stores and rode his wife and daughters mercilessly about their
weight. Rose likely had undiagnosed depression or bipolar disorder but
loved her daughters to the point of worship and did her best to protect
them from their father. My mom—angry at her dad, frustrated with
her mom, and pitted against her sister—learned early on that living in

her own world was her best bet for self-preservation. She threw herself into dance, art, and literature, and was uncompromising in her aesthetics. It makes perfect sense that my dad, an easygoing people-pleaser from the moment he was born, was attracted to this contrarian pixie who unapologetically pushed the limits (and, often, buttons) of everyone around her.

Harold and Anne returned to St. Louis in the fall of 1966—my mom for her senior year of college, and my dad for a postgraduate program he'd enrolled in but dropped out of after two weeks. My mom took her art history classes during the day and worked as an usher for the American Theater at night. Their courtship was uneventful . . . in a very 1966 way. A typical date could range from going to see the newest movie, to grabbing a pizza, to my dad and his friends taking LSD and my mom, stone sober but with a naturally kaleidoscopic brain, leading them on an adventure through the city. "Your mother almost never drank or took drugs," my dad told me, "but everyone else did, and she was a great inspiration. I remember once . . . well, honestly, I don't really remember how we got there, but I know the night ended with a group of us in a little forest, dancing around Anne like fairies in *A Midsummer Night's Dream*. And I'm sure that wasn't the only time." The young couple met each other's parents (both sets approved) and things seemed to be getting more serious, but my mom continued to date other people and my dad started to worry that someone else was going to come in and swoop her up. In January of 1967, she invited my dad to join her as an usher for a production of *The Mikado*, and he proposed to her on opening night. She knew right away that she would say yes but didn't give him an answer until the intermission. And so, six months later, on July 2, 1967, at the tender ages of twenty-one and twenty-two, my parents were married, in a traditional Jewish ceremony, under a chuppah my dad had proudly built himself. My mom had her seven bridesmaids wearing dresses from other formal occasions and my dad's tux may or may not have had ruffles and bell-bottoms. About 150 guests, mostly made up of their college friends and my dad's family, attended the reception at the Bel Air Hotel in St. Louis. My mother, true to form, wanted pie instead of a standard wedding cake, so my dad ordered twenty chocolate pies from a local bakery. He entertained the guests while Mom sat raptly listening to the singer, Sid Selvidge, an anthropology student from Memphis, perform an acoustic set of blues and folk songs. Sadly, there are no photos from this bizarre and blessed event because the photographer forgot to put film in the camera.

Young, in love, and with nothing to lose, they stayed true to their Midwestern roots and moved back and forth between St. Louis and Chicago in their first few years together, following my dad's opportunities for work and my mom's interests for pleasure. They remained close with their core group of college friends, who were largely liberal Jewish artistic types. My parents weren't true hippies but definitely leaned far to the left, politically, at the time. My dad dodged the Vietnam draft in late 1967 by telling the recruiters that he was a gay drug addict (and taking a bunch of speed right before his appointment). He experimented with various types of work and occasionally got hired to sing and play guitar at parties. Though he was interested in pursuing writing and theater as possible careers, he hadn't quite figured out how to break into the creative world. At one point, early in my parents' marriage, he auditioned for a role in *The Importance of Being Earnest* but was told that his looks were "not Dresden enough" (read: too Jewish) and so he didn't get the part.

In spite of his slow start, my dad always credited my mom with pushing him outside his comfort zone and putting him on the path that eventually led to his success. The two instances he always cited in terms of my mother's instrumental role in his career trajectory were her encouragement to perform during open mic night at the Hungry I in San Francisco soon after they first met, and her challenge for him to submit a freelance article for the *Chicago Daily News* a few years into their relationship. "Why not?" was her response to his hesitation in both cases.

My mom lives in a universe where there are no rules, where anything is possible and the more unlikely something is, the better, which is the ideal mind-set for a boundary-pushing creative. And this idea of rules being flexible carried over in all aspects of her life. Once, when my newlywed parents went shopping at the grocery store, my mom kept jumping out of the checkout line for "one more thing." The lady behind them was getting frustrated and tried to scold my mom: "What if everyone did that?" she asked my mom. "If everyone did it, it would be socially acceptable," my mom snapped back, much to my dad's embarrassment and delight. I think he often walked the line between being deeply respectful of her intelligence and creative spirit and frustrated with her refusal to conform or compromise. As much as Dad may have appreciated my mom's extreme out-of-the-box thinking, neither one of them was particularly interested in "dropping out" and running away with the flower children. Despite their countercultural leanings, they were still just a couple of Midwestern, middle-class Jewish kids trying to make their way, and somebody had to pay the bills.

DON'T GO INTO RETAIL

This was the only advice my grandfather ever gave my dad and he took it very seriously. My dad had worked since he was a kid—bagging and delivering groceries in the family business, and stocking shelves in a department store warehouse—but after he and my mom got married, he realized it was time to think about a career. Despite his college theater background and being a natural performer, my dad's path into the entertainment world was a meandering one. After trying grad school for a couple weeks and realizing it wasn't for him, he went on to work several odd jobs, including taxi driver, adult psychiatric worker on a locked ward in the Jewish Hospital of St. Louis, and full-time substitute teacher in the Robert Taylor Homes on Chicago's South Side. In discussing his seven-month stint in the psych ward with Debba Kunk in a 1982 interview for ONTV, he said, "I wanted to compare my own psychedelic hallucinogenic experience to madness to see what the lines were . . . it was a great job for learning a lot quickly about people and about your own madness. You think twice before you say 'I'm going crazy.'" While much of the work was depressing and serious, there were bright spots. In a 1984 *Vanity Fair* interview, he described a non-verbal patient who would respond to questions with "bizarre hand gestures that looked like communication but weren't." "So," he said, "everyone assumed, well, it's madness. I took it as a put-on, and I started giving him hand gestures back that were even more ludicrous than his. It was when he laughed that I knew he was as aware as I was." By allowing himself to get on this person's level, he was able to connect with him in a way that others weren't able to. I think this ability to shift perspective and take an unexpected approach is part of what made him so successful in comedy and film (and everything he did, really).

He brought a similar sensibility to teaching. "Being a full-time substitute is everyone's worst nightmare. You have these kids for one day. You don't know their names, so you only have what they tell you to go on. Every day, I thought the most I could do in those circumstances was to teach them a moral lesson about justice or behavior . . . Rather than try to force something on them, I would try to field whatever it was that they were putting out. There would often—even at ten years old—be a firebrand spokesman for the class who would attack you on racial issues, and in an articulate way, like a young Stokely Carmichael. So I'd try to deal with that in a humane and rational way. Or, if they were into fun and seemed harmless, I'd try to foster it, just make them have the greatest day they ever had in school, so they'd go home and say, 'Well, that was good. I'd like to go back tomorrow'" (ONTV). Although Dad would have made a great psychiatrist or teacher, he was disheartened by his work in the trenches and started looking around for something more fun and creative.

In 1967, after seeing a show at Second City with my mom, my dad thought, *I could do that*, and enrolled in their twelve-week improv workshop. When a spot opened up in the Second City touring company, Dad auditioned but wasn't selected, so he went down the street to the Old Town Players Theater, where he taught improv and staged a small show with his class. Meanwhile, my mom was studying at the Art Institute, training with a Chinese dance troupe, and learning to macramé. She made my father a knotted vest that weighed about twenty pounds and painted the walls of their apartment in bright contrasting colors. My dad, always so crafty, designed and constructed some of their furniture himself—a love seat, a rocking chair, a dining table, and an upholstered stepladder, which my mom then stained and lacquered. When I asked my mom, "So, the stepladder was for sitting?" she answered matter-of-factly, "Yes. I always liked a bird's-eye view. Everything was at a different level in that apartment so you could always have a distinct perspective."

IN A LETTER HE WROTE in 1968 to his college friend Nate Garland, my dad talked about the theater work he was doing prior to joining Second City and his growing desire for fame.

Amid the dramatic social and political upheaval going on in Chicago in 1968, Dad attempted to focus his energy on sorting out his professional direction, chasing the entertainment business in a more direct way. He became a freelancer for the *Chicago Daily News*, writing music, movie, and theater reviews. Around the same time, he was asked to come back to Second City for a live onstage audition and was hired as a member of their new touring company. This is when he first met Brian Doyle-Murray and Joe Flaherty, who both appeared in many of his films and remained close friends throughout his life. Once the company returned

DEAR NATE,   5/18/68

        NICE TO HEAR FROM FRIENDS
IN EUROPEAN COUNTRIES AND WE
DO ENJOY YOUR LETTERS. YALE SOUNDS
LIKE A GUARANTEE OF PROFESSIONAL
SUCCESS AND LEADS ME TO REAFFIRM
MY FEELINGS ABOUT THE POSSIBILITY
OF KNOWING SOMEONE WHO DOES
SOMETHING IMPORTANT ARTISTICALLY.
I'VE REALLY GOT THIS THING IN MY
MIND ABOUT BEING FAMOUS; NOT PURELY
FOR THE GRATIFICATION OF FAME, BUT
FOR THE OPPORTUNITY TO AFFECT
THE AESTHETIC SENSIBILITIES OF A
MASS AUDIENCE. THAT'S PART OF THE
ATTRACTION IN THEATER FOR ME, AND
I EXPECT THAT MOST ARTISTS FEEL
SOMEWHAT THE SAME WAY THESE DAYS.
        MY ACTING WORKSHOP IS GOING QUITE
WELL. I HAVE NINE BEGINNING ACTORS
(INCLUDING BOGATY) AND WE JUST
DID A PUBLIC PERFORMANCE OF 5 ONE ACTS
THAT WAS PRETTY WELL RECEIVED.
I DIDN'T KNOW THAT PEOPLE CREDIT DIRECTORS
WITH SO MUCH INFLUENCE, BUT AFTER
THE PLAYS, PEOPLE WERE COMPLIMENTING
ME EN MASSE WHICH BLEW MY EGO ALL
OUT OF PROPORTION. I LOVED IT THOUGH,

BUT REALIZE THAT ACTING HAD BETTER
COME FIRST BEFORE I CAN APPROACH
DIRECTING IN A COMPLETELY MEANINGFUL
WAY. I DON'T KNOW ENOUGH ABOUT THE
ACTUAL MECHANICS OF ACTING AND SO
WHEN WE MOVE TO SAN FRANCISCO IN
SEPTEMBER, I'M GOING TO TRY TO GET
INTO A GOOD, FORMAL ACTING CONSERVATORY.

I'VE REALLY BEEN SUPER-CONSCIOUS
OF FURNITURE DESIGNS SINCE MY OWN
CAME TO MIND, AND AM REALLY ANXIOUS
TO SEE YOURS. AS FOR FILM, YOU MIGHT
BE INTERESTED TO KNOW THAT MICKEY
FRIEDMAN IS MAKING A FILM. HE'S CASTING
FOR IT NOW AND IT SOUNDS LIKE A POTENTIAL-
LY GOOD EFFORT.

MICKEY SHAMBERG IS ALSO DOING WELL
NOW, WRITING FULL-TIME FOR THE AMERICAN
AND PART-TIME FOR TIME-LIFE. I'M
CONSIDERING FREELANCING SOME THINGS
BUT I HAVE A LAZINESS TO FIGHT THAT
SOMETIMES SEEMS INSURMOUNTABLE.

ANNE'S WORK AT THE ART INSTITUTE
HAS BEEN GREAT. SHE'S LEARNED SO MUCH
THIS SEMESTER AND HAS BEEN TURNING
OUT CONSISTENTLY GOOD PAINTINGS AND
DRAWINGS.

I'LL CLOSE NOW, SO HAVE A GOOD TIME
TRAVELING AND CONTACT US WHEN
CONVENIENT. WE ENJOY HEARING FROM YOU.
SIGNED, HAROLD

to Chicago after their first tour, Dad got himself hired as the party jokes editor at *Playboy*, which would be his "day job" through the remainder of the sixties and early seventies. He read through hundreds of joke submissions every week, surprised by how generally unoriginal most of them were. Talking about his time at *Playboy*, he said, "My defining moment was in the basement in the Grotto when it was on State Street. The entire cast of *Hair* was naked in the swimming pool singing 'Let the Sunshine In.' I was like, 'All right, it's not going to get better than this.'"

IN 1969, Bernie Sahlins ushered in the "Next Generation" at Second City when he replaced the old resident company with my dad's touring company. Reflecting on this transition in the book *The Second City: Backstage at the World's Greatest Comedy Theater* (2000), my father said, "The original companies of the late '50s and early '60s had been Freudian, alienated, post-war, beatnik, bohemian in their philosophy and outlook. We were political in a different way. We were radical, born out of the 1968 Chicago convention. We looked like the guys who were in the streets getting clubbed by the police, but we weren't really in the streets." Even though my dad was too timid to actually put himself on the front line for a cause, he was considered to be one of the most political people in their social circle and was often ribbed for it. "It was always 'your boys' with Joe [Flaherty]," my dad once recalled to me, laughing. "Whenever there was civil unrest, and there was a lot of it back then, Joe would come in with his newspaper and say, 'Well, Harold, your boys in Madrid are at it again,' or 'Tell your boys in California to unchain themselves from those bulldozers and get a job!'" So while my father may have been a radical at heart, he was also an ambitious young performer and libertine who didn't seem to let political sympathies interfere with having fun. I remember him in tears from laughing so hard, telling me a story about the ingenious and infamous Del Close, who had vomited on his cat, decided it would be a good idea to take the cat into the shower to clean up, and was shredded to ribbons by said cat.

But it wasn't all sunshine and applause, and my dad's crazy schedule of nine-to-five at *Playboy* and six shows per week at Second City started to take its toll on my parents' marriage. In 1984, he told *Vanity Fair*:

> Anne was trying to live her life . . . She's much too bright, interested and interesting to want to hang around the theater and watch me get famous, you know? So without any guilt she posed the question of whether we could actually have a life together. And I realized that it was a whole other major life question that I'd been ignoring. I really did believe in having a relationship with another person as opposed to living my life entirely for myself and my career. And it bothered me how one could become so addicted to all the peripherals of being onstage: the groupies, the needing to be famous . . . I just saw myself perpetuating this terrible adolescent fear of not being popular because I felt like a geek or a nerd. Because I didn't want to succeed or fail in life based on whether I could make an audience like me . . . I actually feel that if I'd gone the other way, if I hadn't stayed so strongly committed to my marriage, they might have found me in a swimming pool, facedown.

So he quit his jobs, and they set off on their first major adventure.

. . .

MY MOTHER HAD FIRST READ about the Greek island of Hydra in the liner notes of one of Leonard Cohen's first albums. Cohen was living there on and off and she became fixated on going there to meet him and experience his inspiration firsthand. According to her, the decision to actually go to Hydra was made one night in Chicago when she and my dad took a bunch of acid. Not normally one to indulge in the readily available smorgasbord of substances, my mom had taken the drugs on a full stomach, felt horrible, and started to have a "bad trip."

My dad called Corky the Clown, a local figure who was known within their social circle to moonlight as an LSD guide. The clown fed my mom some maple syrup, talked her down, and left the young couple happily tripping and optimistically planning their future. "It was great," my mom said. "We were like tiny amoebas in this giant world, amoebas with big dreams."

So they started in France and rode the Orient Express, ending up on the rocky island of Hydra in January of 1970. Once there, they fell in with a group of international bohemians, including Cohen, and spent months lounging around in crumbling cottages and crowded cafés talking about art, movies, and poetry. My mom had listened to Greek language records for months leading up to their early visits but still had no idea what she was saying as she parroted phrases like *"Me synchoreíte, kapetánio, boreí na écho aftón ton choró?"*(*Excuse me, captain, may I have this dance?*) My dad, on the other hand, had an ear for languages and would eagerly greet the locals with, *"Geiá sou! I Elláda eínai mia ypérochi chóra!"* (*Hello! Greece is a wonderful country!*) At first, the local women thought my mother was a witch and crossed themselves every time she walked by. The *yiayias* eventually came around, but my mom was indifferent—she just knew she immediately felt at home there. She liked the rocky isolation of the island in winter as much as the warmth of the spring social scene. My dad enjoyed Hydra but never really fell in love with it the way my mom did.

When their money ran out later that year, they returned to Chicago, and my dad went back to Second City in 1971. It was then that he first met John Belushi, who had joined the company in my dad's absence. My dad was excited to be back in Chicago and working with his old friends but started to realize that he was probably better suited to writing and directing than acting. He described this transition in Sheldon Patinkin's *The Second City:* "Every time we'd be improvising, the directors would say, 'Stop writing, just go with what's happening.' I couldn't resist it, because you'd be improvising and the person you might be improvising with would go off on some idiotic tangent that you couldn't imagine. You knew what you wanted them to say . . . But I couldn't psychically influence what was happening on stage. I love the process of improv, but as soon as I had the opportunity, I started writing what everyone else was going to say." My mom, in her way, remained captivated by Hydra and returned there a few years later, alone, while my dad worked. This was typical of their atypical relationship—giving each other space to pursue their individual interests—and probably contributed to the longevity of their marriage, as well as to its eventual ending. In any case, their distance necessitated a lot of letter writing, a lovely example of which I've included on the following pages.

My mom returned to Chicago and rejoined the circus of my dad's Second City life in 1973. Soon after, John Belushi brought my dad

TOOTS SWEET,

IT'S WEDNESDAY AFTERNOON
AND I'M AT THE THEATER WAITING FOR REHEARSAL
TO BEGIN. I IMPROVISED FOR THE FIRST TIME LAST
NIGHT AND IT DIDN'T GO TOO BADLY. I WASN'T
OVERLY FRIGHTENED OR DESPERATE, NOR DID I FEEL
THAT I HAD TO PANDER TO THE AUDIENCE. ALSO, I
WAS SORT OF FUNNY. THE CAST RIGHT NOW IS A
LITTLE SHORT ON IDEAS BUT I'VE GOT PLENTY, PLUS
ENOUGH INFLUENCE AND ENERGY TO IMPLEMENT
THEM (I HOPE). WE WON'T HAVE THE KIND OF
LIVELY TOGETHERNESS WE ONCE HAD AS A CAST—
BRIAN IS OBVIOUSLY NEEDED — BUT IT CAN BE
FUN. I SEE JOHN BELUSHI SOME OUTSIDE THE
THEATER, BUT HE'S A BIT INCOHERENT FOR ME
TO REALLY BE CLOSE TO HIM AT THIS POINT.
JOE IS A LITTLE TIRED OF WORK AND JUDITH
IS TRYING TO GET HIM TO QUIT, SO HIS WORK
HERE SUFFERS A LITTLE FOR IT. BUT I THINK
HE'S EXCITED TO HAVE ME BACK, AS IS FISHER,
SO MAYBE THINGS WILL PICK UP FOR THEM.

DEAR, THE ONLY THING I'LL BE LACKING
HERE IS YOU. I'M LONELY WHEN I'M ALONE
AND REALLY NOT SATISFIED WITH THE RELATIONSHIPS
AT HAND — THERE'S SOMETHING ABOUT

HAVING YOU AROUND THAT MAKES ~~ ~~ LIFE
A LITTLE HEALTHIER FOR ME. IN SHORT, I THINK I
NEED YOU TO TAKE CARE OF ME. IRONIC, ISN'T IT? MAYBE
IT'S NOT SO MUCH THAT I <u>NEED</u> YOU ~~WITH~~ WITH ME; IT'S
THAT I <u>WANT</u> YOU ~~WITH~~ ME. HOW IS IT BEING
WITHOUT ME? MISS ME? ARE YOU FORGETTING WHAT
I LOOK LIKE? DO YOU FEEL DISTANT (NO PUN)? PLEASE,
WRITE ABOUT US, AND NEWS, TOO.

NOT MUCH NEWS HERE. BRIAN CALLED ME; HE'S
SLIGHTLY DEPRESSED OVER LACK OF WORK IN LA. MAYBE
HE'LL COME BACK.

BY THE WAY, I TALKED TO YOUR DAD AND ROSE ON
THE PHONE INSTEAD OF GOING TO ST. LOUIS. YOUR FATHER
IS RELUCTANT TO PROVIDE MONEY UNTIL HE ~~~~ IS
SURE WE'RE COMMITTED TO HYDRA AND NOT JUST
GOING THROUGH A PHASE. HE'S NOT ANGRY OR NEGATIVE
THOUGH— JUST CAUTIOUS. YOU CAN WRITE HIM YOURSELF
IF YOU WANT TO.

I'LL CLOSE AND WRITE AGAIN SOON. I LOVE
YOU WITH EVERY PART OF MY BEING AND DREAM
OF OUR HAPPY REUNION.

                    BLESS YOU,
                    HAROLD

to New York in 1974 to write and perform with the *National Lampoon Radio Hour* and Lemmings touring company. John, Doug Kenney, Joe Flaherty, Chevy Chase, Gilda Radner, and the Murray brothers, Bill and Brian, rounded out the group. What an amazing time that must have been.

Watching the documentary *Drunk Stoned Brilliant Dead*, about this era at the *Lampoon*, I was struck by how different things were during that time. It seems like a small miracle in and of itself that this ragtag group of freakish theater nerds and upstart intellectuals ever found each other, but it's even more amazing that they were able to let their collective genius coalesce into an entirely new form of bawdy and brilliant sociopolitical comedy. While the *Lampoon* style of subversive comedy isn't exactly on par with the invention of the wheel or the development of the polio vaccine, it did change the world in its way, and I am very proud that my dad was such a big part of it. Speaking to journalist Mark Caro about my dad for the *Chicago Tribune* in 1999, Second City founder Bernie Sahlins said, "I always knew . . . that [Harold] would be an important factor in American comedy. He has all the skills and abilities to be funny and to write funny, but he also is a leader, and a very nice guy. He was always looked up to, in Second City to being head writer at 'SCTV.' He was never separate from anybody. He was always one of the boys, but he was the best boy."

Dad kept himself busy writing the script for *Animal House* with Doug Kenney and Chris Miller and was offered the position of head writer for *SCTV* in 1976. Many of the *Lampoon* people had gone on to work for *Saturday Night Live*, but my dad declined. In an interview with Brett Martin for *GQ* he said, "Lorne [Michaels] offered me a job, but at that point I was the head writer on *SCTV*. *SNL* was completely

Best boy, 1975

fueled by cocaine; the show was being written literally overnight. I didn't want to stay up all night writing. And the show had a veneer of New York sophistication—very snide and superior. I thought, *It's just not me.*"

SCTV was the brainchild of Second City Toronto producer Andrew Alexander and writer and improv god Del Close, among others. With the exception of my dad, the original cast—John Candy, Andrea Martin, Dave Thomas, Joe Flaherty, Catherine O'Hara, and Eugene Levy—had all been culled from the stage at Second City Toronto. The premise of the show—a day in the life at the world's smallest television station—allowed for an almost endlessly eclectic mix of characters and setups. Talk shows, game shows, kid shows, news broadcasts, movies, and commercials (for ridiculous nonexistent products, of course) were interlaced with behind-the-scenes footage from the fictional small-town network. Dad performed a lot in the first ten episodes, which are, unfortunately, not included in any of the rereleased DVD sets and are not consistently available online. Some of his more memorable characters included station manager Moe Green, Officer Friendly, Allen "Crazy Legs" Hirschfeld, and Swami Banananananada. I even make an appearance in a commercial for Tiny Tops—wigs for bald babies—*"Your friends won't ask if it's a boy or a girl anymore when she sports the Dolly Parton Top!"* After the first season wrapped, the *SCTV* cast rented a house in Bel-Air for the summer and wrote the second season of shows. "We wrote about sixteen shows in seven weeks. It was one of the happiest times of my life, because they were all so funny and generous and talented in their work," my dad later said (*Chicago Tribune*, 1993). Watching an early episode recently, I was blown away by how ahead of its time the show was, and how prescient my dad and the other writers were about some of the more unsavory directions US culture and politics would take.

From Second City to *Playboy*, *National Lampoon* to *SCTV*, my dad could not have asked for a better foundation of comedy credentials, or better comrades, for that matter. So many of the people he connected with in his twenties remained important in his life for the duration. The lessons he learned from Del and Bernie stayed with him forever: "Work from the top of your intelligence" and "Focus on making the other guy look good" were always his mottos. Although he sometimes projected a sort of indifference to ambition and success, he took his comedy seriously and people took him seriously, in turn. As his career began to really take off, his personal life also flourished, as I prepared to make my big debut—springing like Athena from my father's head, fully formed, armed and ready to take on the world.

HAROLD + ANNE = VIOLET

When my parents decided to have a baby, it was like a big experiment. They didn't read any parenting books, or agonize about whether or not they were ready, or worry about what stroller to buy. They just did it. My dad had a pretty happy childhood by all accounts, and he always knew he wanted to be a father. My mother, with her more complicated family history, had just accepted that she would never be a typical maternal type, but was game for the adventure nonetheless.

I always loved hearing my dad tell the story of my birth every year on my birthday. They were living in a tiny house on Amelia Street in the Cabbagetown section of Toronto, watching *Mary Hartman, Mary Hartman*, when my mom's water broke with a surprisingly loud *pop*. It was snowing. They took a cab to the hospital. My mom's regular OB, Dr. Bean, was on vacation, so Dr. Lickrish stepped in to handle the delivery. My dad hated to see my mom in pain and felt so relieved when she finally got an epidural and started smiling again. After a couple hours of unsuccessful pushing, the doctor started to worry, so he used forceps (and a foot on the edge of the bed) to bring me into the world. The umbilical cord was wrapped around my neck twice and I was very blue. My dad held his breath while they worked on me and then wept when I finally started crying.

"Oh, it was great," my mom recalls. "You weren't breathing so they gave you oxygen and then you pinked up and just stared into my eyes. All babies should get oxygen when they're born. I think that's why you're so smart." Thanks, Mom!

New baby, new parents, 1977

They had decided on Violet Isadora for a girl and Nikolai for a boy, but my mom used to always say that the name runner-ups were Sleeveless and Cinderello. About a week after I was born, my mom developed an infection and had to go back to the hospital. I was readmitted with her but she really wasn't able to take care of me. My dad took care of both of us, and then, even after she recovered, he just kept on taking care of me. My mom was not what I would call an instinctive nurturer and wasn't comfortable with me as an infant. She didn't have any friends in Toronto outside of *SCTV*, and everyone was rehearsing and writing all day. She felt trapped, isolated, and unsure of herself as a mother.

Unfortunately, postpartum depression was not acknowledged or understood at that time, so she would suffer through the days until my dad came home, at which time she would basically throw me into his arms and run out of the house. My dad, in his natural, easy way, just stepped in and took over as primary parent. He was nurturing, was affectionate, and loved to nap—a perfect match for a baby! While my mom thought, *Well, he can do this part and I'll jump back in when she can talk*, he was fine with the extended nonverbal communication. He could goo-goo gaa-gaa all day, and believe me, he did. It wasn't that my mom didn't care about me; I know she did, in her way. Her way, however, just didn't have that cocoon-y feeling of security and warmth that kids want and need. There were times in my life when I resented her for this lack of nurturing but thankfully, she picked the right partner to smooth out her sharp corners, and she and I have a great relationship now. Still, I think what allowed me to be okay with what my mom couldn't give was what my dad always gave: the message I got from him from the day I was born until the day he died—"I am here for you. I am yours. You are loved."

AFTER THE SECOND SEASON of *SCTV* wrapped and just before my first birthday, Harold and Anne returned to Hydra with baby Violet (and a full-time babysitter) in tow. In the following 1978 letter to their good friends the Griecos, my dad reflects on parenting and his career.

When Joe sent me this letter in 2016, I have to admit, I sobbed after

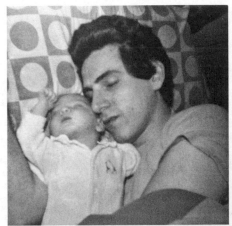

Naps and love, 1977

reading it. Not because it was sad or surprising, but because it so perfectly validated my understanding of my parents and our strange little family. My dad's wisdom, generosity, and humor were evident as he matter-of-factly recounted the mundane news of our lives alongside the personal challenges we faced. That my mom agreed, and was okay with his sharing these intimate details, is also a telling expression of her peculiarity. They were who they were, and they accepted it and loved each other in spite of it. And there I was, the bouncing baby girl, in a castle on a hill, waiting for my parents to come and get me for our next adventure.

DEAR JOE, MARCIA + ADRIAN,   2/3/78
        ANNE AND I ARE NOW ON THE
ISLAND FERRY ON THE WAY BACK TO HYDRA
AFTER A SPARKLING TWO DAYS IN ATHENS.
TWO DAYS SANS INFANT, I MIGHT ADD.
THE SWEET VIOLET WAS LEFT IN THE
CAPABLE HANDS OF HER BABY-SITER, A
STOUT 20-YEAR-OLD FROM MAINE WHO
NOW LIVES WITH US.

        WE TREATED OURSELVES TO 1ST CLASS
ACCOMODATIONS IN CELEBRATION OF ME
FINISHING THE FIRST DRAFT OF MY NEW
FILM, "UNTITLED MONEYMAKER". IT IS
UNTITLED SO FAR BUT I CAN TELL YOU
IT'S A SWORD + SORCERY, FANTASY EPIC
COMEDY. I MAY BE IN L.A. IN MARCH
TO DO THE REWRITE. ANYWAY, "ANIMAL
HOUSE", THE LAMPOON FILM, IS SHOT, EDITED
AND LOVED BY UNIVERSAL. THEY'VE
BOOKED IT INTO THE BEST WESTWOOD
AND NEW YORK THEATERS FOR A SUMMER
OPENING. I'M TOLD, IT WILL BE THE
TAKE-OFF, BREAKTHROUGH WIT OF THE POST-WAR
YEARS, POSSIBLY THE TRIUMPH OF THE
CENTURY. I'M TOLD THIS BY THE PRODUCER.
AH, WELL. WE'LL SEE.

JOE, WHY ARE YOUR LETTERS FUNNIER
THAN MY SCREENPLAYS. WE LOVED YOUR LAST
ONE. IT REALLY BRINGS SWEET MEMORIES
OF YOU ALL TO US. (WHAT A BAD SENTENCE!
"YOU ALL TO US"? YOU KNOW WHAT I MEAN,
THOUGH. WE'RE AWFULLY FOND OF YOU.)

HYDRA IS BEAUTIFUL AND BORING—
BORING TO ME, THAT IS. ANNE IS IN CONSTANT
RAPTURE ABOUT BEING THERE. SHE WANTS
ME TO BUY A HOUSE ON THE ISLAND. I
WILL IF I CAN, BUT I CAN ONLY SEE
LIVING THERE A FEW MONTHS A YEAR. THE
WINTER, ESPECIALLY DECEMBER, WAS AWFUL.
VERY COLD, VERY WINDY, ROUGH SEAS, HENCE
NO FERRY BOAT FOR FOUR DAYS. THE GREEKS
WERE ALREADY FIGURING OUT WHICH
FOREIGNERS TO EAT FIRST IF THE GROCERIES
RAN OUT. BUT IT'S WARM AND NICE NOW.

THE HOUSE WE'RE IN IS A PALACE
BUT IT'S ON A HILLTOP — 400 STEPS UP
FROM THE PORT (I COUNTED THEM). BUT WE'RE
MOVING TO KAMENI, TO A SUNNIER, LOWER
HOUSE. KAMENI YOU'LL RECALL IS THE
LITTLE VILLAGE ATTACHED TO HYDRA WITH
IT'S OWN LITTLE BEACH. WE KEEP THE
SAME MAILING ADDRESS, SO DON'T SCRATCH US

OUT OF YOUR ADDRESS BOOK.

VIOLET IS GREAT — CUTE, BIG, SMART, JOLLY, ALL THE THINGS YOU'D WANT IN A DOG. SHE MAY WALK SOON, HAS 8 TEETH, SOME HAIR AND AN INFECTIOUS GRIN. SHE ALSO SLEEPS UNTIL 9 A.M., HER MOST ENDEARING TRAIT. ANNE HAS TAKEN A VACATION FROM MOTHERHOOD. SHE LOVES VIOLET, VIOLET LOVES HER, BUT ANNE LEAVES ALL THE CHORES AND RESPONSIBILITY TO ME AND LORI (THE BABYSITTER). IT'S ALL RIGHT WITH ME, THOUGH. SHE HAD A ROUGH TIME WITH VIOLET IN CANADA WHILE I WAS OFF AT WORK EVERYDAY AND AT LEAST SHE ISN'T ABUSIVE TO HER. I'M SURE THEY'LL BE FRIENDS WHEN VIOLET IS OLD ENOUGH TO HELP TAKE CARE OF ANNE.

SO, AS I NEAR THE END OF THE PAGE, I'LL HOPE THAT YOU'RE THRIVING AND HAPPY. I KNOW YOU'VE GOT ENOUGH WATER NOW AND I CAN PICTURE THE NICE, MILD WINTER YOU MUST BE HAVING. LOOK FOR US IN THE SPRING AND WRITE AGAIN IF YOU CAN.

LOVE,
HAROLD

Ditto. Anne

It was the Deltas against the rules... the rules lost!

DELTA HOUSE

COLLEGE

NATIONAL LAMPOON'S ANIMAL HOUSE (1978)

Written by HAROLD RAMIS, DOUG KENNEY, and CHRIS MILLER
Directed by JOHN LANDIS

Awkward college freshmen Larry (Thomas Hulce) and Kent (Stephen Furst) attempt to pledge the elitist Omega Theta Pi House, but are unceremoniously rejected. After reevaluating their options and adjusting their standards, they move on to the infamously irreverent Delta Tau Chi House. As the Deltas put their pledges to various depraved tests of brotherhood, the college dean (John Vernon) conspires with the Omegas to have Delta's charter revoked.

> OTTER
> Bluto's right. Psychotic, but
> right. I think this situation
> absolutely requires a really futile
> and stupid gesture be done on
> somebody's part.

                        BLUTO
            And we're just the guys to do it.

The Lampoon people understand the darkest secret of an
American college education: one of the noblest reasons
to go is to spend four years studying sex.
— FRANK RICH, *TIME*

"National Lampoon's Animal House" is by no means one
long howl, but it's often very funny, with gags that are
effective in a dependable, all-purpose way.
— JANET MASLIN, *THE NEW YORK TIMES*

The movie is vulgar, raunchy, ribald, and occasionally
scatological . . . it finds some kind of precarious balance
between insanity and accuracy, between cheerfully
wretched excess and an ability to reproduce the most
revealing nuances of human behavior.
— ROGER EBERT, *CHICAGO SUN-TIMES*

The idea for *Animal House* was born out of the *National Lampoon* 1964 high school yearbook parody, published in 1973, although the content is unrelated. My dad had met Doug Kenney, one of the founders of *National Lampoon*, when he joined the *National Lampoon Radio Hour*, and the two hit it off immediately. My dad adored Doug and their creative work thrived in partnership. They elevated each other's strengths and provided unique perspectives to enhance the overall appeal of their work. He told Tad Friend for the *New Yorker* in 2001,

"[Doug] used to say that 'just because something's popular doesn't mean it's bad,' which I really took to heart, because my stance had always been that people are idiots and sheep. Our other motto was 'Broad comedy is not necessarily dumb comedy.'" The first product of their partnership was a script called *Laser Orgy Girls*, a comedy about aliens and Charles Manson as a high school student. *Lampoon* producers Matty Simmons and Ivan Reitman liked the screenplay but asked them to go back, rein it in a little, and move the story to college. They brought in another *Lampoon* writer, Chris Miller, and the three of them spent weeks writing down every funny college experience they'd had or heard about. It was a truly collaborative process—they each wrote a third of the script and then rotated, so everyone rewrote everyone's work.

Intoxicated by the combination of arrogance, intelligence, and youth (among other things), Dad, Doug, and Chris were convinced they were creating a masterpiece while writing *Animal House*. It's difficult to imagine now, but what they were doing in terms of elevating the under dogs and vilifying the golden boys hadn't been done before. Good was good and bad was bad—from the perspective of the white mainstream, anyway. Somehow, Doug, Chris, and Dad just knew that their new take would work. In a 1999 interview with the AV Club, Dad said, "When Universal read the first drafts of *Animal House*, [executive] Ned Tanen said, 'Wait a minute, these guys are the heroes?' He didn't get it. But we knew that our generation would get it completely." Much like the protagonists of the film, they were driven forward by the momentum of a new generation taking over the (comedy) world and turning the old tropes upside down.

When John Landis was hired to direct the movie, there was some friction between John and the writers. IMDb quotes my dad as saying, "[John] sort of referred immediately to *Animal House* as 'my movie.' We'd been living with it for two years and we hated that." My dad was also mad that John refused to cast him in the movie (*"Fuck that. I'm not hanging around to be an extra,"* I believe were his exact words in an interview years later), but at the end of the day, those were not things he often mentioned when discussing *Animal House*. Overwhelmingly, he recalled what a great time he had writing with Doug and Chris and how the movie was always more to him than gross-out gags and gratuitous sex.

Watching the film now, I find it fascinating how quickly culture can change. What seemed innocently edgy then is borderline horrifying now. Would anyone today laugh at a thirteen-year-old girl getting dead drunk at a frat party and being returned home, naked, in a shopping cart? Maybe a sociopath yukking it up to marathons of *Law & Order: Special Victims Unit*, but the average person, probably not. Or the scene that was supposedly based on an actual experience of my dad's, where Otter and the gang end up in a nightclub filled with scary black people whose physicality and sexuality are so threatening as to cause our heroes to run, screaming, from the building? No, just, no. Now, to be clear, I'm not saying these things out of some knee-jerk PC reaction to humor that walks the line between edgy and offensive. To be honest, I reject the idea of "political correctness" because I think it minimizes the importance of actual sensitivity to racism, sexism, and homophobia, but I do wish my dad were here to deconstruct some of the more problematic choices he made in *Animal House*, and elsewhere.

In any case, the commercial success of *Animal House* provided tremendous validation of the appeal of this new brand of comedy, and an incredible jump-start to my dad's career, however sophomoric it may have been (wink wink). While John Landis's refusal to cast him as Boon may have reinforced the insecurities my dad had about himself as an actor, it also propelled him toward directing as a means to greater overall creative control.

*Dad and Doug, 1980. It makes me happy to think
of them like this now, reunited in the great unknown.*

IT TAKES A VILLAGE . . .

Jews don't really have godparents in the strict sense of the term, as in a person who's officially designated to be responsible for your spiritual life, but I was blessed with two sets: godparents and fairy godparents.

My godparents are Bill Murray and Mary Jane Rosenfeld, my mom's best friend from college. My mom says they chose Bill because he was tall and funny, but then had second thoughts after the fact. "Bill liked to use you as a prop," my mom explained. "He would carry you around like a sack of potatoes and make everyone laugh, but then he wouldn't pay attention to you for the rest of the day."

"But what did you want from him?" I asked. "To be like an uncle?"

"No . . . nothing, I guess. We didn't imagine it would be a very important role . . . maybe we should have given it a little more thought." I'll say! My dad once said of Bill, "It's his job to defy all your expectations," so I guess the bar was set pretty low. Still, I wonder, is there a law against absentee godparents? What if my spiritual well-being were at stake? Can I take Bill to emotional claims court to get retroactive advice on life? Collect on all the ungiven birthday gifts? I joke, of course, but it would have been nice to have him around more over the years.

My fairy godmother was Gilda Radner, who liked to refer to me as a Trick Baby—meaning, I was so cute and easy that I tricked people into wanting to have kids. Gilda died in 1989, tragically, and my memories of her from childhood are few. Mostly, I remember her making funny faces at me, and laughing with my dad. My fairy godfather is Andy Kay, a dancer and painter who teaches Zen brushwork in Hawaii, where he lives with his husband (together for forty

Baby V and Gilda, looking too cute in her pigtails

years). Andy travels the world teaching and making art and generously painted the chuppah for my wedding. Andy is the only godparent who has really been actively involved in my life and it's been a real blessing to have such a magical and loving person looking out for me.

Aside from the appointed godparents (fairy or otherwise), I was lucky to always be surrounded by a lot of smart and funny adults. Doug Kenney was a major presence in the first few years of my life, and I remember him singing me a silly version of the alphabet song where he would just inject random words: "A—b—c—d—e—f—NOSEGAY—h—i—j—k—l—m—n—OHHHHHH GALOSHES—p—q—r—s—t—u—VIOLET! YOU ARE SUCH A PUMPERNICKEL PIE!"

*Bill and Brian, Mary Jane, Dad, and me (in what once passed
for a car safety seat—basically a bucket with a strap)*

Backyard ballet with Andy

He had great energy and I always loved when he was around, as did my dad.

Because I was around adults most of the time, I was what you could call a precocious child. At age two, I could recite "The Owl and the Pussycat" from memory and liked to sing Cole Porter songs with my mom. When I was a bit older, I thought nothing of chatting it up with complete strangers.

"We took you everywhere," my mom tells me. "Once, at a restaurant when you were four, we noticed you had left our table and found you sitting with two men in suits, holding court, talking about who knows what, while they both stared at you, enthralled." On airplanes, my parents let me wander around and would find me, an hour later, sitting with someone, looking at their family photos or telling them about my life. My mom remembers Doug Kenney watching me eat a big bowl of popcorn in front of the TV when I was about three and saying, "She's already an adolescent!"

My dad loved to tell the story of watching the evening news with me when I was four or five when a story came on about gay scoutmasters. "What's that?" I asked.

"Oh, um, well, er, gay is when a man loves a man or a woman loves a woman, like—"

"I know that, Daddy!" I said, cutting him off. "What's a scoutmaster?"

I became obsessed with human reproduction at an early age. When I was around five, someone (probably my mom) had the bright idea to show me *The Miracle of Life*—a PBS documentary that started with infrared shots of people (and their hormones) walking down a busy city street and ending with a close-up shot of a baby's slimy head emerging from a bushy vagina. It was my favorite movie, and I watched it over and over again. At the slightest questioning I would go into a mini lecture on the function of the vas deferens and the epididymis. At some point, one of my mom's artist friends wanted to put me in a little nurse's uniform and have me narrate *The Miracle of Life*, *Mystery Science Theater 3000* style.

This obsession with baby-making led to another favorite pastime of mine—the Birth Game. This was a game I made up that started with the phone call from the doctor's office ("Congratulations! You're pregnant!"), followed by cramming increasingly larger stuffed animals into my dress as I waddled around the house, and ending with me, on my back, legs up, screaming with labor pains until I delivered a teddy bear. "But sound happy when you tell me 'It's a boy!'" I would instruct whoever was lucky enough to get roped into playing the doctor. Maybe that's why we seemed to go through so many babysitters. Can you imagine? Oy!

Another "game," which I would only make my dad play with me, was How Old? It was like the down-and-dirty version of "Que Sera, Sera" (*When I was just a little girl, I asked my mother, what will I be?*) for seven-year-olds. I would say, "What if I like a boy?" and he would say, "But you're too young!" and I would say, "Well, how old do I have to be?" And then he would go through the ages at which things would be acceptable. At twelve, I was allowed to hold hands; at thirteen, I could kiss on the lips; fourteen, French kiss; fifteen, petting (does anyone even say *petting* anymore?); sixteen, sex. Sixteen might seem early but I think everyone was just hoping that I would even wait that long. (For the record, I didn't. Sorry!) I don't know why I liked this game, if you could even call it that. I guess I was looking for some kind of boundaries.

In the early eighties, my parents got connected with this very cool downtown New Wave art scene in LA. Doug Kenney had introduced them to Peter Ivers,* a brilliant musician and performer who had created the TV show *New Wave Theatre*, wrote the soundtrack for *Eraserhead* with David Lynch, and shot some very cool experimental videos for his music. He and my mom were very close and studied yoga together under the same teacher, Alan Finger. My dad coproduced one of Peter's last projects, a musical revue called *Vitamin Pink*, performed at Club Lingerie on the Sunset Strip in June of 1982. I played the part of the Child, and sang with Peter, Rochelle Robertson, and Tequila Mockingbird. We rehearsed for weeks in Peter's huge loft. I can't remember the gist of the show but on my cue, topless in a white satin miniskirt and sequined white turban, I was "born" through a plastic tunnel and right into my solo song—"I Personally Inherited a Hundred Million Dollars" (*and I can do what I want to do what I want, and I may be a child, but I can do what I want to do what I want to do what I want*). I felt so cool going to school the day after the show. I refused to wash the makeup off my face, so I looked like a six-year-old party girl on her walk of shame back to the playground. I yawned often and deliberately that day so people would ask me why I was so tired. "Oh," I would say offhandedly, "I was in a show last night at Club Lingerie, and I didn't get home until after midnight [YAWN]." I loved the whole scene and I couldn't wait for Peter to write the next show so we could do it all over again.

---

* For more on this amazing guy, see Josh Frank's book *In Heaven Everything Is Fine.*

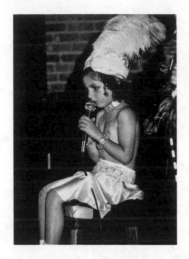

Diva alert!

Vitamin Pink *poster (fans in costume*
half price—love it!)

Tragically, Peter was found murdered in his loft on March 3, 1983, rounding out a heartbreaking trio starting with Doug's death in 1980 and John Belushi's in 1982. My parents were devastated. I will never forget the image of them, standing together in the doorway of my school—my mother's face pale and crumpled, my father looking un-characteristically somber. "Peter's dead," my mother choked out. "No more *Vitamin Pink*?" I asked, thinking only of myself. They both started weeping. "He was such a great guy," my dad sobbed, tears raining down on his turquoise polo shirt. Of course, I had no idea at the time that my dad had been questioned by police for hours that morning, that my mom was completely heartbroken, or that, beyond our family friend, the world had lost a(nother) truly genius creative force.

Being raised in the smoky, coked-up, pre-AIDS pandemonium of early 1980s Hollywood could have been a total disaster for my early development, but it wasn't. I used to think I had saved myself by skipping childhood entirely and going right to mini-adult, but I realize now this isn't really the case, or at least not the whole story. My dad, despite his vices, was committed to being a good father and never seemed to let his work (or play) take priority over me. My mother, for all of her issues as a parent, was at least immune to the superficial bullshit of celebrity life and made sure I was exposed to as many interesting people and things as possible. The hodgepodge of adults who rounded out my coterie of caretakers and role models were, in many ways, often very childlike themselves—exuberant, wild, whimsical, and prone to tantrums. On the one hand, this group of rowdy geniuses meant great fun for me as a kid. On the other hand, it likely skewed my perspective on adulthood, creativity, success, and security, and definitely was an early introduction to the ambiguity that would become a refrain in my bizarre yet normal life. *Famous people are just people. Good people do bad things. Bad things happen to good people. Life is messy!*

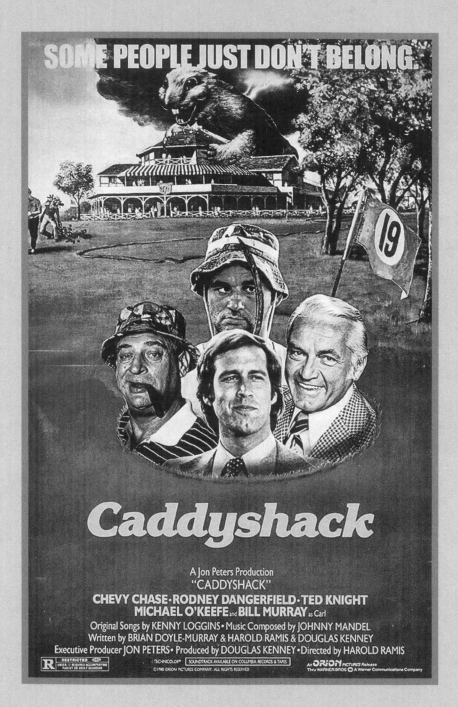

CADDYSHACK
(1980)

Written by HAROLD RAMIS, DOUG KENNEY,
and BRIAN DOYLE-MURRAY
Directed by HAROLD RAMIS

Danny Noonan (Michael O'Keefe), an ambitious teen from a blue-collar family, works as a caddy at the snooty Bushwood Country Club to earn money for college. To increase his chances of receiving a coveted scholarship, Noonan volunteers to caddy for Judge Smails (Ted Knight), an influential, old-money club member who is at war with the crass, nouveau riche Al Czervik (Rodney Dangerfield). As Danny prepares for the Caddy Day golf tournament that will make or break his college dreams, he receives philosophical guidance from eccentric and wealthy playboy Ty Webb (Chevy Chase).

```
              TY WEBB
    There's a force in the universe
    that makes things happen. And all
    you have to do is get in touch
    with it, stop thinking, let things
    happen, and be the ball.
```

The first-time director, Harold Ramis, can't hold it together:
the picture lurches from style to style (including some
ill-placed whimsy with a gopher puppet) and collapses
somewhere between sitcom and sketch farce.
—DAVE KEHR, *CHICAGO READER*

"Caddyshack" never finds a consistent comic note of its own,
but it plays host to all sorts of approaches from its stars, who
sometimes hardly seem to be occupying the same movie.
—ROGER EBERT, *CHICAGO SUN-TIMES*

A pleasantly loose-limbed sort of movie with some comic
moments, most of them belonging to Mr. Dangerfield.
—VINCENT CANBY, *THE NEW YORK TIMES*

Caddyshack came on the heels of the success of *Animal House* and offered my dad and Doug Kenney another chance at developing their nascent brand of what my dad called institutional comedy— basically youth revolting against the establishment. Brian Doyle-Murray (Bill's older brother and a close friend of my dad's from the Second City days) had been a caddy in Winnetka as a teenager, and Doug's father was a tennis pro in Ohio, so they had an inside perspective on the class and cultural dynamics of the country club world. My dad had never golfed before, but as a nerdy Jew, he easily identified with the conflict between "insiders" and "outsiders." While the early drafts of the screenplay focused solidly on the Danny Noonan character, as the star-studded cast came together, my dad saw the story evolving from a standard bildungsroman into being more about the four adult role models, and how Danny would ultimately choose which path to take and what kind of man he wanted to become.

In many ways, *Caddyshack* was also a coming-of-age for my dad. He was confident and ambitious but had not gone to film school, had never directed before, and had to figure out what he was doing on the fly. In a draft of a piece he wrote for the Directors Guild of America, he recalled the first day of shooting.

> I walked on the set of *Caddyshack* and made a total fool of myself on the first setup. We were shooting on a golf course in Davie, Florida, and the AD asked where I wanted to put the camera. I could feel the whole crew staring at me, the first-time director, waiting to see what kind of leader I'd be. I looked around and saw nothing but green, nothing but trees and manicured fairways all around, so I arbitrarily pointed, "That way." The AD looked in the direction I was pointing and squinted. Apparently he noticed something I hadn't. "So you want us to move the generator, the catering tent and all the trucks, 'cause they'll be in the shot." "Oh, is that what all that stuff is? No, let's leave that where it is." I could see the smirks on the faces of the grips and that's when I learned a great lesson of directing—if you don't know, ask. "Where do *you* think we should put the camera?" I asked Steve Larner, the DP. From that moment on everything ran smoothly with the understanding that I knew nothing and should not be consulted on anything technical.

I was only two when *Caddyshack* was being filmed in Florida, but I have rich, if fragmented, memories of our time in Fort Lauderdale: thousands of small frogs clinging to the window of our hotel room

What's my motivation? Me, Mom, and Michael O'Keefe.

during Hurricane David; the day they filmed the explosions on the golf course; playing with Minerva Perez (the young caddy "in drag" in the film); making my big debut in the movie and feeling like a star. (If you blink, you'll miss it, but in the scene on the dock, I'm the pipsqueak in a sailor suit making faces at Michael O'Keefe until my mom comes and carries me away.) According to Mom, I knew everyone's name on the crew, from the caterers to the costumers to the producers to the guy who stocked the vending machine. At the time, I was unaware of the late-night parties, drug use, and other shenanigans going on, but there was a loose, circuslike atmosphere on set that allowed me to ramble around and feel right at home.

After *Animal House*, Dad and Doug expected *Caddyshack* to be a huge success, which it wasn't, and Doug took the criticism very hard. Unfortunately, he died before he could see what a beloved classic it became, but my dad was always amused by how enthusiasm for the film evolved over time: "Back when people used to read *TV Guide*, *Caddyshack* was a two-star movie for the first ten years, then at some point I noticed that it got a third star in the same publication and I thought, *Maybe it's like wine: the longer you keep it, it just gets a little better*. I happen to love *Caddyshack* even though, like *Animal House*, it has some cringe-inducing elements. Could there have been one funny woman with more than a throwaway line? Apparently not. And Lacey Underall? Really? Come on, Dad! Putting that aside, I feel like its messiness is kind of charming and clearly reflects the fact that my dad had no prior directing experience. He often said in his later years that he found it unwatchable because all he could see were the mistakes and missed opportunities, but despite that, he always enjoyed *Caddyshack*'s popularity and endless quotability. After my dad died, even Barack Obama (or whoever wrote his press releases) couldn't help himself, releasing this statement:

> Michelle and I were saddened to hear of the passing of Harold Ramis, one of America's greatest satirists and, like so many other comedic geniuses, a proud product of Chicago's Second City. When we watched his movies—from *Animal House* and *Caddyshack* to *Ghostbusters* and *Groundhog Day*—we didn't just laugh until it hurt. We questioned authority. We identified with the outsider. We rooted for the underdog. And through it all, we never lost our faith in happy endings.

Our thoughts and prayers are with Harold's wife, Erica, his children and grandchildren, and all those who loved him, who quote his work with abandon, and who hope that he received total consciousness.

I know Dad would have loved that.

TELL ME ABOUT WHEN
YOU WERE LITTLE

I always loved to hear my dad's stories of his childhood. He remembered every small detail and acted out stories with voices—like the impression he did of a neighborhood girl who was always trying to get my dad and his brother in trouble, and would yell, "Harold and Steven's MOTHER!" at the top of her nasal voice from the sidewalk in front of their building. He had a real affection for his family and other characters from that time in his life, and it shone through when he spoke about them.

My grandmother Ruth was the second of five children born to Fanny and Hyman Cokee: Rose, Ruth, Harold (who passed away as a child), Jordan, and Shelly. Each of them had two or three children and that generation, in turn, went on to have three to five children each. It was a big, warm, and wonderful family. Bubbie, my great-grandmother, was the heart of the clan. She would beam at her children, grandchildren,

(Clockwise from center of back row):
*Grandpa Nate, Grandma Ruth, Dad, and
Uncle Steven, 1947-ish. (Not sure who
the woman on the left and the boy
in the middle are.)*

and great-grandchildren, her love evident in her eyes. "I'm so proud," she would whisper, "I'm so, so proud." Then she would spit on the floor and say a *kein ayin hora* to ward off the evil eye. Bubbie came from Kiev at seventeen years old and worked in a fish market in Kentucky when she first arrived in the States. She never learned to read or write in English but that didn't stop her from living a full life. My dad told me that once, when she was watching him and his brother, Steven, they had gotten separated from her and taken the wrong El train and got lost. He said he hadn't realized what was going on at first because he couldn't imagine not feeling completely safe and taken care of with her, and that story always stuck with me, because she made me feel that way, too. She was a great lady who made fruitcake and farfel from scratch well into her nineties and passed away peacefully at ninety-seven.

To hear my dad tell it, his childhood in Chicago in the 1950s was like a Jewish working-class Norman Rockwell world, with a little *Lord of the Flies* thrown in for good measure. He and his brother, Steven, roamed the streets with their "gang" like the Little Rascals, collecting bottle caps and other junk that could be used as toys or traded for a few pennies. When Eric Spitznagel asked my dad about his childhood for the *Believer* in 2006, he talked about being independent from an early age: "I was the little guy who knew how to tie a necktie. It came from having absentee parents. They were tremendously loving and caring people who, by circumstance, had to go to work. So my brother and I were latchkey kids, left to ourselves. Instead of turning that into a delightful delinquency, we became overly responsible." As children, he and Steven often cooked dinner to have it ready and waiting when their parents came home from work.

I was endlessly curious about "life in olden times," and Dad would humor me by describing family meals (cheerfully arguing over who would get the last lamb chop), what snacks he ate after school (a gallon of milk, a box of cookies, and a whole salami he would devour like a banana), working in the family store (the time his mother sliced the tip of her thumb off behind the butcher counter), and other neighborhood kids (playing Buck Buck, a brutal game where boys crouched down in a line and then jumped onto each other's backs, digging elbows and knees into kidneys). During my own sadistic phase of fascination with "hurt stories," I asked, "Didn't you ever break any bones? Or have to go to the hospital?" and he recalled that when he was around seven, roaming the streets with his brother and their posse, Steven spotted a piece of chain-link in a pile of ashes and excitedly grabbed it, not realizing that it was white-hot from a fire and severely burning his hands. Ouch! When I was in the mood for stories about romance, Dad offered the tale of his first crush, Joanne Grapey, for whom he gathered all of his savings and bought a rhinestone necklace . . . in second grade. Unfortunately, she did not have feelings for him and threw the necklace on the ground, trampling his little heart along with the rhinestones. I wonder if she later regretted her decision. I have to say, I kind of hope it haunted her forever.

One Moral of the Story fable from his childhood that he told repeatedly was about telling the truth. I first heard the story of the mirror following the only spanking my dad ever gave me. I was about six and thought it would be a good idea to cut my own hair. I stood on the toilet so I could see myself in the mirror and just chop-chopped away. Then I went on about my business and thought that was the end of that. Later, my dad came to me and asked, "Violet, did you cut your hair?"

"No, Daddy."

"Are you sure? I found all of this hair in the bathroom wastebasket. Are you sure you didn't cut your hair?"

"Nope. Maybe Mom did. Yeah, I think Mom cut her hair."

"Okaaaay, I'll go talk to Mom then."

"Okay." Looking back, I don't know how I thought I was going to get away with it; my hair was about six inches shorter on one side and obviously my mom had not cut her hair and was about to tell my dad that.

He came back a few minutes later and said, "Violet, I'm going to ask you one more time, did you cut your hair?"

"No," I said, digging in. "I didn't cut my hair. I'm not even supposed to use the big scissors," I added, as if that was going to help my case.

"Well, I know you're lying," he said tightly, his nostrils starting to flare, "and I'm going to have to punish you. I'm going to spank you, ten times, and you're going to count."

Cue record scratch: *Whaaat?*

My dad had never hit me before and I couldn't believe he was going to now. He led me into the living room, laid me over his knees, and

(Left to right): *Steven and Harold, 1948*

proceeded to spank me on the butt ten times while I counted. It didn't hurt but I cried anyway. Then, when it was done, he sat me up, kissed away my tears, and told me about the mirror.*

When my dad and Steven were six and seven, my grandmother was cleaning their apartment and had pushed all of the furniture to the middle of the room. While she was in the kitchen, they played a forbidden game of indoor tag, jumping from couch to chair to coffee table. A full-length mirror that was propped against the back of the couch tipped over onto the carpet and silently shattered into a million pieces. They stood, open-mouthed, scrambling to think of possible stories of how it happened.

"Maybe someone came in the apartment and broke it!"

---

* I teased him about the haircut incident for years. "How could you have hit me like that? And made me count? So mean!" "I didn't know what I was doing!" he'd laugh. "It seemed like the right thing to do. And it worked, didn't it? You never lied to me again after that, right?" Ummmm, moving right along . . .

"Who?"

"I don't know! A robber?"

"That's dumb!"

"Okay, okay, what if we say we were just sitting there watching TV and it broke?"

"She's not stupid. She'll know we're lying."

So they walked solemnly into the kitchen holding hands and said, "Ma, we broke the mirror."

"Was Grandma mad?" I asked.

"Well, she wasn't happy. But she knew we felt terrible about it and was proud that we told the truth."

"Did you get in trouble?"

"No. She figured we would torture ourselves enough."

This "torture yourself" approach seemed to work for my dad both as a kid and as an adult. It's basically personal responsibility with a dash of Jewish guilt—don't do it because I say so, do it because you know it's the right thing (and I will be so disappointed if you don't). This was his strategy at home and on set, where, as the director, he was like a father to the whole crew. We all wanted to do our best for him, not because *he* would be mad if we didn't, but because we would be mad at ourselves if we let him down.

Maybe my all-time favorite of the Young Harold stories was about my dad's first day of first grade. Little Hershey Ramis (I'm imagining him in knickers and a newsboy cap, but it was around 1950, so more realistically, a little collared button-down) made the mistake of chewing gum in class. The teacher told him, "Oh no! We don't chew gum in first grade. Go back to kindergarten!" He described that he left the classroom and had started walking down the hall when he realized his kindergarten teacher had gotten married and left the school. He felt so humiliated, he started walking home. "But, Daddy," I'd say, "you were really little. That's so sad."

"It was actually kind of a life changer," he said. "There I am walking home, thinking, *Well, there goes college,* and I get home and tell my mother what happened. Well, you know how tough she was. She marched me back to school, went straight to the principal's office, and let him have it. I think the teacher got in some trouble too, but who knows? I certainly didn't have a problem with her for the rest of the year."

"Grandma Ruth to the rescue!" I laughed.

"Something like that." He smiled. "But it made me realize two important things: that getting in trouble wasn't the end of the world, and that authority figures were not always right."

WHILE THESE STORIES OFFER some insight into the formation of my father's parenting philosophies and general worldview, he often spoke about his childhood as it related to the development of his comedic perspective. His standard one-liner when asked if he had been a class clown was "I wrote for the class clown," but he frequently referred to the Absurd Child Syndrome as the process through which his humor originated. He elaborated on the idea in the *Believer* interview, saying, "There was a great construct I once heard about—the Absurd Child Syndrome. Parents tell us things to protect us, or they educate us from their own misinformation or misconceptions. We tell our kids that policemen are good and God protects us and our country is noble, and at a certain point—for some of us, it comes quite early, at five or six years old—we start to realize that it's all a façade. So the child says, 'Well, geesh, the institutions that I'm supposed to respect are telling me things that don't appear to be true. Either I'm crazy or they're crazy.' That creates the Absurd Child. The Absurd Child is one who says, 'Well, I think *they're* crazy.' So you live in this state of alienation from your culture and your society and your family because you see this rampant bullshit around you [. . .] Some people have a fear of rejecting all the security that comes with family, church, and state. They become funda- mentalists. In a lot of ways, every child is a miniature fundamentalist. They need to believe in these things. It's too terrifying otherwise. It takes maturity to embrace all that ambiguity. Once you're alienated, you're on your own."

This absurdity—the hypocrisy of authority, arbitrary morality, and, often, societal expectations—was a major theme throughout my dad's personal life and is clearly reflected in much of his work. It significantly influenced his parenting choices with me and shaped my worldview in an entirely different way. Whereas he grew up with (and eventually rebelled against) standard, binary, black-and-white models of thinking and living, I was raised in an endless gray area, left to form my own conclusions about right, wrong, and the kind of person I wanted to be. Thankfully, both of my parents provided distinct and dynamic models of how to do this, and although I am probably more of a fundamentalist than either one of them, their encouragement to draw outside the lines made me the person I am today.

GROWN-UP STUFF

My dad smoked. A lot. Vantage 100s by the carton, and pot, pretty much by the pound, throughout my early childhood. Say what you will about irresponsible parenting, but I think smoking grass helped him be the infinitely patient, playful, and peaceful dad that he was. It's not that he *had* to be high to play dolls with me for hours, but I'm sure he enjoyed it more with a little buzz. I remember watching him cleaning seeds and stems out of a big plastic baggie and then effortlessly rolling joint after joint until he had a little collection neatly lined up in front of him—always a perfectionist. He called them French cigarettes. When I was young, I didn't really have an understanding of drugs; I just knew it was a part of what he did and so I never questioned it. While I climbed around on the rickety swing set in our backyard, he lovingly tended to a scrawny little pot plant that never quite took off. At night, I often faked a stomachache so I could get out of bed and sit with him on the couch while he got high and watched movies. Long before I had any clue what it was all about, I would switch into that

holding-in-smoke voice to make a joke, much to the amusement or confusion of my audience, depending on who they were.

Once, someone dropped off a big plate of brownies that I, of course,
was very excited to eat after dinner. When I'd finished my standard
evening meal of hot dog and Tater Tots, I asked my dad where they
were and he told me, "I'm sorry, baby. Those are for grown-ups only."
After that, whenever offered sweets, I would ask, "Are they grown-up
cookies or are they okay for kids?" Looking back, I wonder what my
friends' parents made of this. I guess if it wasn't a secret from me it
wasn't a secret from anyone. Now the fear of being reported to Children's Services is so strong, I can't imagine being as open with my kids
as he was with me.

Admiring the greenery in the backyard of our
house on Eleventh Street, 1981

Since we're talking about drugs, we might as well round out the
twin pillars of parental discomfort and talk about sex, too. I guess you
could say that my parents had an "arrangement" or "understanding"

74

when it came to their marriage. My dad had been my mom's first boy-friend, and they got married so young, neither one of them had had much opportunity to get out there in the world on their own.

As I've said before, my mom was (and is) unconventional to the core. For her part, she honestly was okay with Dad having sex with other women as long as he came home to her. From his perspective, he wanted her to be happy and didn't take it personally if she was turned on (intel-lectually, creatively, or sexually) by other men. I think it also made him feel less guilty about his own behavior if she was doing it too. In any event, he slept with a lot of women outside their marriage and she had a couple of long-term affairs. They each knew what the other person was doing and each respected the other enough to let them be who they needed to be and do who they needed to do. Although there were some "special friends" who would be around for a while and then disappear, I, rightfully, was not privy to any of these details as a kid and didn't fully understand the inner workings of their relationship until long after they had divorced.

What I was aware of, and what became an ingrained part of my own belief system, was the fluidity and acceptance of deviation when it came to social norms. This is not to say that my parents' relationship was all roses or that no one ever felt hurt or confused or angry. I am also not saying that everyone should do drugs around their children and damn the consequences. What I'm saying is this: My parents had beliefs, needs, and habits that fell outside of the generally accepted boundaries of marriage, home, and family. Because of this, they modeled behavior and set expectations around honesty and authenticity rather than blind acceptance of the Rules. I mean, let's face it, it was never going to be *Leave It to Beaver* with these two. They were who they were, warts and all, and those warts were as much a part of their parenting as anything else. I've made different choices in my own life and family, but I appreciate their example of an alternative lifestyle because it gave me an expansive view of the gray areas of life and a much wider definition of what is "okay" and "acceptable" than I ever could have had otherwise.

STRIPES
(1981)

Written by LEN BLUM, DANIEL GOLDBERG,
and HAROLD RAMIS
Directed by IVAN REITMAN

Chicago cabbie John Winger (Bill Murray) is failing at life. His response to being fired from his job and dumped by his girlfriend is to enlist in the U.S. Army with his best friend, Russell Ziskey (Harold Ramis). After they barely make it through basic training under the watchful eye of Sergeant Hulka (Warren Oates), Winger's and Ziskey's military skills are put to the test when their oddball platoon is captured and held prisoner behind enemy lines.

                    RUSSELL
        You could join a monastery.

                     JOHN
        Did you ever see a monk get wildly
        fucked by some teenage girls?

                    RUSSELL
Never.

                    JOHN
So much for the monastery.

An anarchic slob movie, a celebration of all that is
irreverent, reckless, foolhardy, undisciplined, and
occasionally scatological. It's a lot of fun.
—ROGER EBERT, *CHICAGO SUN-TIMES*

Mr. Murray hasn't yet reached the point at which his
routines can be sustained for more than 10 minutes
at a time. But he has achieved a sardonically
exaggerated calm that can be very entertaining.
—JANET MASLIN, *THE NEW YORK TIMES*

Stripes, originally written for Cheech and Chong, attracted the attention of Ivan Reitman, who had just come off directing *Meatballs*. He wanted Bill to star and figured that if he could get my dad involved, Bill would be more likely to commit to the film. According to the *New Yorker*, Ivan thought, "Harold is my secret weapon . . . Bill is this great improv player, but he needs Harold, the focused composer who understands setting a theme and the rules of orchestration. So I told Harold, 'One, I want you to co-star in my movie and two, I want you to rewrite it for two really intelligent guys—you and Bill.'" So, Dr. Jokes, as my dad was known from his *Playboy*/Second City days, agreed to get on board and turned a generic army/buddy/fish-out-of-water comedy into something more thoughtful and relatable.

Russell Ziskey is my personal favorite of all of my dad's on-screen roles, because I can really see him acting. Even though he is playing Bill's reasonable sidekick, he is clearly doing his version of "cool." Next time you watch *Stripes*, notice all that head bobbing, those sly glances, and the many small gestures and expressions that you wouldn't pick up on if you were paying attention to anything other than him. There are a lot of great performances in *Stripes* (John Candy, John Larroquette, Warren Oates) but for me, Dad steals the show. When discussing the character, he said, "I hear people describe that character as a nerd, but he wasn't a nerd at all. He was a cool guy! I got Sean Young in that movie!" That Ziskey was my dad's version of a "cool guy," and that Sean Young was such a prize back then should tell you a lot about what was going on in 1981.

Stripes was filmed in Kentucky on the Fort Knox army base, at an abandoned distillery, and in Louisville proper. I was almost four and wasn't on set as much as I had been with his other films. I do remember

Dad on the set of Stripes

Little V soaking up some love from Sean Young and P. J. Soles

spending time with "the girls," P. J. Soles and Sean Young, in the hair and makeup trailer, and I remember being devastated and hysterical the day my dad cut his hair. My dramatic response was partly because I was an obsessive "twiddler," meaning I loved to play with hair, my own and others'. My dad always had great hair—thick, soft, and lots of it. I would suck my thumb and wind my fingers into his curls, and that was all I needed in life. So when this person walked into our rented house, with my dad's face and voice but with this weird short hair, I couldn't understand it. I cried and ran from him when he tried to pick me up. Not only was I sad to lose my "security blanket," I was also terrified by how foreign he suddenly looked.

Again (surprise, surprise), there was a lot of drug use going on at the time that I wasn't aware of, but which my dad told me about later. For example: One morning, Dad, John Candy, and John Larroquette were done with hair and makeup and were all hanging out in my dad's trailer, waiting to get called to set. My dad brought out a joint and they all smoked. Then someone decided it would be a good idea to drink a bottle of cognac. So they did. They were so out of it they weren't sure if they'd be able to do their scene, so someone suggested they do some cocaine to sober up. Feeling better after that, my dad looked at his watch and it was only eight a.m. Do wah diddy diddy dum diddy do!

The success of *Stripes* kept my dad's string of hits rolling, but I don't think he felt the same ownership of it that he had with *Animal House* and *Caddyshack*. It was Ivan's movie, Bill was the star, and my dad was there, as usual, to provide the brainy straight man for Bill to play off of. In many ways, *Stripes* seems like a warm-up for *Ghostbusters*. They just needed that less cynical outlier and a more original story, both of which Dan Aykroyd provided, to push them to the next level.

MY DAD, MY HERO

Whenever I was sick as a child, my dad was the best nurse. He would hold my hair back as I threw up, murmuring reassurances while I cried. I have a very vivid memory of him, cigarette dangling from his lips, as he wiped down the bathroom walls after a particularly virulent stomach bug. Once my nausea settled, he would make me his special "socky eggs." They were really soft-boiled eggs, which I misheard as *sock*-boiled and then shortened to "socky." For a long time, I actually thought that he boiled the eggs in socks. Either way, it was yolky and delicious and always made me feel better. Incidentally, it's also good for a hangover if you can stomach the runny egg.* My mom, no Florence Nightingale but doing her best, would recycle

---

* Harold's Sick Kid Socky Eggs: Make toast. Butter the toast. Cut toast into small squares. Soft-boil 2 eggs (2–3 minutes in boiling water). Scoop out the runny eggs and mix with the toast squares until everything is nice and yolky. Add salt. Eat. Smile.

the same get-well card every time I got sick. It was a painting of a distinguished-looking black cat in bed with an ice pack on his head and a thermometer sticking out of his mouth. In it, she wrote in her sprawling, loopy script, "Hope you feel better real soon! Love, Annie."

Strangely, I don't have very many significant memories of my parents together. We lived together in a little house, 437 Eleventh Street, in Santa Monica until I was six (1983). There was a huge evergreen tree and hydrangeas in the front yard and avocado and lemon trees in the back. A rickety redwood swing set (with exposed nails) was the only real concession to childhood outside of my room. I played in the mud and ate the small, tart strawberries that grew alongside the driveway. Mom converted the garage into an art studio, and I would skip and dance around, often alone, in a fantasy world. There were three other families that made up the bulk of our family social sphere—the Shambergs, the Ruckers, and the Griecos. They all had kids around the same age and we'd get together often for barbecues, Easter egg hunts, and Fourth of July picnics.

My parents and I took vacations together and did day-to-day stuff, but I don't have a picture in my mind of the two of them together when I think "parents." They separated when I was about eight, so maybe it's because they tag-team parented me that the three of us weren't actually together very often—or maybe it's just that my dad's light burned so bright, it eclipsed pretty much everything else. Either way, the memory of them together that stands out most in my mind is of a fight.

When I was about five, my parents and I went to someone's art-themed birthday party, where the parting gifts were crayon-shaped soaps. I had an idea to try to trick someone into attempting to draw

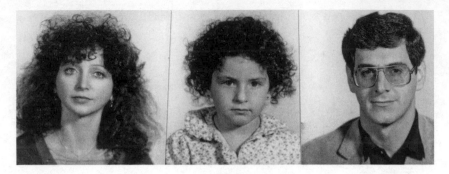

Passport photos or mug shots? 1981.

using the soaps, but I needed to cover the large "SOAP" on the label. I went into the junk drawer and cut two one-inch pieces of double-stick tape off the roll. I took the crayons to my mom with a glimmer in my eye, asking her, "Will you draw me a picture with these?"

She immediately homed in on the tape and demanded, "Where did you get this?"

"From the tape drawer," I answered tremulously, taken aback by my mom's sudden anger.

"Who said you could use this tape?"

"No one."

She demanded that I give her two dollars to replace the tape, which was about all I had in my piggy bank at the time. Whimpering, I walked into the kitchen to give her the money.

My dad, as usual, was writing at the table, with legal pads everywhere and his customary coffee and full ashtray. "What happened?" he asked.

"I used two pieces of double-stick tape and Mom got mad and said I have to give her two dollars." At this point, my mom took the money from my hand and walked out of the room. My dad told me not to cry, picked up the tape, and followed my mom into their bedroom, where he unraveled the entire roll in her face. Enraged, she charged back into the kitchen and attempted to sweep all of his papers onto the floor. He grabbed her from behind as she flailed around and I hid behind the wall, partially confused, partially terrified, and partially pleased as pie that my dad had stood up for me. My knight in shining . . . khakis? This kind of physical fight was definitely a one-off for my parents. Sure, they argued from time to time, but mostly they seemed to cut each other a lot of slack. I think this particular fight stands out so vividly for me because it was so uncharacteristically intense and seemed to come out of nowhere.

On a happier note, our semi-nomadic lifestyle brought us to New York often when I was small for a mix of business and pleasure. I remember being so excited and feeling very much like Eloise, superimposing my imaginary world over the city. We always went to Tender Buttons (an amazing store full of nothing but buttons) and "the Dead Zoo" (also known as the American Museum of Natural History). Brian and Ann McConnachie, friends of my parents from the *Lampoon* days, were a staple of the smart, funny, cool cadre of adults in my world. Brian, years ahead of his time, would greet me with "Hail to thee, computer generation!" and taught me to respond, "Hail to thee, baby boomers!" We spent a lot of time with them and their daughter, Mary, who was a few years younger than me, whenever we were in the city.

During one visit, the Ann(e)s went to see a show and Brian and my dad took Mary and me to a maze at Lincoln Center. I remember the bright primary colors of the plastic tunnels against the endless gray concrete of the plaza. Lost, and unable to find my way out of the twists and turns, I panicked, sat in a corner, and peed in my pants. Someone saw me crying and led me out. I flung myself into my dad's arms as if I had been on the brink of death. "What's wrong, baby? What happened? Did someone hurt you?" I shook my head, too embarrassed to say, and pointed to my dripping pants. I could see he was trying not be annoyed as he hugged me. "Don't worry," he said. "It happens."

"Did it ever happen to you?" I asked hopefully.

"Oh yeah!" he said. "All the time. In fact, I just bought these pants because I peed in the other ones while I was waiting for you."

"Oh, Daddy, that's not true!" I laughed. I begged him not to tell Mary or her parents. He threw my pants in the garbage, belted my little London Fog overcoat into a makeshift dress, and promised not to tell anyone.

Walking down Columbus Avenue later that evening, I was feeling like the happiest, luckiest girl in the world. I looked down and saw a ruby, glittering on the ground. I bent to pick up this precious gem and was shocked when it turned out to be the glowing ember of someone's discarded cigarette. Brian and Ann laughed at my grandiose imagination, and again, my dad was there to kiss the tears away. They remember this story as an anecdote about a quirky girl, a fish out of water in the big city. I used to joke about it with my dad as an early step in the lowering of my expectations of life. For better or worse, my dad was always my rock and I never grew out of running to him to kiss away my tears, even when the problems got more complicated than peeing in my pants.

First day of school, 1982

TICKET TO RIDE

My parents didn't give up their adventures just because they had a child. My dad always joked that I'd traveled halfway around the world before my first birthday and all the way around it by the time I was five.

They first took me to Hydra when I was just nine months old, and for the last time when I was around four. My memories of our trips are fuzzy but vivid: I remember staying in a stone house that seemed like a castle and provided an amazing backdrop for my fantasy play; eating a huge piece of spanakopita in a café and the cook coming out to pinch my cheeks and give me candy; and walking through the ruins of the ancient amphitheater at Epidaurus, where we could hear each other whispering from two hundred feet away. I wish I could remember more from that magical place and time.

The Hydra story that does stand out in my mind will not endear my dad to animal lovers, but I loved hearing him tell it because it reminded

me of the song "The Cat Came Back," where Mr. Johnson tries everything to get rid of his cat but it keeps coming back. (Think Wile E.
Coyote and the Roadrunner.)

Hydra was overrun with feral cats. They were everywhere. There
was an orange three-legged cat that would come around the house we
rented, looking for food. The cat had a very loud and irritating meow
that would wake my dad up at the crack of dawn almost every morning. "NNNGWAAAOW," he would wail as he told me the story, while
pantomiming grumpily getting out of bed to shoo the thing away, as I
dissolved into giggles. Unwilling to just accept the early wake-up call,
my dad wrapped the cat in a blanket and carried it to the other side of
the island, hoping it would find a new house to beg from. But the cat
came back.

My dad would swim in the ocean almost every day and noticed a lot
of tied-up plastic bags in the water. A local fisherman at the dock told
him that the bags were full of stray cats, so one day, after the yowling,
he wrestled the cat into a plastic bag and started walking toward the
cliffs to toss it in. The cat clawed its way out of the bag and was back the
next day. Finally, one night he and my mom were having a dinner party
and the cat showed up: "NNNGWAAAOW...NNNGWAAAOW...
NNNGWAAAOW."

"Pardon me for just one moment," my dad said, ever so politely, ex-
cusing himself from the table. Then he went outside, filled a garbage
can with water, threw the cat in, put the lid on, and went back to his
guests. He would cringe guiltily as he recounted his Final Solution but
I, weirdly, liked that side of him. Behind the sweetness, there was this
other thing—I guess what Robert Bly would call the Shadow. I think

of it as more naughty than cruel but I guess my mean streak sought validation in his. Mr. Nice Guy wasn't always so nice after all.*

WHEN I WAS FIVE YEARS OLD, my mom, my dad, and I traveled to Bali for two weeks. My mom, as always, was a real adventurer and had us traveling all over the country on crowded buses to see a certain temple or wood carver or shadow-puppet maker she had read about. Toward the end of our trip, we met up with P. J. Soles, whom Dad had acted with in *Stripes*, and her then husband, Dennis Quaid. While walking around near Ubud, we happened to encounter a large funeral procession for a local priest. There were hundreds of people in the streets,

Bali, 1982

---

* This is also why I loved his road rage and would cheer as he yelled, "You're a FUCK-ING MENACE!" out the window of his little BMW 3 Series as he sped east on the 10 freeway in LA.

carrying offerings and playing instruments. An elaborate funeral tower was carried down the street on a bamboo frame and then set on fire, and Dad put me on his shoulders so I could see better. I remember being so shocked that someone was being cremated in public.

Around the same time we were in Bali, Bill Murray also visited the Indonesian island. Dad recalled this trip in the 2004 *New Yorker* article "Comedy First":

> "One of my favorite Bill Murray stories is one about when he went to Bali. I'd spent three weeks there, mostly in the south, where the tourists are. But Bill rode a motorcycle into the interior until the sun went down and got totally lost. He goes into a village store, where they are very surprised to see an American tourist, and starts talking to them in English, going 'Wow! Nice hat! Hey, gimme that hat!'" Ramis's eyes were lighting up. "And he took the guy's hat and started imitating people, entertaining. Word gets around this hamlet that there's some crazy guy at the grocery, and he ended up doing a dumb show with the whole village sitting around laughing as he grabbed the women and tickled the kids. No worry about getting back to a hotel, no need for language, just his presence, and his charisma, and his courage. When you meet the hero, you sure know it." He smiled. "Bill loves to get lost, to throw the map out the window and drive till you have no idea where you are, just to experience something new." And you? "Oh, I'd be the one with the map. I'm the map guy. I'm the one saying to Bill, 'You know, we should get back now. They're going to be looking for us.'"

So while my dad may not have been the type to get lost in the jungle or wander aimlessly through the world, he was always game to try something new and did enough research to know how to get himself out of any sticky situation that might arise.

The memories and experiences of our early travels fill me with a sense of nostalgic longing now. Things seemed so much simpler when I was just a kid, along for the ride. I didn't have to worry about making arrangements or paying for anything or the colonialist impact of my presence in countries dependent on (and exploited by) tourism. So while I wouldn't say I have a persistent wanderlust, like my mom, I am curious about the world and happy to get in there and experience it from the comfort of a decent (and reasonably priced) hotel.

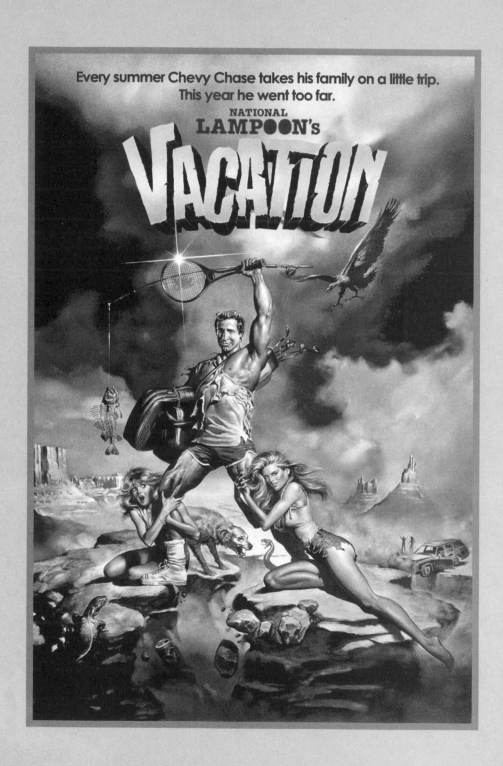

NATIONAL LAMPOON'S
VACATION
(1983)

Written by JOHN HUGHES
Directed by HAROLD RAMIS

Nothing seems to be going right when Clark Griswold (Chevy Chase) takes his family (Beverly D'Angelo, Dana Barron, and Anthony Michael Hall) on a cross-country road trip to Walley World. When Clark starts to crack under the pressure of making his wife and children happy, he becomes entranced by a beautiful woman in a red convertible and is distracted by his fantasies. As Clark's carefully planned itinerary unravels, the Griswolds are forced to deal with marital problems, car problems, the death of a family member, and one final speed bump that threatens to ruin the whole vacation.

```
            CLARK GRISWOLD
      Hey, hey, easy, kids. Everybody
      in the car. Boat leaves in two
      minutes . . . or perhaps you don't
      want to see the second-largest
```

ball of twine on the face of the
earth, which is only four short
hours away?

Despite plenty of gross-out gags and dumb slapstick bits,
the careful viewer can occasionally detect some acrid
and original satire in this 1983 film.
—DAVE KEHR, *CHICAGO TRIBUNE*

. . . confident humor and throwaway style that helps sustain
the laughs—of which there are quite a few.
—JANET MASLIN, *THE NEW YORK TIMES*

Director Harold Ramis, who went on to make *Groundhog Day*,
keeps the silliness coming at a fast and furious pace.
—JOANNA BERRY, *RADIO TIMES*

National Lampoon's Vacation was based on "Vacation '58," a story written by John Hughes that appeared in the *Lampoon* magazine. As *Lampoon* alums and fellow Chicagoans, my dad and John knew each other, but weren't really friends. Hughes's short story was focused on the experiences of the thirteen-year-old son, but my dad was more interested in the father's character, "the guy who wants to be a good dad, wants to be a good husband, but only has two weeks a year to do it." My dad is not credited as a writer on *Vacation*, but he and Chevy did a lot of work on the original Hughes script. Of that time, Chevy said, "My favorite thing about Harold was when we were rewriting 'Vacation.' I'd sit there with a yellow legal pad and he would sit and do two *New York Times* crossword puzzles. We'd agree on the basic

"She was born without a tongue, Clark."

writing and I'd say, 'Okay, I've got it,' and hand it to him. And he'd just say, 'No.' And he'd re-do it, to my chagrin. I'm doing the writing, and he's doing the puzzles, and then he'd change it, after we already agreed. It's not something that bothered me, it's just funny. It points out the looseness about him."

During the filming of *Vacation*, in 1982, my dad pulled me out of Montessori school and took me with him on location. The cast and crew traveled across the southwest United States for two months like a Gypsy caravan, covering fifteen cities in four states. My seventeen-year-old cousin Pam was my babysitter, and lucky for me, she was very irresponsible. Pam was not much older than Dana Barron and Anthony Michael Hall, and we spent hours plotting various pranks against each other. Beds were short-sheeted, notes were stashed in cereal boxes, and wet toilet paper fights were waged in motel hallways late at night. I was over-the-moon excited to be cast as Daisy Mabel, also known as the Girl Without a Tongue. I thought it was going to be my breakout role. The

Hanging out with Dad in the director's chair

truth is, I got that part specifically because there were no lines, so I didn't have to be paid or credited. Also, I was a pretty terrible actor because I totally stick my tongue out during the scene. Something in me just couldn't resist, or maybe I was worried about getting pigeonholed as that young actress without a tongue; either way, my acting failure is there on camera for all of eternity.

My dad was both proud of and a little embarrassed by *Vacation*. The (mostly) tidy narrative showed his growth as a director, but there were moments in the film I know he wasn't satisfied with. They shot a few different endings and I think it never quite pulled together the way he wanted it to. He was also genuinely distressed by the "lost in St. Louis" scene and used to cringe and apologize every time it came on. Still, Chevy and the supporting cast were fantastic and it remains, in my mind at least, the quintessential family road trip movie. Dad and I would often quote lines from *Vacation* to each other because so much of it captures the ridiculousness of family dynamics. The franchise continued without him, but I have to admit I've never seen *Christmas Vacation* or the recent reboot. Watching *Vacation* with my kids when they were young, it was as if things had come full circle. Now I'm the idiotic but (hopefully) endearing parent pointing out silly landmarks and doing everything in my power to give the kids memories to last a lifetime. Walley World, here we come!

Dad at Warner Bros. Studios during post-production, 1982

NO MORE TANGLES

Before there were American Girl dolls, there were Cabbage Patch Kids. In 1983, when I was six, all of my friends had gotten them for Christmas (which my family didn't celebrate). I begged my parents for one for weeks. My mom thought they were ugly, and neither parent was the type to jump on the latest trend, even less the type to fight the crowds at Toys "R" Us on my behalf. By the time they relented, every store in Southern California was sold out. There was no Internet then, no eBay, no Craigslist. There was only the *Recycler*, a weekly magazine of classified ads that sold everything from cars to baseball cards to "dates." I remember my dad sitting at the Formica kitchen table, chain-smoking his Vantage 100s, circling all the ads for Cabbage Patch dolls with brown hair. My mom could not have been less interested in fulfilling this "need" of mine, so my dad and I drove more than a hundred miles that weekend searching for my doll. Twice, the people had already sold their goods by the time we got there. At one of our stops in Pasadena, a guy tried to pass off a redhead as a brunette. "Well, you must be fucking colorblind!" my dad yelled at the guy as he pulled me down the driveway. We finally got lucky on a Sunday afternoon in Downey. I'll never forget the pastel floral pattern of the woman's house-dress as she placed the doll in my arms. Her birth certificate said Ava, but I called her Cara Alicia. I felt like the proudest little mama in the whole world and my dad smiled down at me and said, "You better love that goddamn doll until you die."

Because I grew up in Los Angeles, many of my childhood memories seem to take place in the car. Whenever we had something to do down-town or on the east side of LA, my dad would drive down to "the Nickel" to show me all the homeless people and junkies. Just like that super-offensive scene in *Vacation* when they take a wrong turn and end up in the "bad" part of St. Louis, and Chevy's character, Clark, says, "Ellen, it's good for them. We can't turn a blind eye to the plight of the inner city. Kids, are you noticing all this plight?"—that was my dad. "The Nickel" was the nickname for Fifth Street in downtown LA, which, at the time, looked like a cross between *The Walking Dead*, *New Jack City*, and *Slum-dog Millionaire*. One time, when I was about seven, we turned the corner and almost ran into two men in the middle of the street beating the crap out of each other. "Shit!" my dad gasped—part fascinated, part horri-fied, part terrified—as he threw the car in reverse and sped the wrong way down the one-way street until we were clear of the melee. When we would visit Chicago, he would make a detour to show me Cabrini-Green, one of the most disenfranchised and crime-ridden housing projects in the country at that time. I don't really know why he did this. Was it a voyeur thing? Was he trying to teach me about poverty and systemic rac-ism? Was he feeling nostalgic about his year of teaching in the projects? Was he somehow attuned to my interest in social justice before I even knew what it was? I never asked him directly, but I always "enjoyed" these little windows into other worlds and he seemed to, too.

Hopefully by this point it goes without saying, but my dad was great at making things fun that might otherwise have been a drag. When I would get out of the bath at night, he would transform into Mr. Charles, a flamboyantly gay hairdresser. "Well, hello, little girl! What a gorgeous head of hair you have! Would you like a side part, middle part, or should we take it straight back?" he would ask as he liberally doused my curls with No More Tangles. I hated having my hair combed. Hated it! It always knotted up overnight and by the end of the day, it would look like a rat's nest. I would cry every time my mom did it, but of course, her tactic was to say, "Keep crying! Don't stop! I'm going to get my camera!" which would usually make me stop crying immediately.

Those Jewy curls, which I have since learned to love, were endlessly trying for all of us, and even Mr. Charles had his limits. Apparently no one had ever told Mr. Charles that peanut butter could get gum out of hair, so my dad once used turpentine when I fell asleep with a mouthful of Big League Chew. I was not happy about having to sit still for two hours while he worked the gum out of my tangles with a smelly rag; he was not happy about

One of many bad hair days

You can't make this stuff up!

not being able to smoke while dousing my head in flammable solvent. Another time, Mr. Charles forgot to brush my hair for a week when I had the flu and then had to pay some nice ladies at the hair salon to spend half a day combing out my massive dreadlocks. Mr. Charles also sometimes became Mr. Schmendrick, the shoe salesman, who would inquire, in a thick Yiddish accent, "Can I interest you in a moccasin today? How about a nice Mary Jane?" I was like my dad's little doll, and he was my own personal one-man show.

Sweet as they were, these theatrics left little time or energy for some of the other concrete requirements of parenting. Like, say, feeding your kid. In a 1983 article in the *Chicago Tribune Magazine* my dad discussed our unorthodox habits. "We eat like animals. We basically stand around the refrigerator eating uncooked food. We lost the habit of sitting down together. Anne is not a housewife by any stretch of the imagination. I'll roast a piece of meat like a caveman and eat it with some Diet Pepsi.

Violet eats mainly frozen waffles and hot dogs . . . I gotta tell you, we don't bother with plates. We don't have to wash them. Anne eats chicken about six or seven nights a week. Mainly chicken and pineapple." My mom had a complicated relationship with food, so she was often on one fad diet or another and preferred to eat alone. At home, I ate mostly cold cereal, hot dogs, and anything that could be made in a toaster oven—waffles, Tater Tots, French bread pizza. My dad was always a voracious eater (even as the string bean he was in his late thirties), so if he didn't feel like making himself a steak and baked potato, we went out for Chinese food at Hunan Gardens or to McDonald's. My dad would eat a McRib, Quarter Pounder with cheese, six-piece Chicken McNuggets, and chocolate shake. I would get a Happy Meal. I know McDonald's is disgusting, but thinking about the joy on my dad's face as he slurped sweet and sour sauce out of the little white tub ("Free dessert!") still makes me smile.

Clearly, I grew up with few rules and very little structure, and it didn't just extend to meals. Bedtime? What was that? After I took a bath and Mr. Charles did my hair, my dad and I would watch TV until one or both of us started to doze. If he fell asleep first, I would finish watching whatever was on, then wake him up to tuck me in. He would put me in bed and say, "I'll be back to check on you in ten minutes."

"How many seconds is that?" I would mumble into my pillow.

"Six hundred seconds," he would say, kissing the back of my head.

"Okay." I would count dutifully but always passed out before making it to six hundred. To this day, when I can't sleep, I start counting and think about my dad, just in the next room, coming back in to check on me soon.

OUR AV CLUB

My childhood was full of singing. From Sam Cooke to Simon & Garfunkel; Ella Fitzgerald to Elton John; James Taylor; Bob Dylan; Leonard Cohen; Eric Clapton; Harry Nilsson; Peter, Paul and Mary; Sweet Honey in the Rock—you name them, my dad sang them. He had a beautiful acoustic guitar and sweet, warm singing voice. As a lifelong Beatles fan, he loved to play their songs—"In My Life," "Yesterday," "Here, There and Everywhere," and "You've Got to Hide Your Love Away" were some of his favorites. When I was very small, he would do verse after verse of "Hole in the Bucket," hysterically acting out Dear Henry's haplessness and Dear Liza's increasing frustration. Later, I would bring home songs from school or camp and he would pick them out on his guitar. "The Cowboy's Lament," depressing as it was, was on heavy rotation for years.

I used to love it when my mom and dad sang together—especially this random Czech folk song, "Stodola Pumpa," that started out very soft and sweet and then came in with a surprisingly loud and boisterous polka chorus. At six years old, I couldn't get enough, and it was nice to see them enjoy something together too, however small. I don't really know what my parents' relationship was like at this point. From where I stood, they seemed to have pretty separate lives; they had come a long way together but just didn't seem to have much overlap anymore. My mom was focused on her art and my dad on his work. This isn't to say that I was neglected, but we just didn't spend a ton of "family time" together. Singing in the car on the way to a party or friend's house was the exception.

By far, my dad's and my favorite thing to sing together had to have been *Les Misérables*. We saw the stage show several times, listened to different cast recordings (he liked Patti LuPone as Fantine; I was not as enamored), and we watched all of the anniversary specials on PBS. We always put a lot of heart into our renditions, switching back and forth between the characters, alternately laughing and crying as the story progressed. After my dad got sick, I would sing *Les Miz* to entertain him. I'd make my voice extra nasal or add in ridiculous choreography—anything to make him smile. Now I still sing it sometimes, but it mostly makes me cry. "You will live, Papa, you're going to live. It's too soon, too soon to say goodbye." "Yes, Cosette, forbid me now to die. I'll obey, I will try."

Movies were also a big part of my life from an early age. Dad and I would go to the Warehouse, our local video store, every Friday after school to rent movies for the weekend. As I'm sure you can imagine, there wasn't a lot of discussion about age-appropriateness, so I was exposed to a lot of things early on that, looking back, are hard to believe. *Midnight Express, The Elephant Man, Quest for Fire, Eating Raoul, The Dresser, Flashdance, The Cotton Club, Never Cry Wolf, After Hours,* and

Blue Velvet were all movies I'd seen, many in the theater, by the time I was ten. Violence was fine, apparently, but Dad did try to cover my eyes when Linda Hamilton's breasts popped up on-screen in *The Terminator*. Thanks, Dad, for trying to spare me the trauma!

One of my favorite early eighties movies was *Coal Miner's Daughter*, starring Sissy Spacek as Loretta Lynn. I probably watched it five times every weekend for a couple months when I was around six. Superficially, I suppose I liked that Lynn fell in love with a boy her parents didn't approve of, ran off with him, had a bunch of babies, and still became a big, glamorous star. Her abusive husband and eventual issues with addiction only made it that much more dramatic and alluring to me. I would put on my fanciest nightgown (shiny, synthetic material with an empire waist and ruffled cap sleeves) and sing my little heart out into a hairbrush in front of the full-length mirror in my parents' bedroom. My dad thought it was adorable . . . for a few weeks. Then he kindly but firmly suggested we rent something else when Friday rolled around. Reflecting on it now, I think I was comforted by Lynn's unbreakable connection to her dad. No matter how big her life got, no matter how far she strayed from home, even long after he died, in her heart, she was still just her daddy's little girl. It's not very feminist, I know, but it was true for Loretta and it's true for me, and I'll keep singing it into a hairbrush for as long as I live.

After my parents separated, my dad and I would go out, alone, once a week to dinner and a movie. I called it Divorced Dad Night. It usually involved Sizzler or good old Hunan Gardens and whatever was playing at the Aero, Wilshire, or Laemmle theater. Whether I was living with him or my mom, or switching back and forth, Divorced Dad Night was our time and I cherished it. When I was fifteen, we went to see Abel

Ferrara's *Bad Lieutenant*. You'd think that after all of the other twisted movies I'd seen, neither one of us would bat an eye, but my dad turned to me in the theater, as Harvey Keitel masturbated on a teenage girl's face, and mouthed, "I'M SO SORRY." It was one of the more awkward Divorced Dad Nights, I admit, but I didn't care. It was all part of the mess. And it wasn't all sex, drugs, and depravity. We laughed hysterically together over *Love and Death*, *Noises Off*, *Three Amigos*, *Monty Python's Life of Brian*, *Unfaithfully Yours*, *A Night at the Opera*, and other classics, too.

For better or worse, I've carried on the tradition of Wildly Inappropriate Cinema with my own kids. Some of the highlights include *21 Jump Street*, *Kill Bill*, *White Men Can't Jump*, and *Working Girl*. Now, when I suggest a movie to my daughter, she immediately asks, "Is there nudity? How many times do they show boobs?" One of my favorite movies as a kid was *The Blue Lagoon*, and when I showed it to my daughter Carina a couple years ago, I was a little shocked. How did they even get away with *making* that movie? Of course, she loved all the things about it that I had loved as a girl: children on their own, nudity, sex, and of course, childbirth. Now she's moved on to *Law & Order: Special Victims Unit*. At first, I tried to limit which episodes she would watch. "Mom!" she yells from her brother Keon's room. "Can I watch the next episode? It's about hate crimes, not rape!" "Um, okay, I guess," I stammer. "Mother of the Year," my husband jokes, mouthing, "YOU'LL BE SORRY."

Although my taste in music and movies may have changed over the years, I was always grateful to my dad for giving me such a solid foundation in both. He wasn't someone who had the radio on all the time, but there was music in him always. And he cried at every movie, no matter how corny it was. I think both of these things were important to him because he was such a balanced, reserved person in every other area of his life. So belting out "Bridge over Troubled Water," weeping through *Legally Blonde*, or growling along with Jack Nicholson in *A Few Good Men* was not just entertaining, it was my dad's emotional outlet. Despite his firsthand, nuts-and-bolts knowledge of the production process, Dad was always a sucker for the magic of movies and remained an ardent and sentimental cinephile throughout his life.

THEY'RE HERE TO SAVE THE WORLD.

BILL MURRAY   DAN AYKROYD
SIGOURNEY WEAVER

GHOSTBUSTERS

COLUMBIA PICTURES PRESENTS
AN IVAN REITMAN FILM
A BLACK RHINO/BERNIE BRILLSTEIN PRODUCTION
"GHOSTBUSTERS"
ALSO STARRING **HAROLD RAMIS**   **RICK MORANIS**
MUSIC BY **ELMER BERNSTEIN** "GHOSTBUSTERS" PERFORMED BY **RAY PARKER, JR.** PRODUCTION DESIGN BY **JOHN DE CUIR**
DIRECTOR OF PHOTOGRAPHY **LASZLO KOVACS,** A.S.C. VISUAL EFFECTS BY **RICHARD EDLUND,** A.S.C. EXECUTIVE PRODUCER **BERNIE BRILLSTEIN**
WRITTEN BY **DAN AYKROYD** AND **HAROLD RAMIS** PRODUCED AND DIRECTED BY **IVAN REITMAN**

GHOSTBUSTERS
(1984)

———

Written by DAN AYKROYD and HAROLD RAMIS
Directed by IVAN REITMAN

After being booted from their plum positions at a New York university, three paranormal scientists (Harold Ramis, Dan Aykroyd, Bill Murray) go into business as "ghostbusters," capturing and containing supernatural beings all over the city. A fourth "buster" (Ernie Hudson) joins the team as spectral activity soars and the business becomes wildly successful. While investigating a disturbance on the Upper West Side, the team discovers a gateway to another dimension, and must ultimately battle Gozer, an ancient god of destruction, to save New York City from annihilation.

```
                        EGON
          Print is dead.


                        JANINE
          That's very fascinating to me. I
          read a lot myself. Some people
```

```
think I'm too intellectual but I
think it's a fabulous way to spend
your spare time. I also play
racquetball. Do you have any
hobbies?


                    EGON
I collect spores, molds, and
fungus.
```

On balance, "Ghostbusters" is a hoot. It's Murray's picture,
and in a triumph of mind over matter, he blows away the
film's boring special effects with his one-liners.
— GENE SISKEL, *CHICAGO TRIBUNE*

This movie is an exception to the general rule that
big special effects can wreck a comedy.
— ROGER EBERT, *CHICAGO SUN-TIMES*

Whoever thought of having evil's final manifestation
take the form of a 100-ft. marshmallow deserves
the rational mind's eternal gratitude.
— RICHARD SCHICKEL, *TIME*

The original idea for *Ghostbusters* arose out of Dan Aykroyd's life-long interest in the paranormal. An early draft, intended for himself and John Belushi, opened in a future world, where Ghostbusters was an established and franchised company with paramedic-like teams all over the country. Dan's story was intergalactic and very technical, heavy on action sequences and light on character development. Ivan wanted to focus the story on the origins of the Ghostbusters and pull the action down to earth, so he brought my dad in to add structure and differentiate the three leads. Dad frequently described the three of them as the Brains, the Heart, and the Mouth—I'll let you figure out who was who. Working on a very tight schedule, my dad and Dan wrote separately and then rewrote each other, with major input from Ivan. Dan Aykroyd was always quick to acknowledge what my dad brought to the writing table. "Harold added the irony, the heart, the romance with Sigourney Weaver, and all the adult writing as well as the structure. And he knew which passes to throw to Bill, so Bill would look funny throughout," he said in the *New Yorker* in 2004.

The mood surrounding *Ghostbusters* was reminiscent of the confidence around *Animal House*. My dad recalled, "When we were doing *Ghostbusters*, Dan, Ivan and I had the feeling that this was going to be huge. People were going to love it. We had a great sense of each other and what we could contribute . . . I'm sorry if it sounds arrogant to say that it wasn't a surprise, but it's really satisfying because it didn't feel that surprising." It's odd because this confidence could easily read as egotism, and yet my dad was always such a grounded, humble person. I guess when you're part of a comedy dream team, there's no use denying it.

During the filming, my dad and I lived at the Sherry-Netherland hotel in New York City while my mom stayed in Santa Monica for most of the summer. I loved the Sherry because it was very fancy and being there made me feel like a little princess. And being in the city was endlessly fascinating to me. New York in the 1980s was very different than it is today—just map the trajectory from Basquiat to Bloomberg to de Blasio—but some things never change. The energy of the city was exciting and edgy and I loved bopping around with my babysitter, a young woman from upstate named Joey. After our mandatory hour of school-work, we would eat hot dogs and pretzels and go to a museum or to Central Park, and then go visit the set. I had been on movie sets before, but this one felt different somehow, even to six-year-old me—like they knew the movie was going to be huge, but no one wanted to jinx it by acting too cocky. There was a sense of excitement and it was an infec-tious feeling, even extending to the extras. The crowd scenes in the movie with groups of Mohawked punks, Wall Street suits, Orthodox Jews, and fancy rich ladies may seem now like caricature, but it really reflected part of what New York City was at the time: an edgy mix of cultures, classes, and lifestyles playing out their differences to the extreme.

On the day they filmed the exterior scene where the Ghostbusters run out of the New York Public Library, a crowd had gathered to watch, as usual. Bill, Dan, and my dad, dressed as Venkman, Stantz, and Spengler, came tearing through the doors and down the stairs on the first take, but a lens cap went flying off the camera Stantz wore around his neck. "Cut!" Ivan shouted, and they reset the scene, making sure that cap was on tightly. "Action!" Ivan yelled, and they came bar-reling through the doors again. This time, one of the gadgets around my dad's neck fell off and went bouncing down the steps. "Cut!" Ivan yelled again as a props person scurried to secure the piece. "Action!" he called again once everything was in place. Again, something came loose and went flying as they charged down the steps. "CUT!" Ivan said, get-ting annoyed. "Let's get it all locked down now, come on!" The props people went through everything, shaking and jostling to make sure nothing was loose. The spectators were giggling and making friendly bets that something else would fall off. I remember feeling worried

because my dad had the most gadgets and therefore the most potential to drop something, and I didn't want Ivan to be mad at him. I held my breath as he called action and crossed my fingers that everything would hold. It did. The trio made it to the bottom of the stairs with all their gear intact, and when Ivan called cut with a big smile on his face, the crowd let out a round of applause. It seemed like New Yorkers were rooting for *Ghostbusters* from the start, and I think that New York feeling is one of the things that makes the film really great. At the end of the movie, when Winston Zeddemore yells, "I LOVE THIS TOWN!" you can't help but love it too.

That feeling of being on the verge of something really cool carried back to the soundstages in LA, where they finished the shooting schedule. Even though I went back to my "normal life," I still visited the set

 often and got to see some of the iconic scenes being filmed (Dana, possessed by Zuul, floating above the bed à la *The Exorcist*; Gozer, played by a hot androgynous Yugoslavian supermodel, coming down the "crystal" staircase). The special effects team was doing some really innovative stuff and everyone seemed eager to show off their new toys. Being able to see behind the scenes may have dampened my appreciation for the movie when it actually came out, but everyone else was going nuts.* When people would ask me if I liked the movie, I would say, "It's not my favorite." I was definitely in the minority on that, but to be fair, 1984 was a great year for moves (*The Karate Kid*, *Footloose*, *Breakin'*, *Splash*, *Romancing the Stone* . . . I mean, come on!). All the boys in my third-grade class were obsessed with *Ghostbusters* and would swarm around my dad when he came to pick me up. "Egon! Egon! Can I have your autograph?" Even though he wasn't the cool guy in the movie, he was the coolest dad at school, hands down. We both loved every minute of it.

Because *Ghostbusters* was such an iconic movie, it created an enormous and passionate fan base. My dad did several Make-A-Wish visits

---

* I don't think I actually really enjoyed *Ghostbusters* until I was about fifteen and watched it at my friend J's house. All of a sudden, the jokes I was too young for in 1984 were hilarious, and those scenes I had watched them shoot over and over and over again seemed fresh and fun. I called my dad at his office when the movie ended and told him, "Okay, *Ghostbusters* was really good. I get it now." "Phew," he chuckled, "glad you finally came around."

as Egon and received ardent letters from awkward brainy people (and those who loved them) from all over the world. Even twenty years after the fact, *Ghostbusters* was the thing that my dad was most often recognized for and asked about. Whereas other people may have been frustrated by having their life's work reduced to a Twinkie, he never seemed to tire of it and proudly worked to keep the *Ghostbusters* legacy alive.

CH-CH-CH-CHANGES

In 1983, my parents decided to upgrade their lifestyle in anticipation of the success of *Ghostbusters*. They bought a new house a few blocks away from our little Eleventh Street cottage and my mom got a new car to replace her enormous Pontiac Bonneville—a boxy Volvo station wagon that she had painted in a ballet-slipper pink. For my sixth birthday, my mom decided to throw me a huge party in the new place, since it was empty and waiting to be gutted. We went wild—drawing all over the walls, smooshing potato chips into the orange shag carpet, and digging our fingers into the birthday cake. I was allowed to invite everyone in my school, and all my parents' cool friends were there. It was awesome. Eventually the house was redesigned and renovated by my mom and the wonderful architect Brian Murphy. It was a 1980s fantasyland—pink, black, and aqua tiles everywhere, carpet made to look like pink and aqua tiles, splatter-painted couch, glass brick–and–turquoise dining room with a glass table and stainless-steel chairs, green corrugated fiberglass, deco accents. Truly, it was like living through the looking glass.

Me and Mom in the Vegetable Kingdom dining area

At the time, I was going to a small (about sixty kids, K–6) private school in Santa Monica called PS1. There weren't really grade levels or report cards, and we called the teachers by their first names. I have fond but chaotic memories of PS1. When the whole school went on a camping trip to Leo Carrillo State Beach, my parents forgot to pack my pajamas, so I froze all night in my leotard, jeans, moccasins, and flimsy sleeping bag as I looked enviously at my classmates, cozy in their long johns and actual camping gear. The next day, I gathered hundreds of tiny tadpoles in a jar, excited to bring them back home and watch them turn into little frogs. Sadly, the jar wasn't closed tightly and when I opened my duffel bag to show my dad our new pets, all we found were hundreds of squished tadpoles.

I went to PS1 until what I thought was third grade but then ended up doing third grade again at Franklin Elementary, our local public school. My parents were concerned that I was falling behind and needed a more structured environment. Going from a "pluralistic school" with about sixty kids in a converted house to a public school with more than three hundred students was a big adjustment and didn't go particularly well. At eight, I didn't have the social skills to integrate myself smoothly into an established group of friends, plus, I was tall for my age with a big, unruly head of curls. Kids teased me—about my name, about my hair, about being an "early bloomer," even about my dad. What had once been an unquestionable asset was now a liability. "Hey, Purple! Hey, you big hairy mountain! Who's your dad? Kurt Rambis? Purple Rambis? No? Oh yeah, he's that other nerd." So fucking mean.* This was probably the first time that I recognized how my unusual upbringing, while enriching and entertaining, was not really giving me the tools that I needed to function in the world. It's easy to be an oddball when your whole life is like a sideshow, but try being a little bearded lady in a sea of perky blond ponytails and see how it works out for you. My dad would always tell me, "Different is good. Don't worry about what everyone else is doing," and while this seemed to be a winning formula for him, all I wanted to do was blend in and have some semblance of a normal life.

---

* Other kids definitely had it worse, but I wasn't used to the harsh(ish) reality of public school in the wealthy north side of Santa Monica. Unfortunately, this experience made me both more compassionate and more cruel. Once I had overcome the hump of being the new kid—i.e., easiest target—I still got shit from people but I wasn't the lowest on the totem pole anymore. I then turned on other vulnerable kids, and probably made some people pretty miserable over the years. Hopefully no permanent damage was done, but if you're one of the people whom I unleashed my rage on and tortured mercilessly at any point from 1984 to 1995, I'm truly sorry.

It was around this time that I first met my stepmother, Erica Mann, when she came in to interview at Ocean Pictures, the production company my dad ran with Trevor Albert and, at that point, Michael Shamberg. My dad and Michael met on their first day of college at Wash U and became fast friends. Michael was one of the founders of the TVTV (Top Value Television) collective in the 1970s and my dad collaborated with them, as an actor and a director, on a series depicting the fictional history of television for KCET. Trevor was a production assistant on *Caddyshack* and was also the man behind the gopher puppet in several scenes. He and my dad had gotten along so well, they decided to keep working together for the next twenty-five years. Ocean Pictures' first project was *Club Paradise*, and my dad needed an assistant who could do the high-intensity work of coordinating pre-production and picking me up from school.

Although Erica had worked in the film industry for several years and was very clear in her interview that she was not comfortable doing personal errands, once she got the job, she quickly realized that she was okay with adding me into the mix of her other responsibilities. "I was so adamant about the job description," she recalled. "I was at a point where I really wanted to be taken seriously and I knew that wouldn't happen if I was running around picking up dry cleaning. But then when I met you, I just couldn't help myself. I told your dad, 'I know I said no personal stuff but if you ever need me to pick Violet up or watch her, I'd be totally fine with it.'" What can I say? I was irresistible!

When Erica started at Ocean Pictures, she was twenty-nine, chain-smoked Larks, and looked like a hippie version of Katharine Hepburn. She would pick me up after school and bring me to the office to play and hang out, or to her apartment, where she would fry up chicken livers for her cat, Ming. A few times, she took me to lunch with her father and made me promise not to tell him she smoked. I liked having a secret with her and, even more, liked the power that the secret gave me. I considered spilling the beans a few times but she would catch my eye, see my impish smile, and make a funny monster face, so I just let it be.

Erica temporarily took on more of a nanny role in addition to her production duties during an extended scouting trip we took to the Caribbean while my dad and Brian Doyle-Murray were finishing the script for *Club Paradise*. We spent about three weeks on the island of Nevis, at the Nisbet Plantation Inn. It was pretty much paradise for

Erica in Jamaica, 1985

me—no school, hanging on the beach every day, and a group of local kids to play with. The manager of the hotel was a cranky old Brit who taught me to play cricket and tend bar. The local kids—Tesson, Winky, Clive, and Desiree—were a few years older than me but would come to the hotel beach after school. The hotel manager, being a classic old-school colonial-style racist, didn't like them and threatened to have his dogs chase them off the property. When he saw how horrified we were by this, he backed off and the kids were allowed to hang out with us as much as they wanted while we were there. Clive especially loved my dad and would just stand next to him, sometimes reaching out to touch the hair on his arm, but mostly just observing while Dad and Brian smoked, wrote, and made each other cry with laughter.

Erica and I had a lot of fun together during those times. She didn't have much experience with children, but I wasn't exactly a typical kid, so it worked out well. She liked my spunk and sass, and I appreciated her sweetness and easy laughter. The whole trip seemed like heaven to me but was probably not so idyllic for Erica, because as you can probably imagine, I was used to doing whatever I wanted and not always very easy to take care of. Take, for example, my attitude toward maintaining a clean space.

"Why don't you pick up your clothes and toys off the floor before we go to dinner?"

"No. I'm *not* going to."

"Violet, I'm the adult and you have to listen to me."

"No I don't. I'm gonna tell my daddy."

"You can tell him," she said, "but I think he'll agree that—"

"No," I explained, "I'm gonna tell my daddy to fire you."

And then I would run right to my dad, take hold of his hand, and smile sweetly at Erica over my shoulder as he escorted me to dinner. What a brat, right? Well, all my threats obviously backfired in a major way. They were ultimately married for twenty-five years and had two wonderful children together, so I guess I learned my lesson.

CLUB PARADISE

The vacation you'll never forget–
no matter how hard you try.

WARNER BROS. PRESENTS A MICHAEL SHAMBERG PRODUCTION A HAROLD RAMIS FILM
ROBIN WILLIAMS · PETER O'TOOLE · RICK MORANIS "CLUB PARADISE" JIMMY CLIFF · TWIGGY
ADOLPH CAESAR AND EUGENE LEVY AND JOANNA CASSIDY STARRING ANDREA MARTIN · BRIAN DOYLE-MURRAY
EXECUTIVE PRODUCER ALAN GREISMAN STORY BY ED ROBOTO & TOM LEOPOLD AND CHRIS MILLER & DAVID STANDISH
SCREENPLAY BY HAROLD RAMIS & BRIAN DOYLE-MURRAY PRODUCED BY MICHAEL SHAMBERG
PG-13 DIRECTED BY HAROLD RAMIS

CLUB PARADISE

(1986)

Written by HAROLD RAMIS and
BRIAN DOYLE-MURRAY
Directed by HAROLD RAMIS

Retired Chicago firefighter Jack Moniker (Robin Williams) takes off for the Caribbean and teams up with reggae singer Ernest Reed (Jimmy Cliff) to open a resort. As the first group of guests arrive, ready for luxurious fun in the sun, Jack scrambles, against all odds, to keep them happy. Instead of being able to kick back and enjoy the island life, Jack and Ernest have to contend not only with their unhappy customers but with civil war, as greedy land developers collude with corrupt politicians to take over the island and put Club Paradise out of business.

```
            MR. ZERBE
Ernest, I know this business . . .
a guy who just paid $32 for a bad
Veal Oscar doesn't want to know
the band is angry.
```

The movie is painless, and everybody associated with
it is good company, but considering the obvious
effort and the expense that went into it, the result
should have been much, much better.
—VINCENT CANBY, *THE NEW YORK TIMES*

A frenetically unfunny and charmless movie.
—SHEILA BENSON, *LOS ANGELES TIMES*

What's fresh about Ramis and Doyle-Murray's brand
of comedy is that they're not one-liner wordsmiths,
they're social satirists. They find humor in the
subversion of a stable social community.
—CARRIE RICKEY, *PHILADELPHIA INQUIRER*

The premise of *Club Paradise* was inspired, in part (and improbably) by Gillo Pontecorvo's 1969 film *Burn!*, starring Marlon Brando. During his newspaper days, my dad had flown to Colombia on assignment to interview Brando and write an article about the production. *Burn!* addressed issues of colonialism, political intrigue, and corporate exploitation of native people in the context of a sugar plantation on the fictional island of Queimada. My dad, still in his "institutional phase" of comedy, wanted to explore some of these same dynamics in regard to tourism in the modern-day Caribbean—sort of like *Caddyshack* but on an island and with black people—so he and Brian Doyle-Murray teamed up again to write the script. My dad told the AV Club that as they wrote, they envisioned Bill Murray and John Cleese as the leads, "with Bill as the laid-back guy and Cleese as the over-the-top guy, and we ended up with Robin Williams and Peter O'Toole, with O'Toole as the laid-back guy and Robin the over-the-top guy. The polarities shifted, and it was probably not as interesting or as solid as it might have been if Bill and Cleese were there." The rest of the ensemble cast was filled out with Jimmy Cliff, Twiggy, and some hilarious *SCTV* alums. Both my mom and Erica have silent little cameos (travel agent and bar hottie, respectively), but sadly, I didn't make it into this one.

I did, however, get to spend about three months in Port Antonio, Jamaica, during the filming of the movie. My mom came to visit for a few weeks, but I was mostly on my own there for the duration of the shoot. This didn't seem at all unusual to me at the time because I was used to being alone with my dad, and I enjoyed a rich social life on the set and at the resort where we were based. My mom was content to be at home, doing her art, and never loved hanging around the set waiting in line for my dad's attention.

Since Erica was busy doing actual production work now that filming had started, I had a new babysitter, Rachel, and the intermittent company of Robin Williams's son Zak; Twiggy's daughter, Carly; and Michael Shamberg's daughter, Caitlin. I'm sure we were expected to do a few hours of schoolwork every day, but I don't remember much work getting done. We went to the beach a lot and took trips into town to go to the markets, visit old sugar factories, and hike up to various beautiful waterfalls and caves. Some weekends we would do big group excursions to other areas, or take rafting trips down the Rio Grande, stopping along the way to eat jerk chicken from flimsy outdoor kitchen stands in the middle of nowhere.

Early on in the production, and unbeknownst to me at the time, my dad and Brian were arrested by Jamaican police for marijuana possession. "Oh, well, we were being stupid and driving around at night with

Just hanging out . . . with Peter O'Toole, 1985

a half pound of ganja in the car," my dad told me, years after the fact. "I'd heard stories about the Jamaican police so I tried to slip them some money with my license but they did not like that at all. It was bad. We were cuffed pretty quickly and taken to a cell in the local police station." After a nerve-racking few hours in jail, they were allowed to access a production folder that Erica had prepared with a list of local contacts. Number one on the list was the prime minister. Needless to say, they were released immediately. Like the movie itself, the production was a bit of a mess but lots of fun.

Club Paradise, unfortunately, flopped. My dad attributed this partly to a glut of "island movies" that came out around the same time but since none of those movies did particularly well either (anyone seen *Water* with Michael Caine? No?) I think that probably wasn't the main reason for its lukewarm reception. Don't get me wrong, *Club Paradise* was definitely underappreciated, but something about it just didn't work. Even though movie-making is a completely collaborative effort, as the captain of the ship, my dad was clearly not on his A-game. In retrospect, my dad was probably reaching burnout status in terms of drug use and was likely distracted by the impending changes in his personal life. I don't say this as an excuse, but just to provide context for the faltering of his previously spot-on comedic and commercial instincts.

THE SPLIT

After we got back from Jamaica, my dad said he had something important to talk to me about. We sat down on the pastel-colored splatter-paint-covered couch in the living room, and I nervously began picking at a stray blob of pink near my right knee. He took my hand, cleared his throat a few times, and asked, "How would you feel if your mom and I separated?"

"Fine," I answered quickly, relieved that no one had died. In my head, I remember thinking, *Finally! Now I'll have him all to myself!* I didn't know what a midlife crisis was, let alone that my dad seemed to be having one.* I understood the concept of divorce and was okay with the idea of it (or at least I thought I was), in part because I thought it

---

* I don't use the term "midlife crisis" in a flippant way. There is something developmental/existential about reaching a point—let's say turning forty—where you seriously re-evaluate the choices you've made in life and perhaps decide that this is the time to make a change. To mark this turning point for himself, my dad wrote the words "NEW LIFE" on an index card and taped it inside a kitchen cabinet.

would mean that I would get more of him without my mom there to interfere. I didn't realize that it really meant that I'd get less of him than I'd ever had before.

"I'm in love with someone else," he said. "I'm in love with Erica, and I'm not going to live here anymore."

Ohhhkay. The mini-adult me nodded, smiled, and assured my dad that I understood and was fine with what he had just told me. I could tell he was nervous and worried about me, and I didn't want to add to his stress or be seen as a "problem" that needed to be fixed, or worse, avoided. The child me had no idea how much this change would transform my life, for both the better and the worse.

Oddly, my mom was completely taken by surprise. She had been fine with their marital arrangement of low-key and respectful nonmonogamy but says now that it never occurred to her at the time that he would leave. "He was always so dependable and we had been together for so long. I didn't think it would ever change. Looking back, I guess we were more like brother and sister than husband and wife, but I was okay with that and I thought he was too." Perhaps my parents could have gone on in their patchwork way for a time, but my dad was clearly not getting what he needed from the marriage and was starting to worry that if he didn't make a change in his life, he would end up losing it to drugs, depression, or some combination of the two.

I knew a lot of other kids whose parents were divorced, and so I didn't feel any stigma around the news, but I wanted to be sure to maximize the opportunity for drama. The next day at school, I gathered my little posse in the bathroom, and cried and told them what had happened. One of my too-smart-for-her-own-good friends said, "He's leaving your mom for the secretary? Typical." I guess she read more gossip mags than I did, because at that age I had no clue what a cliché it was.

Cliché or not, Dad and Erica were crazy about each other and wasted no time settling into a semi-traditional domestic situation. I think their romance had started in Jamaica, but they always maintained that they did everything aboveboard and waited until my dad told my mom. Regardless, the transition happened quickly. Erica retained her apartment for a few years, but in reality, they moved in together right away, living in a series of hotels and efficiency suites, some nicer than others. There was the Sovereign Inn, where I slept on a squeaky cot in the living room and watched the roaches run around on the ceiling after the lights went out. Then there was the Oceana, with the daybed in the living room covered in a polyester disco print. Next up was the Shangri La, which we stayed at for about six months. Eventually they ended up renting an apartment in the Penthouse, a building that is literally stuck to the side of a cliff overlooking the Pacific Coast Highway and the Pacific Ocean. It was a cool apartment and they stayed there for about three years before buying a house in Santa Monica Canyon once my parents' divorce was finalized.*

Unlike my parents, Erica was not from the Midwest and was at the other end of the baby boomer spectrum. Born in 1955, she was raised in Santa Monica, the middle child and only daughter of Daniel and Catherine (Cate) Mann. Daniel, a lauded film director, was something of a tyrant, and Cate, an actor and artist who had grown up poor in Okla-

---

* The divorce itself was very civilized. My dad was generous and fair and my mom was not interested in cashing in, so there was no haggling over money. Same with custody. We should all be so lucky to divorce as well as they did.

New love, new look, 1987

homa, battled her own demons throughout her kids' childhoods. Erica had taken on the role of protector of her mother and younger brother, and learned early on to be finely attuned to the moods and needs of those around her. Coming of age in the late 1960s, she embraced the flower-child spirit and used to ask Cate to drive her and her best friend down Sunset Boulevard while they leaned out the windows yelling, "Peace!" and "Love!" to the hippies on the street. She had not been a wild teenager herself, but had seen enough of her friends' drug use to feel that the risks far outweighed the rewards when it came to substances. Financially abandoned by Daniel after a messy divorce, Cate and Erica lived in the Zen Center in downtown LA in the late 1970s. Downtown LA in the seventies and eighties was a far cry from the hipster haven it is now, and Erica decided that she had to find a way to make a saner and more stable life for herself. Like my mom, she had gone through this very difficult and dysfunctional childhood, but whereas my mom came out of it all edges and angles, Erica was like a soft, warm blanket . . . that wrapped itself tightly around you and tried to snuggle you to within an inch of your life.

Erica was not only completely different from my parents, but once she got together with my dad, she was unrecognizable from the fun companion she had been to me when she was getting paid to play. I think she must have read some books about step-parenting that warned not to let the children from the first wife interfere with your new relationship, because right off the bat, she had a lot of Rules and Boundaries. There were to be no secrets—meaning, I couldn't tell my dad anything without his telling her. I was no longer allowed to get in their bed if I had a bad dream (she still apologizes for this one). She was always very concerned with what was appropriate or not appropriate and did everything she could to "un-parentify" me. Having gone through several years of therapy around her own childhood, specifically the way in which the parent-child relationships had been inverted as Erica became like a mother to her own mother, she wanted to protect me from as much of that as possible and was determined that I be treated age-appropriately.

My feelings on this were mixed. On one hand, I liked having what I thought was a more traditional family structure than I was used to. *Maybe she'll bake cookies*, I remember thinking optimistically. On the other hand, I did not like being treated like a child, even though I was one, and moreover, I did not like having my relationship with my dad regulated by *her*. I couldn't believe how he just went along with everything she said. Where was my hero now?

Prioritizing his own happiness for a change, I guess. It was tough. The loss of Erica as my friend only added to my confusion and sense of betrayal. I suppose I felt abandoned by my dad and angry with him for turning my already upside-down life on its head, but since he was all I had, it was Erica who bore the brunt of my emotional upheaval. To be fair, it couldn't have been easy for her to make the transition from employee to girlfriend/stepmother, and I know we were all doing the best we could in a complicated situation.

DURING THIS TIME, I bounced back and forth between equally uncomfortable worlds as we experimented with a lot of different variations of joint custody. The first iteration was Monday with Mom; Tuesday, Wednesday, and Thursday with Dad; Friday, Saturday, and Sunday with Mom—reverse, repeat. Eventually we went to alternate weeks, then switching every two weeks, and ultimately, I would stay with one parent until I couldn't take it anymore and then move. It didn't bother me at the time but I guess, in retrospect, it was a lot to deal with. For some reason, no one thought to get me doubles of anything, so I would go to school on my Switch Fridays with a huge duffel bag filled with my clothes for the week.

Erica and my dad were happy, were in love, and had a very active social life. My mom, on the other hand, was mostly depressed and alone. One night, a few of her friends decided to throw a divorce party and someone brought a three-tiered wedding cake with a bride on top and the groom's feet sticking out from under the bottom layer. My dad, mensch that he was, even made a brief appearance at the party to toast my mom and thank her friends for their support. My parents did some joint therapy at the time, and we had a few family sessions. Erica and my mom even went together once. There weren't any knock-down drag-out fights between my mother and father, or any malicious bad-mouthing between my mom and Erica, but it was not a happy time for me or my mom. Although things were amiable between them, my mother had hoped to remain close friends with Dad and was very hurt that he rarely spent time with her or sought her out on an individual basis.

"Are you sure you don't want to get back together?" she would ask jokingly when he called—even twenty years after they'd split up.

I vacillated between feeling left behind by my dad, displaced by Erica, and stuck, alone, with my mom, who was going through her own turmoil and could not be there for me in the way I needed. Long after the fact, Dad told me that he briefly considered filing for sole custody to try to shield me from my mother's sadness and unpredictable moods, but worried, rightly, that if left completely alone, my mom would not survive the separation. So, like all children of divorce, I did the only thing I could—I adapted. I struggled to make sense of my former, now fractured, family and did my best to fit into the two new ones that had taken its place.

Because of their highly different parenting styles, there was a fair amount of code switching required by me as I traveled between the two homes. My mom let me paint my nails and wear what I wanted, while Erica forbade nail polish, dangly earrings, and any clothing she felt was too "sexy." My mom's house was very solitary—generally just the two of us, with me watching TV in the living room and her listening to the radio and painting in the kitchen. My dad and Erica, on the other hand, were much more social, and would host lively dinners and parties with lots of people. My mom was very unpredictable and I could never be sure what kind of mood she would be in or what little thing could send her into a rage (remember the double-stick tape?). Sometimes I would tread lightly around her, and sometimes I picked fights, depending on my own mood. My dad and Erica were much more stable and nurturing, but there was something oppressive about the amount of communication that was expected. (Does it look like I care how *my* messy room makes *you* feel, Erica? So what if I'd rather roll my eyes a million times than share my feelings about being forced to eat broccoli? And no, I'd rather not do a five-minute free-write about how I felt when you wouldn't let me wear a tube top to school. Thanks, though!)

True to their usual nonconformist style, my parents bought a house in Ojai together as they were separating. They got an amazing deal on the seven-acre property and historic Wallace Neff home as Ojai was just starting to emerge as a spiritual, natural, and artistic sanctuary. My mom wanted to be there as much as possible after the divorce, which meant we drove out there every weekend—listening to her eclectic mix of cassette tapes of Terence McKenna, James Brown, *Kiss of the Spider Woman*, Ram Dass, and the soundtracks to *Out of Africa* and *The Last Emperor*. My mom made this house her project and would spend hours in antique shops and flea markets while I sat in the car reading and pouting. *A Tree Grows in Brooklyn*, the Sweet Valley series, anything by Judy Blume, and those creepy V. C. Andrews novels were my go-to books, and I read them all obsessively several times. Did I mention that I spent *a lot* of time waiting in the car for my mom? She could spend hours going through boxes of doll parts or old postcards or fabrics until she found that one magical item to complete her decorating vision.

Once, trying to scare her, I lied that a policeman came to the car and asked me where my mother was. I said that I'd told him I didn't know where she was but that she was short with curly hair and bright blue Reebok high-tops. Her response to this was not "My God, maybe I should stop with the antique shopping so my daughter doesn't get kidnapped by a psycho," as I'd hoped. It was, "What do you mean 'short'? I'm taller than you!" My feisty little mama was not buying my girl-in-pink-Volvo-in-peril story at all. And truthfully, I was fine . . . But there was something about the orphan anxiety fantasy that I kept going back to during that point in my life. *What if she never comes back?* I would think. *Would I eventually walk back to Santa Monica on my own? How would I feel as a motherless child? Would people feel sorry for me? What if someone shot her while robbing the store? How would anyone know she had a child waiting for her in the car? Antique stores can be dangerous!*

Once the Ojai house was furnished, my dad and Erica also used it occasionally. They would invite friends up for the weekend and cook a big brunch and walk around the property picking wild blackberries, but they never really loved it the way my mom did. I didn't like being there because I didn't want to be away from my friends, my shows, and civilization in general, but to her credit, my mom did everything she could to try to make it fun for me. My friends were always invited, she installed a tetherball pole, and she even got a little rabbit-ear TV set that never quite worked. Still, I think I just wanted the security and consistency of "home" while she, understandably, just wanted to get away.*

---

* In 2007 they sold the Ojai house to an interior decorator, who stripped it and flipped it to Reese Witherspoon. *"Better Homes and Gardens* . . . ha!" my mom sneered as she clicked through the online gallery of the house. "Better for who? It was perfect just the way it was!"

My mom, for better or worse, has never changed. She is still the same whip-smart, quirky, confrontational, artistic, and adventurous person she always was. While this has not always made things easy in terms of our mother-daughter relationship, we've learned, over time, how to appreciate our respective strengths and weaknesses and are now very close. Still, at eight or so years old, I would have traded in her out-of-the-box brilliance for a little tender loving care any day of the week.

MYSTERY BABY

One afternoon in September of 1985, in the midst of my parents' separation and the official beginning of his relationship with Erica, my dad picked me up from school and told me we were going to visit a friend of his, Amy, at the hospital.

"Who is she?" I asked, knowing the name sounded familiar but not able to place it.

"Amy's a friend from work," he said. "She directed *Fast Times at Ridgemont High*."

"Oh yeah," I giggled, waggling my eyebrows and making kissy faces. "I liked that one. Is she sick?"

"Nope, she just had a baby."

"Oooh, can I hold it?" I asked, still enamored with all things reproductive.

"Probably not," he said. "She's brand-new and very tiny and we're just going to say hi and then leave."

"Can we go to McDonald's after?"

"Sure."

When we got to the hospital, I remember seeing Amy, pale and exhausted, looking down at me from the bed and a tiny baby sleeping in a bassinet by her side. After a couple minutes, the nurse came to take the baby to the nursery and the three of us walked down the hall together to look at the other babies in the unit. All the infants were crying, and it distressed me. "Isn't anyone coming to pick them up?" I asked my dad and Amy. "Doesn't anybody care?" There was uncomfortable silence. I was only eight, but I could tell that something weird was in the air. Amy was nice enough but did not seem particularly happy to see us, and my dad was definitely in a hurry to get out of there.

About a year later, I was snooping around in Dad and Erica's room—*The Joy of Sex* in the nightstand drawer? Check!—and, opening Erica's diary to a random page, I came across the following sentence: "We just found out that Amy Heckerling's baby is Harold's baby, too." Say *what* now? Harold's baby? *I* was Harold's baby. How could there possibly be another? Despite my shock, I didn't say anything to my dad or Erica about it. I did bring it up to my mom, however, over our respective breakfasts of Grape-Nuts with four sugar cubes (me) and half a watermelon (her) when I was ten or so. I don't know if I was compelled by genuine curiosity and a need to process or if I was just being my usual troublemaking self, but all of a sudden, I just blurted out of nowhere, "Did you know about Dad and Amy Heckerling?"

"Yes," she said carefully, "I knew. They had an affair, and she was really in love with him but then he and Erica got together and . . . why do you ask?" She looked at me unwaveringly with her clear green eyes but swallowed audibly. I remember hoping she wouldn't cry.

"Did you know they have a baby together?" I asked sharply.

"Oh . . . I thought he wasn't sure." She looked away. "He told you?"

"No, I overheard him talking to Erica about it. Don't tell him I told you."

She agreed, we both hastily dropped the subject, and I tried as best I could to put the whole thing out of my mind. For all my precociousness, I was confused by the whole situation. How could my dad have another baby but not be with it? Did that mean he wasn't really its dad? Was the baby part of our family? Why didn't he tell me it was his baby when we were at the hospital? Why did my mom seem so sad? I could have asked these questions but I didn't. I preferred being in the dark, scared of whatever the answers might reveal. I figured as long as everyone else was keeping the secret, I would too.

When I was about twelve, my mom and I went to a good friend's performance art show and party in downtown LA. As soon as we walked into the courtyard of the theater, my mom said, "Violet! Amy Heckerling is here . . . with the girl." *Oh great*, I thought, *this is the last thing I want to deal with right now*. Visiting Amy and the baby in the hospital and then talking to my mom about the situation had been enough of this Other Daughter to last me a lifetime. I was already annoyed about being at the show in the first place, and this encounter threatened to push me over the edge. "Can we leave? Please?" I moaned. "I didn't even want to come." My mom completely ignored me, too curious to care that I was not in the mood.

The girl, who was probably around five, had a mop of fiery red hair and danced around among the partygoers. I could barely look at her. "Ooh, she looks just like Harold, doesn't she?" my mom whispered conspiratorially.

"I don't know, maybe," I said sulkily.

It was true but I didn't want to accept it. My dad and I were fighting a lot during that time and here was this sweet little sprite who could just dance into his life at any time. It worried me, but I couldn't admit it. I don't know if I was also somehow ashamed of this mess he'd made, but I had emotionally distanced myself so much from the issue that it didn't sink in at all that this little girl was my half sister. I was at the height of my preteen angst and just didn't want to think about or deal with any one else's drama when I had so much of my own going on internally at all times.

After that close encounter, I managed to put this little mystery sister out of my mind for the most part. She had her life and I had mine. It seemed strange to leave such an important loose end flapping around in the breeze, but I had no control over the situation and no interest in sharing my dad with anyone else. If all of the adults in the situation were fine with ignoring it, who was I to stir the pot? Nothing to see here, just move along . . .

ONE IN THREE

Between the ages of nine and ten, I was molested by my mother's boyfriend Adam.* This was her first real relationship after she and my dad split, and it was nice to see her happy with someone. It's hard for me to say "molested" because I felt, at the time, like an instigator, maybe even a willing participant, or at the very least, a curious kid. He was fucked in the head (obviously) and "primed" me with European art books showing naked kids, articles about parents having romantic relationships with their children, and whatnot. I knew it was wrong but I didn't really care. I had always been very curious about sex and was partly caught up in the excitement of it. I was also partly scared of what would happen if anyone found out, especially since I had clearly "asked for it" by being a flirty, pubescent tween who was looking for love in all the wrong places.

I felt like I was getting a real education in the thirty minutes here

---

* Not his real name.

and there when my mom was busy or at the store. Mostly, he would tell me stories of his sexual experiences and I would partially undress while he jerked off. Occasionally, he touched me or asked me to touch him. I started to get increasingly uncomfortable with the situation but didn't know what to do. How could I just arbitrarily stop what I had started?

Finally, after witnessing a nasty fight between this douchebag and my mom, I told her. I think I actually wrote it down on a piece of paper because I couldn't bring myself to say it. *Adam wants to have sex with me.*

She immediately told my dad. The police came to interview me at school with those anatomically correct dolls so I could show them exactly what happened. We talked to the Santa Monica DA and my dad asked if I wanted to go to trial. I said no. Later, in the parking lot, he said, "Do you want me to kill him?"

"Not really," I said, relieved he didn't want to kill me.

He hugged me hard and said, "Everything is going to be okay."

Thus began years of forced psychoanalysis with a parade of oddball therapists. My mom usually took art classes in the afternoons so whatever unfortunate assistant my dad had at the time would drive me to my sessions after school. (Lin, Whitney, Dawn, Trish, and Suzanne come immediately to mind, but I'm sure there were more—thanks, ladies!) One after another, I resisted these counselors and their years of experience, their postgraduate training, their buddy-buddy approaches. Sure, I had issues, but I'd be damned if anyone could make me deal with them against my will.

First there was Barbara, whom I remember as an older woman with a slight tremor who would wear mauve skirt suits with a wispy gray/blond bun. She would start the sessions by putting out paper and markers, and I would draw page after page of dark rainclouds and small boats in the middle of rough seas. Eventually I got so tired of her frowny "I know you're hurting" face that I would just sit in sullen silence or yell nonsense at her until the clock struck five. Sorry, Babs. Then we tried Stephanie, who had kids of her own and saw clients in her home. She was probably in her late thirties, had dark curly hair, wore jeans, went barefoot, and tried to be cool. She was into play therapy so we cycled through weeks of board games and dollhouse scenarios. My favorite game was always Dungeons and Dragons (nerd alert!). One day she brought out her Batakas—basically lightweight, heavily padded baseball bats—and handed them to me, saying, "So you can get some of your anger out." I pretty much beat the shit out of her (as much as you can with a pillow on a stick) and she never suggested we play with the Batakas again.

Then there was Carol, who was part tutor, part therapist. We were supposed to work on my homework together and just talk if we felt like it. I don't remember much about her except she taught me how to make egg salad and showed me her mastectomy bra with a fake boob in it. I think I made her cry once.

I eventually found a therapist I could connect with when I was about fifteen—Dr. Paul Hyman. I was dealing with the standard hostile and rebellious teenage issues and it helped me to have a sympathetic adult I could be open with who would then reassure my parents that I was generally okay. Paul was a classical-guitar-playing MD psychiatrist who looked like a cross between Anthony Bourdain and Lurch from *The Addams Family*. Psych 101 says I liked him because he reminded me of my dad and was a perfect recipient of my transference, but I think it was because he was smart, let me smoke cigarettes on his balcony, laughed at my jokes, and never tried to bullshit me. Okay, okay, I guess he was a substitute dad in many ways, but he was a good one and we were all grateful to him.

Years later, in a five-hundred-student Intro to Feminism lecture, the professor asked everyone who had been sexually abused to stand up. Women rose up all around me, looking around the room curiously. Some were crying, some were hugging, but all were standing tall, appearing proud to be counted as survivors. I did not stand, unsure if what had happened really counted as abuse or not. The professor went on to explain that one in three women has experienced some type of sexual abuse and that she knew by looking that there were probably at least fifty more people in the auditorium (like me) who preferred not to be counted. It was in the discussion section for that class that I first entertained the idea that that asshole had done something to me that had nothing to do with my curiosity or invitation. He was a predator and I was his prey. Nothing more. Sadly, this realization was validated the following year when I was called to the Ventura County courthouse to give a deposition for a new case being brought against the same guy by a woman he had been dating who had a twelve-year-old daughter.

He had shown her the same books, given her the same articles, and done the same things. I felt horribly guilty that we hadn't gone to trial and possibly saved this other girl from being hurt, but I also felt relief. I don't think all the therapy in the world could have helped me understand the situation at the time, but once I did, I stopped blaming myself and admitted that I was not at all in control of the situation even though I thought I had been.

He was sick. I was a kid. It wasn't my fault.

A SWIFTLY TILTING PLANET

Things began to change quickly in my dad's life as he prepped for *Ghostbusters II* and began to lay the foundation for spending the rest of his life with Erica. He bought a big, beautiful house in Santa Monica Canyon, which they decorated in what came to be "their" signature style of ethnic potpourri meets modern elegant comfort. Her old friends became his new friends, and his old friends all seemed very happy for him. I can feel my dad's disapproval as I write this, but I'm going to go ahead and say that this was the time in his life when he really started to embrace the materialism and luxury that his success afforded. In my child's mind, this was a departure I had a hard time accepting, but looking back, I understand that he was really just seeking greater comfort and ease in all areas of his life. He got a new car and wanted to get Erica one as well. She was driving a truly crappy fifteen-year-old brown Honda Civic at the time but said she could not accept a car from him unless they were married. Soon after, he took me shopping with him to pick out her new car/engagement present and excitedly planned out exactly how he would propose. When the car arrived a couple weeks later, he put it in the garage with a big red bow on it and after dinner asked her to come outside to take a look at something. As soon as she saw the car, she knew what it meant and started crying. He got down on one knee and said, "Erica, I'm so in love with you. I've never been happier than I am with you. Will you marry me?" She said yes and fell into his arms, and I inched my way out of the garage and up to my room with a mixture of excitement, relief, and resignation.

Then the wedding planning began and with it, many trips to Beverly Hills, where they registered for fine china, silver, and crystal at Gump's. "Two hundred dollars for a spoon?" I asked, incredulous. My mom's kitchen was filled with plastic plates from the 1970s and a toaster oven that she received as a wedding gift in 1967. "Why do you need this stuff?"

"These are special things for special occasions," they said, as if that explained anything.

I couldn't wrap my mind around it but was along for the ride and enjoyed looking at all the little tchotchkes and lovely things that seemed like they belonged in a museum—not in our living room.

I was still shuttling back and forth between my mom's and dad's houses during this preteen period and could never seem to get comfortable at either place as I struggled to synthesize all of the changes going on, deal with the aftermath of the situation with my abuser, and ride the waves of my own hormonal and developmental shifts. My mom vacillated between giving me almost total freedom and being relentlessly demanding of my time and energy. My dad and I started having little fights here and there, and with Erica in the mix, soon everything became a battle: I left my room a mess, argued belligerently about what I was and wasn't allowed to do, and, honestly, tried to make things as generally unpleasant for them as I could, without being so awful they would tell me to get lost. Erica and I still had great moments together, but things between us were becoming increasingly contentious and I began digging psychological trenches for what was shaping up to be a long and drawn-out war, with my dad running interference between sides. As the reality of my dad's new life with Erica seemed to draw more sharply into focus with the upcoming wedding, my own identity and place in the family continued to blur.

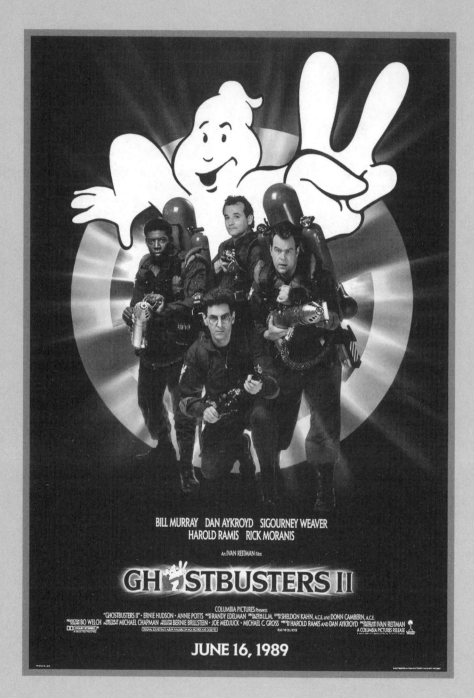

GHOSTBUSTERS II
(1989)

Written by DAN AYKROYD and HAROLD RAMIS
Directed by IVAN REITMAN

Five years after saving New York City from supernatural destruction, the Ghostbusters (Bill Murray, Dan Aykroyd, Ernie Hudson, and Harold Ramis) have returned to battle a new spiritual villain—Vigo the Carpathian, a medieval tyrant who is preparing to make his own comeback by feeding on the negative energy of New York until he can take physical form in Dana Barrett's (Sigourney Weaver) baby, Oscar.

> PETER
> Let's suck in the guts, guys. We're
> the Ghostbusters.

The film gets by on the sheer good-naturedness Reitman is
able to place in all of his efforts, though it doesn't seem likely
to inspire the same level of affection as the original. Innocence
is one quality that can never quite be recaptured.
—DAVE KEHR, *CHICAGO TRIBUNE*

Jumbo budget and the same talent notwithstanding, the
element of surprise is missing. And ghostbusters, it seems,
need that every bit as much as their targets.
—MIKE CLARK, *USA TODAY*

Here, the comedy breathes, and the illusion that it's not a
factory-assembled product (which it most certainly is) is a
nifty one. For a major studio blockbuster, the thing is darned
chummy, and above all, that rare, modest thing, a good show.
—HAL HINSON, *WASHINGTON POST*

G*hostbusters II* came out in 1989, when I was twelve, and the circus of publicity and excitement started all over again. I was old enough by that point to have read several drafts of the script, and was happy that the Egon character got a little more love in the sequel than he had in the first film. As much as my dad was interested in my thoughts on the *GB II* screenplay, I was really not his target audience, and I told him so. "I think you need a teenage boy to read this," I said.

"I am a teenage boy, Violet," he chuckled. "Just tell me everything you think is funny or if something doesn't make sense or if you get bored, okay?" He watched me as I read, eagerly asking, "What? Where are you?" every time I laughed, looked up, moved, or breathed audibly.

"Relax, Daddy. It's good. Funny. Scourge of Carpathia—hahaha. Can I keep reading?" He was trying to walk the fine line between making the sequel different and interesting enough to set it apart, and maintaining the things that people loved about the original.

As usual, my dad was most excited by the Big Ideas behind the film, and he was happy to be back together with Ivan and the rest of the cast. In the writing of the film, he wanted to tap into the idea of negative human energy accumulating in urban areas and, basically, coming back to bite people in the ass. I believe there is a shot in *GB II* of a fur coat attacking its owner on Fifth Avenue, but my dad's initial fantasy for the film went even further. He told Brett Martin for *GQ* in 2009, "I wanted the Statue of Liberty to be inhabited by the evil spirit, so that they'd have to destroy it. My image—how socialist is this—was that the Statue of Liberty ends up lying on Wall Street with her skirt up over her knees. A Marxist comedy!" While it didn't end up being quite the political statement he envisioned, he was satisfied that the sequel remained true to the original and still had something more to say than the average action comedy.

Artistic integrity aside, I was just happy that I got to meet Bobby Brown. Even though I had been around actors and famous people my whole life, I remember being *so* nervous to meet him on set.

"I can't, I can't," I told my dad.

"Why not? You weren't nervous when you met James Taylor, right?"

"Yeah, but, Dad, Bobby Brown is *cool*."

"Oh yeah, of course. Well then, just pretend he's like any other person you ever met . . . because he is."

Bobby Brown!

And he was. Pre-crack Bobby seemed like a regular, super-good-looking, talented, and successful guy. He was sweet, but clearly more interested in his entourage than in the blushing, gushing twelve-year-old daughter of Egon. He hugged me, posed for a quick photo, and then disappeared in a sea of tracksuits.

On release, the movie was far less successful than the original *Ghostbusters* and the reviews were mixed. Some critics called it lazy and mechanical, others said it was actually better than the original. There was another round of toys and merchandising, but a lot of kids seemed to have moved on to Batman, Ninja Turtles, Game Boys, and the new Sega Genesis by that point. The die-hard fans of the original film still turned out and in the end, everyone was happy enough, but the lightning-bolt popularity that characterized the 1984 film just wasn't there.

HAROLD AND ERICA, HUSBAND AND WIFE

Harold and Erica got married on May 7, 1989, at a beautiful property in Malibu overlooking the ocean. It was pretty much picture-perfect. The happy couple shone brightly, clearly in love and ready to take the plunge. The interfaith ceremony covered all the bases of their respective spiritual and ethnic backgrounds (a rabbi, a Buddhist monk, and a Native American ceremonial drummer walk into a bar . . .) but the drinks flowed freely and the mood was light. My uncle Steven was the best man and I was the maid of honor. I wore a lacy pink dress with dyed-to-match low-heeled pumps as I stood near the chuppah, holding Erica's bouquet of calla lilies while they read their vows. There were probably three hundred guests, including Erica's family and friends, my dad's whole family from Chicago, his college friends, industry people, and a few celebrities (Bill and Brian Murray, Sigourney Weaver, Robin Williams), but it wasn't a flashy, star-studded *Us* magazine centerfold by any means. In full late-eighties yuppie glory, Dad and Erica worked their way through the crowd schmoozing as guests nibbled Wolfgang Puck–ish pizzas, sushi, and tacos from little kiosks scattered around the great lawn. Later, a DJ played the Beatles, the Rolling Stones, funky soul oldies, and the obligatory "Hot Hot Hot," while people got (very) loose on the dance floor.

Meanwhile, I snuck champagne from behind the bar and ran around with the other teens, making an overly enthusiastic toast for the videographer and pretending that this was the happiest day of my life too. My mom had been invited . . . then uninvited, as Dad and Erica worried that her presence might make people (including me and them) uncomfortable, and I dreaded going home to her when it was all over. She didn't say or do anything to make me feel guilty but I did anyway. I knew how much she loved my dad and how hard it must have been for her to lose him again, in a way, as he committed his life to Erica in front of many of their mutual friends.

I hadn't been particularly anxious leading up to the wedding, but looking back, I realize this is a protective strategy I still use to this day. Even in the face of major changes, or perhaps especially in the face of major changes, I do my best not to stress in advance. My dad's positive outlook and the privilege of my life have allowed me to assume that things will work out for the best. If, for whatever reason, they don't, you deal with it, but there's no point in making yourself crazy over something that may or may not happen. In this case, Dad and Erica were already so solidly together that I didn't think that much would change once they tied the knot. I was right . . . wrong. My dad had stayed unhappily married to my mom for more than fifteen years. Now it was clear that my dad was not only happy but completely committed to a new life with Erica. I suppose that I had pushed aside my feelings of loss, abandonment, and displacement in order to be "a good sport" but as the happy couple flew to Paris to officially kick off their new life together, I mourned the official end of my own honeymoon with Dad.

TERRIBLE TWEENS

My tween years were not particularly kind to me. For sixth grade, I went to Lincoln Middle School in Santa Monica and had one of the hardest and most confusing years of my life. I had been branded a "slut" in elementary school because I had big boobs and, yes, I was curious about sex. Back then, instead of "hooking up," we called it "scamming" or "getting together," and while I had scammed with a few boys, I had nowhere near as much sexual experience as everyone thought I had. It was like a self-fulfilling prophecy, because the more attention I got around my sexuality (negative or positive), the more I experimented with using that power. I started to drift from many of the friends I'd made in elementary school but found that all of the girls who didn't already know me hated me. Then someone started calling me the Happy Hooker and it was like my fate was sealed. I got threatened daily and beat up semi-regularly by small groups of Latinas with carefully sculpted gravity-defying bangs, who were mad that I had been "talking to" their boyfriends. If only they knew how much I envied their toughness and wanted to be like them. If only I had been more self-aware around the effects that being molested was having on my developing sexuality and self-esteem. If only the movement against slut-shaming had been active then, I might have felt empowered to say, "Hey! I'm just experimenting, and aren't we all? Give me some time to figure this shit out before you decide to hate me or not but until then, how about a little love?" If only.

Instead, I started going to the nurse's office every day to avoid lunch period and my afternoon classes. I faked fevers, stomachaches, and fainting spells, and even slammed my own arm in a door so I wouldn't have to face the girls who despised me or the boys who both wanted me and told me I was ugly, dirty, or nasty. I was too scared to use the bathroom at school so I wouldn't go all day. Once, I couldn't hold it anymore and peed in my seat in class during last period. Thankfully, no one noticed (sorry, janitor!) and I just tied my jacket around my waist once everyone had left and ran to the car of whoever was picking me up to take me to my dad's. A few other times, I would practically run the five blocks home to my mom's house, only to fumble with my keys and pee in my pants on the doorstep. Pathetic, right? I didn't talk to my parents about what was going on, again, because I figured I'd brought it on myself and didn't want them to know how bad it really was. Ultimately, someone told the guidance counselor that I had birth control pills in my backpack. It was, in fact, just my retainer case, but my parents were called in for a "What to do about Violet?" meeting (not the last, I'm sorry to say).

The summer after sixth grade, while I was at camp, my mom, my dad, and Erica got together and decided to pull me out of Lincoln and send me to private school. I was furious. I had been miserable at

Lincoln but in my eyes, it was *my* problem, not theirs, and I wanted to deal with it in my own way.

"You can't do this!" I screamed. "Don't I have any say in my own life?"

"Most of the time, yes. But not on this one." My dad held firm. "We've spoken to an educational consultant and I'll go with you to meet with her tomorrow."

"I'm not going. You can't make me."

"Violet, you told your mom that one of the girls you fought with had a razor blade hidden in her bangs. That's terrifying for us and it can't feel very good for you either."

"Well," I began, not wanting to admit he had a point, "it should still be my decision."

"Well," he said with a bite, beginning to lose his temper, "it isn't, so get over it!"

"This is so unfair! It's total bullshit! I'll never forgive you for this!" I ranted as I ran upstairs and tore up a photo of my dad and me hugging on the beach in Carmel. I can now (grudgingly) concede that it was probably the right decision to take me out of Lincoln, but it felt awful at the time.

The next day, the consultant laid out some options, and we went home to discuss. Erica really pushed for Windward, a seventh-through-twelfth-grade independent school with about 250 students that was known at the time for being artsy. She had gone to high school there when there were only fifty students and felt it would be a good fit for me. There were other kids of actors and artists, and the teachers were a mix of creative eccentrics and enthusiastic nerds. My mom was okay with this because she trusted my dad and was also at a loss about what to do with me.

So we decided I would go to Windward, but it wasn't a cure-all by any means—there were a couple of boys who knew people from Lincoln, heard about my reputation, and teased me cruelly, plus I developed an inappropriate relationship with a young male teacher*—*but* without being scared for my safety, and in an environment where I didn't feel I had quite so much to prove, I had a little more psychic space to breathe and grow. This allowed me to reengage with my education, push boundaries in more positive ways, and make some great friends, without whom I would not have survived the next five years.

Even though Windward provided me with a better structure than I'd had before, I still rebelled in my own ways. It was around this time that I started smoking cigarettes for real. When my dad and Erica smoked, I would sneak one here and there—mostly just to watch myself in the mirror—but once I started hanging out with the "cool" older kids at Windward, I started buying my own packs. My friends and I would spend hours in Burger King, Zucky's, or Fatburger, just endlessly smoking our Camel Lights or Marlboro Reds, talking, laughing, and feeling like we would live forever. I tried to hide it for a while—even going so far as to blame my stinky, smoky clothing on the drama

---

* No, the teacher and I did not have sex. There were a lot of long late-night phone calls and some pretty amazing and intense letter writing, but the most that ever happened physically was one very awkward kiss. Eventually I got bored and stopped taking his calls and he took up with a classmate of mine, who told her parents what was going on, prompting them (understandably) to call the school and demand immediate action, ultimately resulting in his being fired.

teacher—but no one was buying it and I eventually just 'fessed up. My dad, who had started smoking as a young adolescent, didn't have much to say. Erica and my mother didn't like it but they accepted it. I think they were just relieved to have me out of trouble at Lincoln. This was the kind of trouble they could relate to, at least.

In 1990, when I was thirteen, my brother Julian was born, which took some of the pressure off me at home but also reinforced Erica's need for order and control. I loved babies, so I was happy to hang out and coochie-coo with him, and I didn't feel any kind of resentment or sibling rivalry. It all seemed to fit in with the new life my dad was creating, which, to me, may have looked like an endless episode of *Thirtysomething*, but to him provided the stability and comfort he'd been seeking.

My dad took some time off from moviemaking and he, Erica, and baby Julian basically just stayed in bed, cocooning, for two years. At this point I was going back and forth weekly between homes and still experiencing a kind of culture shock every Friday when I made the switch. My mom and I gave each other a pretty wide berth but at my dad's, it felt like there was nowhere to hide. Dad may have been the man of the house, but it was Erica who ran the home (including everyone in it). She set the rules and expectations, and he backed her up. I don't mean to vilify her, really. We all have our issues, and I do believe that her need to control me came (mostly) from a genuine love and concern about my well-being. But I was the first kid she had to deal with and I was no shrinking violet. I chafed under her ever-expanding list of rules: no Westwood, no Venice, no beach at night, and (the worst) they had to talk to a parent before I could go to anyone's house. She assumed that everyone was on drugs all the time, was "concerned" about anyone who wouldn't make eye contact with her, and had very strong opinions on what was and wasn't "appropriate" (her favorite word).

I had tried pot a few times by this point but it wasn't a habit, yet. Still, as soon as I walked in the door, she would be in my face, with a knowing look in her eye.

"Are you stoned?" she would ask. "Your eyes are red."

"No," I would answer honestly, so paranoid about her invasive welcome-home evaluation that I didn't dare give her anything to catch me with. "It's from my contacts."

"Something is going on with you, Violetti. I can always tell."

"Do we have to do this every time I come home?"

"Well, if you would just communicate with me, then I wouldn't have to ask so many questions."

"Well, maybe if you stopped asking so many questions, I would communicate more! God!"

Classic teenage Catch-22, right? My dad used to say, "Trust is something every teenager wants and something that no parent in their right mind can give." Still, he was never the one interrogating me. I don't deny that he was concerned about me, or that there were reasons to be concerned, but he was just not a helicopter parent by nature, and if he'd been left to his own devices, I know we wouldn't have gone through anywhere near as many power struggles as we did.*

Luckily, I had some close friends I could also go to for escape. One of these friends was Ethan. We met in seventh grade through a mutual

---

* Years later, watching similar scenarios play out with my brothers, he acknowledged that he favored a more "hands-off" approach but felt that he had to support Erica as the primary parent. "Happy wife, happy life?" I asked. He smiled wryly and said, "That's the goal."

friend and hit it off right away. He was a smart, funny, shy little skater boy who taught me about good hip-hop, didn't make me feel bad for being a busty oversexed mess, and never let attraction get in the way of our friendship. There was a whole awesome group of guys like this, but I was closest to Ethan. In my mind, it was like Dorothy Parker and the Vicious Circle but with pot, baggy pants, and baseball caps.

Unfortunately, the only part that my dad and Erica seemed to see back then was the baggy pants and the tops of the baseball caps, as the boys avoided all contact (eye or otherwise) with my comparatively square parents. My dad would try to cajole them out of their resistance by saying dumb/funny things like, "Hey, guys, nice pants. How many people can you fit in there? I'd be happy to recommend a good tailor if you're interested." Or, once when I was playing music in the car as he drove a group of us somewhere, "Did he just say 'Too Short baby, all in them guts'? Nice. Great song. Really dopey, right, guys?"

"Dad, it's dope, not dopey, and you can stop."

"Stop what?" he said cheerfully. "I'm just talking to the guys about my friend Mr. Short."

"Dad!" I said through gritted teeth while my friends snickered in the backseat.

"Oh all right, Violet, I'll stop. But remember what Mr. Short said, 'Big butts, not big mouths,' okay?"

And the boys died laughing, while I pretended to die from embarrassment. What I was really thinking was, *Yes! Why can't you just be a dork like this all the time?* It was a nice change of pace from the dutiful-husband-and-concerned-father role he had taken on in his new life.

My mom was always more than happy to provide a reprieve from the restrictions of Dad's house. She was "cooler" because she did her own thing and didn't insist that my friends talk to her. If my mom wasn't gardening, she was parked in the kitchen with her art supplies and her radio blasting opera or KPFK, largely oblivious to anything else going on in the house. I could do whatever I wanted in my room and she was okay with it. My walls were covered with my friends' tags and graffiti and there were overflowing ashtrays everywhere. It was this time where my two homes really could not have felt more different. I appreciated different things about each of them but had a really hard time navigating the extremes. Why couldn't I have had the warm, nurturing environment *and* the freedom to do what I wanted? Why couldn't there have been some comfort and consistency to balance out the aesthetic and emotional envelope-pushing? It was a lot to deal with, so I did what most teenage girls do: focused on boys and friends and pretty much tried not to care about anything else.

Me and Julian, après swim, 1992

GROUNDHOG DAY
(1993)

<hr />

Written by DANNY RUBIN and HAROLD RAMIS
Directed by HAROLD RAMIS

Self-centered weatherman Phil Connors (Bill Murray) is on assignment in Punxsutawney, covering the annual Groundhog Day festivities. When the town is hit by an unexpected blizzard, Phil finds himself caught in a metaphysical timewarp that has him reliving the same day over and over again, and learning how to be a decent human being along the way.

```
            PHIL
You want a prediction about the
weather, you're asking the wrong
Phil. I'll give you a winter
prediction: it's gonna be cold,
it's gonna be gray, and it's gonna
last you for the rest of your life.
```

There were a lot of ways for this film to go stupid;
it succumbs to none of them.
—LOUIS BLACK, *AUSTIN CHRONICLE*

For once, the audience isn't forced to surrender
its intelligence (or its healthy cynicism) to
embrace the film's sunny resolution.
—HAL HINSON, *WASHINGTON POST*

"Groundhog Day" may not be the funniest collaboration
between Bill Murray and director Harold Ramis . . . Yet this
gentle, small-scale effort is easily the most endearing film of
both men's careers, a sweet and amusing surprise package.
—KENNETH TURAN, *LOS ANGELES TIMES*

Groundhog Day is probably the most widely loved and respected film of my father's career. It makes every list of great movies and was embraced by religious and spiritual leaders of all stripes. He was so proud of and delighted by its reception by these communities. He told the AV Club in 1999, "People of every religion and spiritual discipline wrote me, saying, 'This movie expresses the philosophy of yoga better than any movie ever,' or the philosophy of Zen Buddhism. Jesuits were writing me, rabbis were preaching sermons on the High Holy Days about it, psychoanalysts were saying the movie is about psychoanalysis. So everyone got it, you know? It's interesting that everyone tended to think that they got it exclusively. The Buddhists would say, 'Well, no one else would understand it, but this is really a Buddhist movie. You must be one of us.'" *Groundhog Day* was the only film of my dad's to be recognized in any way by the film establishment, too—it won a British Academy Film Award for its screenplay.

I was lucky to be able to read many drafts of the script, including Danny Rubin's original, which opened with the story already in motion, with Phil punching Ned Ryerson in the face, then explaining why it happened via voice-over. My dad initially loved how the story began in media res, but then went back and changed it because he felt the more abrupt start would limit the audience's investment in the characters. Danny and my dad also went back and forth about explaining why the repetition was happening—Gypsy curse? Glitch in the space-time continuum?—but ultimately decided to leave it a mystery. Good choice, guys!

Groundhog Day was filmed, on location, in the town of Woodstock, Illinois, which stood in for Punxsutawney, Pennsylvania. I was fourteen during the production and visited the set with my friend Lauren for about a week. My dad joked at the time that the people of Woodstock were so happy to be featured in the film, he probably could have run for mayor (and won) if he'd wanted. In spring of 2016, the town's local movie theater, Classic Cinemas, hosted a three-day Harold Ramis film festival and showed many of his films in the . . . Harold Ramis Auditorium.

As has been widely documented, *Groundhog Day* was the film that broke the friendship between my dad and Bill Murray. Bill was going through a difficult time in his personal life, and he and my dad were not seeing eye to eye on the tone of the film. They had a few arguments on set, including one in which my dad uncharacteristically lost his temper, grabbed Bill by the collar, and shoved him up against a wall. Eventually, Bill just completely shut my dad out . . . for the next twenty-plus years.

My dad did his best to be diplomatic about the whole thing and tried not to take it personally, but it bothered him. He described feeling variously heartbroken, confused, and yet unsurprised by the rejection, explaining, "Bill would give you his kidney if you needed it, but he wouldn't necessarily return your phone calls." Some people hypothesized that Bill may have been resentful of my dad's influence on his career or wondered if my dad had offended or betrayed Bill in some way, but truly, the root of his decision remains a mystery to this day.

"I've had many dreams about him, that we're friends again," my dad said in the 2009 AV Club interview before he got sick. "There was a great reunion feeling in those dreams. Bill was a strong man. [John] Belushi had that before, too. He was a rock for us. You'd do a movie with Bill, a big comedy in those early days, just knowing he could save the day no matter how bad the script was, that we'd find something through improvisation. That was our alliance, kind of, our big bond. I could help him be the best and most funny Bill Murray he could be, and I think he appreciated that then. I don't know where that went, but it's there on film. So whatever happens between us in the future, at least we have those expressions." Privately, he was only slightly less generous about the estrangement. "I've reached out. He won't respond. What can I do? Make myself crazy? Not worth it," he told me.

I was more bothered on his behalf. "Curse him out! Send him a big box of shit! Something! He's a jerk, Daddy. What could you possibly have done to deserve fifteen years of the silent treatment? It's fucking disrespectful and cruel."

"I love your loyalty, my baby, but it's fine. I watched him turn on people before for virtually no reason. Maybe it was only a matter of time." Honestly, it still pisses me off, but what can I do, make myself crazy? Not worth it.

Bill, to his credit, eventually did come around toward the end of my dad's illness. In classic Bill fashion, he showed up at the house, unannounced, at seven a.m., with a police escort and a dozen dough-nuts. My dad wasn't able to talk much by that point, so they didn't get into the nitty-gritty of what happened or go back and rehash any of the old stuff, but they spent a couple hours together, laughed a little, and made their peace.

I've reached out to Bill a few times since my dad's death but, apart from one brief text message, haven't gotten a response. In my fantasy, he tells me he's sorry for shutting my dad and me out of his life and offers to "be there" for me in whatever way I need. In reality, I know this is an impossible ask, so I guess I'm stuck with my own unresolved feelings until he resolves them or I die, whichever comes first.

SO YOU WANNA BE
A GANGSTA?

I went through several awkward stages in my teens—hippie, goth, artsy, raver, gangster, girlfriend. Some of it was purely ornamental—purple hair, a tattoo, combat boots and baby-doll dresses, enormous baggy pants, Aqua Net hair spray for days, and some very heavy lip liner—but other aspects of my rebellion and search for identity ran deeper.

When I was fifteen, I was in love with the son of one of my teachers. Let's call him Oscar. I had a steady boyfriend at the time who was a wonderful guy, but I was inexorably drawn to Oscar—a bad boy lite with a twinkle in his eye and a way with words. So I cheated on my boyfriend with Oscar, and we had a secret and exciting relationship that went on for a few months. Oscar was going through his own adolescent-boy-without-a-father stuff and had recently been "jumped in" to a gang. My friend Lauren and I would sneak out of my mom's house late at night and take cabs to Culver City to go to parties with Oscar and his friends. It was fun and nothing really bad happened, but it could have easily gone another way. There were alcohol and guns and boys with big chips on their shoulders, and it all seemed a million miles away from my own privileged yet unsatisfying life.

Our affair was destined to flame out, though, and one day, Oscar stopped calling me back. About a week later, he was shot and critically injured by a rival gang. I was devastated and concerned for him, but also still so hurt by his rejection. My parents, understandably, flipped out. My mom had met Oscar a few times and knew I was head over heels for him. She may have been worried about the circumstances, but compassion was her primary response to the whole situation. I really appreciated her gentle and nonjudgmental approach, especially since, as a result of the shooting, my boyfriend had found out about my cheating and all of his friends were angry with me and were very vocal about it. In a school of two hundred people, there's really nowhere to hide when the tide turns against you. As was my unfortunate pattern, I took everyone's negativity and criticism in and turned it into fuel for my own anger toward others.

Instead of being "scared straight," after the shooting, I grew increasingly more fascinated and infatuated with gang life in LA. I guess I just had no idea who I was or wanted to be. I had all of this rage, but I didn't know why. I was privileged but didn't feel it. It was like Little Orphan Annie in reverse—I had Daddy Warbucks, but I wanted the hard-knock life. After several years of therapy, I think I understand it a little better. On an emotional level, I wasn't able to deal with my own feelings—about my mother's depression, about my parents' divorce, about being molested. I was sad but didn't want to be vulnerable, so I got angry instead. But then there was nowhere to put the anger because my family was largely supportive and my issues just felt insignificant in the big picture. So I sought out people and situations that seemed to justify these feelings—poor people had a right to be sad and people of color had a right to be angry. I aligned with these groups in order to validate myself, and that somehow made sense in my adolescent mind. Not to mention that there was a cultural moment happening in music and film that celebrated, or at the very least romanticized, the strength and power of the bonds within these communities, along with the rage and hopelessness that so many were experiencing.

I LEFT WINDWARD AFTER ninth grade and went to Concord, an even smaller private school for kids who had been kicked out of or couldn't hack it in the more respectable private schools. The administration at Windward was tired of dealing with my behavior (cutting class, arguing with teachers, dressing provocatively, etc.) and I had basically checked out of most of my coursework. At the time, Concord had about sixty students and was housed in an office building at Pico and Cloverfield. There were no extracurricular activities (unless you count smoking cigarettes in the parking lot) and the teachers were used to dealing with "difficult" kids. Still, the academics were rigorous and the small class sizes meant that everyone got a lot of attention. It was there that I met Selena,* who was in the school on scholarship and had the life I thought I wanted. Looking back, it's embarrassing the way I fetishized her poverty, her toughness, her "Mexican-ness," even the recent death of her brother, who had been killed in a neighborhood shooting. But in spite of my awkwardness, we became close friends. She would do my hair (sprayed to the heavens) and makeup (thick black eyeliner, blood-red lips, long curved cherry-colored acrylic talons), and together we would

---

* Not her real name.

go to the cemetery to put flowers on her brother's grave before we drove to Hollywood to "cruise the boulevard" or to Alhambra, a neighborhood in East LA, to meet boys. From the outside, we were in some pretty risky situations—two sixteen-year-old girls, driving all over Los Angeles in an unreliable car, alone in unfamiliar neighborhoods with guys we didn't know, our parents having no idea what we were doing—but everything turned out fine, miraculously. Selena had strict rules about what we could and couldn't "do" with these guys and for whatever reasons, none of them ever pushed it. My parents weren't in love with my new best friend or my new look, but they didn't try to forbid me to see her. There was no phone at her apartment and her mother didn't speak much English anyway, so I would bring my giant, cinder-block size cell phone with me, check in once, and then do whatever I wanted. Sadly, my friendship with Selena ended when she left the school, unexpectedly, in the middle of tenth grade. We kept in touch for a few weeks but eventually stopped talking altogether. I don't know if she was tired of me, or if I was ready to move on, or if, without the commonality of school, there just wasn't enough holding us together, but I have thought of her often over the years, and hope that life has been good to her.

When I was sixteen, my reckless behavior caught up with me, and I got pregnant by a twenty-one-year-old sleazeball. I can't even remember now where I met him or what I liked about him. Eddie* was Italian but looked Latino and affectionately called everyone the N-word. He was minimally employed, lived with his girlfriend and one-year-old baby, and treated me like shit. (I know it's awful. Believe me, I'm cringing as I write this.) We were "together" (in the loosest sense of the word) for

---

* Not his real name.

about four months. I was working at the TCBY frozen yogurt shop on Montana Avenue at the time and I knew something was wrong almost immediately when I almost puked into someone's hot fudge brownie sundae. I had been on birth control pills but I wasn't great about taking them consistently. I had fantasized about being pregnant and having a baby since I was practically a baby myself, but this was not at all how I'd pictured it. I told my close friends right away but wouldn't have been able to hide it anyway since I was throwing up all morning at school. They would leave class to go get me ginger ale and saltine crackers and covered for me with the teachers by saying that a stomach bug was going around. In a school of only sixty students, there was actually another girl at school who, I found out through the grapevine, was pregnant at the same time. She and I were not friends but we would smile weakly at each other on our way to lunch with our respective crews. I toyed with the idea of having the baby but knew that Eddie was bad news and couldn't imagine having to deal with him for the rest of my life. I was planning to go to Planned Parenthood and "take care of it" without telling anyone but I made the mistake of disclosing the situation to one of my brother's babysitters and she threatened to out me if I didn't come clean. It wasn't that I was afraid or thought my parents would be mad; it was more that I was embarrassed, didn't want to deal with the fallout of their "concern," and just wanted it all to go away with as little fuss as possible.

The night before the babysitter's deadline, I gave myself a pep talk in the mirror. "Just do it. What's the worst that can happen? They're not going to be mad. You got yourself into this shit and now you have to go through them to get out of it. Just go, now!" I walked into the living room, where my dad and Erica were sitting watching TV. They both looked up at me expectantly as I leaned against the door frame. "I have to tell you something," I said, then froze and started crying.

"You're pregnant?" my dad asked gently as he walked over to me and guided me back to the couch. I nodded through my tears and let him hold me while I sobbed. "Everything is going to be okay, baby. We're going to take care of it and we're going to take care of you." Before I could even say "shmashmortion," Erica was on the phone with my doctor, scheduling the appointment. Both my mom and Erica had terminated pregnancies in the past so there was no stigma, no shaming, and no question of what my "choice" would be.

Dad drove me to the appointment a week later. I knew I was doing the right thing but I still cried bitterly. It wasn't that I wanted to be a mom at sixteen, but there was a small, defiant part of me that thought, *I could do it*. This was also the first real, palpable consequence from my irresponsibility, and I felt like this poor (peanut-size) baby was paying the price for my carelessness. As I waited for the anesthesia to wear off, I hummed Sinéad O'Connor's "Three Babies" and hoped that I would get another chance to be a mom someday. After it was all over, I walked silently with my dad to his car and then sobbed into his shoulder as he drove. He made comforting sounds, patted my leg, and stopped to buy me a giant box of maxi pads on the way home. He expressed no judgment (even if he was feeling it), just comforted and reassured me. I vowed to myself that day that I would never be so irresponsible with birth control again.

In many ways, this signaled the end of my teenage rebellion. If I wasn't actually going to be a teenage mom with a gangster boyfriend, what the fuck was I doing? I needed to find a way to accept myself and my life for what it actually was, while still staying true to the people and things I cared about.

PASS THE PIPE

Long before he was giving Seth Rogen his fatherly pearls of wisdom in *Knocked Up*, my dad was giving me his bottom-line advice about drugs—"no powders, no pills"—and for the most part, I listened. He often said that he felt like his most important role as a parent was to get me through high school without a disease or addiction. Given the pervasiveness of both of those things among adolescents, and my unplanned pregnancy, it turns out this was a pretty solid goal.

Because I had been exposed to so much as a kid, there was no way he could take a "drugs are bad" approach. Instead, he would tell me honestly, "Look, drugs make you feel really, really good—the first time you do them. After that, you'll try to take more and more just to get that feeling back but you never will. If you're lucky, you'll quit. If you don't quit, you'll probably die. You already know lots of my friends are dead because of drugs, and they were smart, talented, successful guys, with their whole lives ahead of them, so . . . just please be careful." Although he had quit all drugs when he got together with Erica as part of his New Life, I'm glad to say that he never really lost his stoner sensibility.

Without turning this into Cheech and Chong's Guide to Parenting, I will say that many of my favorite stories about my dad involve drugs. Once, in his early twenties, he and a friend bought a "lid" of grass and were driving around smoking joints. A police car pulled up behind them and flashed the lights, and Dad's friend told him to eat the weed so they wouldn't get caught. I'm not really sure how much a "lid" is but I guess it was a lot, because he said he was stuffing his face with pot, trying to get rid of it all, and when the cop approached the car, my dad smiled up at him with a mouthful of marijuana. "Hello, officer," he said, with seeds and stems basically falling out of his mouth. He was beyond relieved that they didn't get arrested but did not enjoy the crippling high that lasted for the next two days.

Or there was the time in college when he had a term paper due the next day so he took a bunch of speed and stayed up all night filling the little blue composition books with what he thought was a brilliant essay, only to get an F and realize, when it was handed back, that it was completely illegible and made absolutely no sense. Or when he dropped two tabs of acid before a New York–to–LA flight in the seventies and was listening to classical music on the headset when suddenly there was all this turbulence and dinner trays went flying and stewardesses were falling down in the aisles and he wasn't sure if it was real or part of the trip, so he just kept his headphones on and tried to go with it.

One time when he was visiting Hydra in the seventies, my dad had gotten high with some friends and gone to a movie with a walnut-size ball of hash in his pocket. Halfway through the movie, police started walking up and down the aisles. *Oh shit*, my dad thought. *They can't be looking for me, can they?* His friends were like, "Just be cool," but his heart was pounding in his chest. All of a sudden, the movie stopped and the house lights came on. *Oh God!* he thought. *I can't go to prison!* There were always stories floating around their group about this or that guy who'd been caught with drugs and gone to jail in some very scary place. He was starting to sweat and feel woozy so he ducked out one of the exits, certain that the cops would be right behind him. *I can't go to prison. I can't go to prison. I can't go to prison*, he repeated in his head as he tried to walk casually toward the cliffs, looking over his shoulder every other step. He got to the cliffs, took the hash out of his pocket, and threw it as hard as he could over the edge. "As soon as it left my hand, all my fear evaporated instantly," he said. "*You idiot!* I thought. *No one is after you!* And then I thought, *I wonder if I could climb down this cliff.*"

"Then what did you do, Daddy?" I asked.

"Went looking to buy more hash, of course," he laughed. "I joke now, but it seemed so real at the time . . . which is a great example of the fact that people on drugs do a lot of dumb shit. Oh well, live and learn." Even though it was not exactly his intention, this story, combined with gallons of Visine, always saved me from the unnecessary paranoia that seemed to afflict so many potheads. Good looking out, Dad!

Part cautionary tales, part joyful reminiscences, these stories capture something important about my dad and his equanimity. He wasn't afraid to push the limits, but he always kept one foot firmly on familiar ground. In a 1983 interview with ONTV he said, "[Drugs are] really just a symbol of the expectation that you can have everything in life, that you can be totally euphoric all the time. Part of growing up is realizing that there's no way you can feel great all the time. It just doesn't happen, and every high has a hangover that comes with it."

When my dad and Erica got together, he was still smoking a lot of grass and doing cocaine semi-regularly, mostly at parties. She didn't do drugs and didn't think they were doing him any good. The way he told it, they were at a party together, people started cutting up lines, and Erica said, "I'm going to do some."

"Why?" he asked. "You don't like it and it's not good for you."

"Well, it's not good for you either, and if you're doing it, then so am I."

"Okay, I won't either then," he said, and never did hard drugs for the rest of his life. That was that.

I wasn't much of an adolescent drinker or "partier," so we basically had a deal when I was in high school that as long as I kept my grades up, my parents wouldn't bother me about smoking weed. They were still suspicious of my behavior, though, as evidenced by the mayhem that broke out when I was sixteen and stupidly took one of my grandmother's insulin syringes to play with. I know that sounds ridiculous, but I swear to God it's true. The cleaning lady found it and told my parents, and all hell broke loose. Suddenly everyone thought I was a junkie and I had to go for weekly drug tests. "I'm not going to stop smoking," I told my dad. "We had a deal."

"I know," he said. "And I know you want me to trust you, but I just can't. I love you too much and it's too scary."

So I would drive to my doctor's office every Monday and pee in a cup, and on Wednesday, I would get the report from my dad: "Okay, no opiates, but your THC levels were very high this week. Are you smoking right before you go in or what?"

"Sometimes," I replied casually. "But I got an A on my chemistry test." That was me—rebel with a conscience. I actually liked school at that point and got along well with my teachers at my new high school.

They were used to dealing with all kinds of fucked-up kids and my issues were nothing new. My friends and I were largely "motivated stoners" and despite being high pretty much all day throughout high school, we still graduated, went to college, and are largely functioning, productive adults. Go figure.

One spring day during my senior year after eight a.m. physics, Ethan and I had an hour break before our next class. We drove to get coffee, then came back to the school parking lot to smoke a joint. As we were pulling into the lot, Ethan said, "Isn't that your dad's car?"

"No," I said, "I'm pretty sure he's out of town." So we smoked and were sitting in the car listening to music (probably Del the Funky Homosapien or Steel Pulse) and Ethan looked in the side-view mirror.

"Your dad is not out of town. He's walking toward the car right now."

I jumped out of the car and a big cloud of smoke puffed out behind me. My dad hugged me, laughed, and said, "I can't believe you're getting high at nine in the morning. I'm going to go now. I dropped some papers off for you inside. I love you."

As I got back into the car, blushing and beaming, Ethan asked if everything was okay. "Yeah," I said, "he's cool."

"Then you should have asked him to join us! I want to get high with Harold. Oh well. Maybe some other time."

Many years later, my dad and I finally did get stoned together. I thought it would be weird, but it was actually not at all. We smoked, we laughed, we talked Big Ideas, we snacked, we smoked some more. It was great. He and Seth Rogen had gotten high together after *Knocked Up* and Seth said, in his taped message for my dad's memorial, that it was like a dream come true (and that my dad still owed him money for the weed). My younger (half) brothers, not having experienced my dad's drug use firsthand, were kept in the dark about it throughout their childhoods and adolescence.

When Tad Friend's article "Comedy First" came out in the *New Yorker* in 2004, the boys were fourteen and ten, and I was given strict instructions not to discuss the article or show it to them. I guess the concern was that it would seem hypocritical to forbid them from doing drugs if Dad appeared to be celebrating his own drug use. Raised at opposite ends of the spectrum—total openness vs. total secrecy—none of us have developed serious addictions or problems related to drugs, which is obviously the most important thing. But the second-most important thing is that I got to get high with my dad, which was awesome.

YOU GO YOUR WAY,
I'LL GO MINE

The birth of my brothers—Julian in 1990, and Daniel in 1994—bookended the worst of my rebellious teen years. I was living with my dad at least part-time for most of Julian's childhood, but by the time Daniel came along, I was pretty much out of their house for good. It wasn't that they didn't want me; I didn't want to be there. Part of it was that I never really felt that I fit into their world and was tired of being the black sheep. Their lifestyle was so different from what I'd grown up with, and frankly, it made me uncomfortable. The vagabond caravan and eclectic assemblage of my early childhood had been replaced by luxury cars and Power Rangers parties and even though I was no Cinderella by any means, I couldn't help but feel left behind by these changes.

My dad also took on some interesting hobbies in his New Life. He got interested in Robert Bly and the men's movement, and for a while he held a weekly group called the Roadkill Council of Men that met in the garage for African drumming, ritual craft making, and spiritual

Me and Dad with the boys, 1995

affirmation. I found it partly hilarious and partly mortifying, but my dad took it very seriously and every Wednesday, these very earnest, middle-aged, chino and sneaker-wearing white guys would chant and drum their hearts out amid the shelves of tools and extra toilet paper, and then come in after for lemon squares and Perrier. It still makes me laugh, actually, but if that's what it took to fulfill their primal urge to connect with each other, who am I to judge?

After the mess I'd gone through with Eddie, I started thinking more seriously about my own primal urge to connect and what kind of relationship I might like to have. These questions were answered right around my seventeenth birthday when I met a great guy, Diego Jones,* and settled down with him for the next five years. When Diego and I got together, I moved back to my mom's house permanently, needing

---

* Not his real name.

more privacy and fewer rules than were possible at Dad and Erica's. Soon after, Diego essentially moved in with us, although he kept a room at his parents' house (it was more of a shed in the backyard, really), which he used for band practice and beat-making. Diego was a mix of crazy and super traditional, which was exactly what I needed at the time. He was romantic and sweet and creative and funny but also liked to drink Colt 45 and get in fights. He was half black and half Mexican, played guitar in a heavy metal band, and knew every word to every Nat King Cole song. His parents, Dr. and Mrs. Jones, were both physicians who ran a clinic primarily for undocumented Latinos out of their home. Dr. Jones was an amazing and hard man who had lived an amazing and hard life. Diego was the youngest of five children and they all adored their father despite how cruel he could be with them. "Hey, asshole, how's that white Jewish bitch of yours?" Dr. Jones would call out from the clinic when we came in the house; that was on a good day. Mrs. Jones was the sweetest, most loving woman, who once stuck a suppository up my ass after I had vomited for twelve hours straight from the flu. Needless to say, this was the moment when I really felt I had been accepted as part of the family.

Diego and I spent a lot of time with his siblings and nephews, and he grew very close with my family, too. My mom loved Diego and enjoyed having him live with us. He got along with her in a way that I could not—he was endlessly patient as she showed him old movies, took him to art galleries, or held him captive in the kitchen listening to Ralph Nader on the radio. She didn't much care what we did as long as we kept her posted about where we were and when we'd be back. She even let Diego get a dog, bringing the household total of dogs to four—a motley little crew of two cocker spaniels and two German shepherds that would bark their heads off any time someone rang the doorbell.

I imagine that many fathers would not be happy about their under-age daughters being in any serious relationship, let alone one with a tattooed, non-college-attending rock musician of another race, but thankfully, in this case, my dad was not like many fathers. He saw that I was happy and didn't let the rough exterior prevent him from develop-ing a warm and close relationship with Diego. Dad really took an inter-est in supporting his music and education, and they would make each other laugh hysterically with their mutual enjoyment and mastery of the art of passing gas. While there's no doubt that my dad and Erica genuinely loved Diego, I think they were also relieved that my life had turned a corner and felt grateful that I had found someone stable and positive. Our relationship was pretty damn wholesome, from my per-spective: We made art for each other and took his nephews to Disney-land; I would do my homework while he practiced with the band. We even got tattoos of each other's names. This is not to say that he and I didn't do our share of dumb things together—getting in fistfights with random people who "disrespected" us, going on car chases through Hollywood, eating magic mushrooms and seeing *Natural Born Killers*— but we took care of each other in a very loving way and provided each other with the kind of home base we both needed. Whereas before, I was just kind of ambling around, trying things out and attempting to "find myself," this relationship gave me an identity that no one could mess with. I was part of a team now, and we were a pretty kick-ass duo if I do say so myself.

STUART SAVES HIS FAMILY (1995)

Written by AL FRANKEN

Directed by HAROLD RAMIS

Twelve-step enthusiast and self-help personality Stuart Smalley (Al Franken) struggles to follow his own advice as he deals with his dysfunctional family and their issues of emotional abuse, alcoholism, and co-dependency. A comedy.

> STUART
> You're good enough. You're smart
> enough. And, doggone it, people
> like you!

The idea [for the movie] came from someone with no S.N.L. connection, though he'd worked with several alumni: Harold Ramis. As Franken remembers it, the director of *Caddyshack* and *National Lampoon's Vacation* read the *Daily Affirmations* book that was published in the fall of 1992, then contacted Franken about the possibility of turning it into a film. Michaels

signed off and lent his support, but, Franken said, "It was
really done on the West Coast. It was Harold's baby . . . I think
Lorne trusted Harold, and I think Lorne really liked the movie."
—ERIC D. SNIDER, *VANITY FAIR*

The beauty of "Stuart Saves His Family," written by Franken
and directed by Harold Ramis, is that it's somehow true to
Stuart at the same time it sees the humor in him. You'd think
he might become obnoxious at feature length, but he becomes
more likable, especially because of his unforgiving self-
criticism ("Listen to me! I'm shoulding all over myself!"). The
movie is also unobtrusively wise about the real nature of
the problems in Stuart's family, and doesn't offer easy
solutions or a phony happy ending. I not only enjoyed
Stuart Smalley, doggone it, I liked him, and that
attitude of gratitude ain't just a platitude.
—ROGER EBERT, *CHICAGO SUN-TIMES*

In the summer of 1994, I worked as a production assistant on *Stuart
Saves His Family*. *Stuart* was a spin-off of the *SNL* character Stuart
Smalley, a formerly obese asexual self-help addict who had a show on
the public access channel and ended every episode with the line "Remember, you're good enough, you're smart enough, and doggone it,
people like you." My dad rewrote Al's original script but was not credited as a writer.*

During the making of *Stuart*, Dad and Erica were expecting their

---

* The Writers Guild of America (WGA) states that a director/writer has to contribute
more than 50 percent of the writing to an original screenplay in order to be credited.

second child and she and I were not getting along. I was living with my mom full-time and Dad figured my working on the set would give us a good chance to spend some quality time together . . . twelve hours a day, for three months. Whether I sucked at the PA gig or they just expected very little from me, it's hard to know. Either way, it was better than dishing out fro-yo at TCBY, because I basically got paid to hang out with my dad and a bunch of other awesome people, smoke cigarettes, and gain ten pounds eating Bit-O-Honey at the craft service table.

Oddly, I was probably more starstruck by the actors in *Stuart* than in any other of my dad's movies. Apart from Al Franken, who had been a part of such a great *SNL* cast over the previous five years, my friends and I were obsessed with the movie *Scarface* at the time, so getting to bring Harris Yulin bottles of water was like a dream come true. Throw in Vincent D'Onofrio, whom I loved from *Full Metal Jacket* (and *Adventures in Babysitting*—shhh), Laura San Giacomo from *Pretty Woman*, and Lewis Arquette—unbelievable mensch and father to Rosanna and Patricia—and I was genuinely in awe.

Although I did have a line in the film ("Stuart, phone!"), being on the set made me realize I was not interested in following in my dad's footsteps. The Hollywood life simply did not fit in with my worldview and I lacked the blind self-confidence that seemed essential to most of the aspiring actors and filmmakers I knew. Also—and this may sound ridiculous—I have a "lazy eye," which I assumed would prevent me from ever being successful as an actor. Rather than facing the inevitable rejection, I just decided that the entertainment biz was not for me.

It was great to watch my dad in action on a movie set, though. Directing really brought out all of his best qualities—his creativity, humor, intelligence, organization, leadership, and compassion were ever present. He knew everybody's name on the crew and made sure to keep the shooting days short so people could still have some semblance of a life outside of the typically grueling production schedule. Everyone appreciated his approach and often said that his sets were the most pleasant work environments they'd ever experienced.

Stuart Saves His Family did not do well at the box office and was largely panned by critics. Some friends of mine even confessed that they'd walked out of a free test screening—thanks a lot, guys! I guess dramedies about twelve-step programs and dysfunctional families weren't "in" yet. My dad said in an interview with the *Believer* in 2006, "It had some painful stuff in it. When we showed it to focus groups, some of them actually said, 'If I want to see a dysfunctional family, I'll stay home.'"

Although Al hadn't made the leap to politics yet, he was friends with the Clintons, and we all got to go to Washington, DC, for a special screening in the White House theater. Hillary said she loved the film, so I guess even then she was a little out of touch with the wider audience. In any case, my dad really loved this movie, and having watched it recently with my kids, I think it holds up. Putting the Stuart Smalley character and twelve-step context aside, it's well written, full of heartfelt and genuine performances, and tells an important story about moving beyond family trauma, building healthy relationships, and learning to love yourself. If you haven't seen it, do yourself a favor—grab a pound cake and a box of tissues, curl up on the couch, press play, and let the healing begin!

White House screening, 1995

YOUR WALLS WILL NOT
PROTECT YOU

When I was a senior in high school, my dad and brothers were robbed at gunpoint in their Brentwood home. Erica was out to dinner and my dad was asleep in bed with both boys. Julian was about four at the time and Daniel was just a baby. Two young guys, reportedly Crips, had followed one of the neighbors' Mercedes home, intending to rob them, but were thwarted by a speedy automatic gate. They reported later that they had no idea where they were and decided to look for another house. My dad's house was dark and there was a big wall around it, and while there was an alarm system, it wasn't on. They hopped the wall, found an open door, and went inside. My dad said he was half-asleep when he heard a loud click. He opened his eyes, saw a gun pointed at his head, put his hands up, and slowly got out of bed. As the mattress shifted, four-year-old Julian woke up.

"Who are those guys?" Julian asked sleepily.

"Oh, they're just here to get something and then they're going to leave," my dad said calmly. "Put your head down and go back to sleep."

"Where are your guns? And where is your safe?" the guys demanded.

"We don't have any guns but I'll give you everything else. Please. My kids. I'm not looking at you. I'll give you whatever you want."

He went on to give them several expensive watches and all of his cash and credit cards. As they were arguing about what to do next, the phone rang. It was Erica calling to let my dad know she was on her way home.

"Okay!" he said in an unnaturally bright voice. "Thanks for the info. Just keep doing what you're doing."

"Harold, what's wrong?" she asked.

"Oh, nothing! You're doing great. There's no hurry."

"Harold! What's going on?!" She was panicking, imagining that something terrible had happened to one of the boys. "Is everything okay?"

"Oh, not really."

"Is there someone in the house?"

"Yep."

"Should I call the police?"

"Yeah, that would be great! Okay, bye!"

By the time the police came, the guys were long gone. They were caught later that night after pointing their guns at a cop car parked near their neighborhood in South Central LA. As the police chased them, they started throwing my dad's credit cards out the window. The next morning, after he told me the story, I cried, knowing how easily it could have gone badly and how close I'd come to losing him and my brothers. We joked later that he should have offered them some of his pricey sculptures and paintings, but he said he had a feeling they were not art lovers. Through the whole ordeal, he maintained amazing compassion for the robbers. He said they were basically just kids themselves, and as scared as he was in the moment, he had a sense that they had been touched by the sight of him curled up with the boys and knew they didn't want to hurt him.

Except for a quick item in one gossip mag, the story did not get picked up. Maybe now, in the age of the relentless twenty-four-hour news cycle, it would have, or maybe my dad was never really that kind of celebrity. He used to say he was "just the right amount of famous," meaning he was known enough to get a good table at a restaurant but not so well-known that he couldn't fly under the radar. He was also a vocal supporter of gun control and didn't want his experience turned into propaganda for armed self-defense. In any case, this was an incident he was more than happy to leave quietly behind him. Even though I wasn't living with him anymore, there was no doubt that my dad was the most important person in my life and the close call of the robbery was like an admonition from the universe—*Hey! Anything can happen at any moment, so don't waste time fighting the people you love. Just love them.*

CONCORD CLASS OF 1995

As my high school years drew to a close, my relationships with all of my parents were in a relatively good place. Erica and I were still hot and cold—light and sweet one minute, oppressive and intolerable the next—and my mom was still her unpredictable and challenging self, but it was much better with both of them than it had been in years prior. Though our conflicts had never been *that* serious, my dad and I had let go of whatever tension we had, reinstated our old Divorced Dad Night, and tried to make the most of our last few months of living in the same city before I went off to college.

My dad and I were both asked to speak at my high school graduation, along with my pal Ethan and his dad, Reverend Jim Conn. Jim made a great speech that day about Jonah and the whale, in which he encouraged everyone to go out into the world and get swallowed up by something. My dad loved Jim's speech and quoted it often over the years. "It doesn't really matter what you do," he'd say. "Just get out there and get into it—anything! Get passionate! Get in that whale!" Ethan mumbled something about how much he was looking forward to going to college and how our high school experience had prepared him well for a life of creativity and critical thinking. I spoke about what I thought would appeal to the students, parents, and school—finding balance after the tumult of adolescence and how Concord had offered me an environment that was the perfect mix of challenging and nurturing, structured and flexible, rigorous and relaxed. I think it was good, but who knows? My dad, of course, knocked it out of the park. Below is his speech from that day.

CONCORD COMMENCEMENT
June 12, 1995

Thank you _____. I'm very happy to be here and very, very proud of my wonderful daughter. When Sonya asked me to speak here I had no idea what I'd say, but I started thinking back on the last four years and wondered if most of the families here today didn't have the same experience. I once heard it said that God made teenagers so parents wouldn't feel bad when their kids finally left home. Violet was about thirteen at the time and I laughed when I heard it, but by the time she turned fourteen, I stopped laughing. She'd always had a mind of her own, but now it was getting ridiculous. She was rude, disrespectful, hostile, and rebellious. She questioned every decision, challenged every rule. She knew everything, I knew nothing. It was almost impossible to have a conversation without one or both of us getting hurt or angry. I felt like I was being tested every day. "I want a tattoo." "I want to get my nose pierced." "You don't trust me." "Who says you have to finish high school? Not everyone's like you, you know." One battle after another. (Don't worry. I asked her if I could talk about these things and she said it was okay.)

I remember she once told me, "I want to paint my room black." "You can't paint your room black." "Why not, it's my room." "Don't you think a black room might be a little gloomy?" I asked her. She rolled her eyes. "Dad, kids are into gloom." Boy, was she ever.

Then a wise friend told me there were three keys to getting along with teenagers. One, don't be punitive: "Do what I say or you're staying in for the next 147 weekends," or whatever. Two, don't be judgmental: "You're not wearing that to school, you look like Madonna," etc. Three, don't be moralistic: "So I suppose if everyone else jumped off a cliff, you would too?" I thought, if I can't be punitive, judgmental, or moralistic, what have I got left?

Then I started to realize that what I had left was my deep, abiding love for my daughter. My concern for her health, her safety and her well-being. My desire to see her grow and learn and flourish. My wish that she would find something to do in life that she loved, and then have the opportunity and good fortune to earn a living at it. That she would be socially responsible, helpful, concerned and productive. That she would form warm, caring, wholesome relationships with people she respected, who respected her.

From that point on I backed off, maybe not far enough for Violet, but as far as I could. I tried not to be critical, I started to trust her for better or worse. I tried to focus on feelings and wishes, mine and hers, and little by little, things started to get better. We didn't agree on everything, we still don't, but I think the war ended some time ago and we've enjoyed a couple of years of relative peace. It's fun again.

Mark Twain said something like, "When I was fourteen, I realized my father didn't know anything. Then when I turned eighteen I was amazed how much he'd learned in four years." I think Violet is getting to that point. She actually asks me for advice now—she even takes it sometimes.

So what advice would I give her now? I'd say to her what I want to say to all of you graduating today. I remember a study done many years ago. A group of little kids were surveyed about what they wanted to be when they grew up. You can imagine the responses— cowboy, astronaut, ballerina, fireman, pilot, professional athlete, movie star, the usual dreams we all have as kids. Then they asked the same children the same question when they were seventeen or eighteen. Now the answers were lawyer, doctor, MBA—much more practical, and certainly useful, but I hope you all keep in mind that we still need cowboys and ballerinas. Somebody's got to do it and it could be you. I guess I'm saying if you have a dream, give it a try. You might just make it.

I'm not going to tell you that you're the hope of the future or that it's up to you to save the world. That's up to all of us. But I think you have to do good wherever and whenever you can.

And get educated. It might happen in a college or university, but the important thing is to keep learning. Can't get enough of that at any age.

And of course, just do it, go for the gold, be all that you can be, but remember, as the Zen poet said, "The miracle is not to walk on water. The miracle is to walk on the earth."

So let me conclude by returning to that statement I heard five years ago. That God made teenagers so parents wouldn't feel bad when their kids left home. Now I know—it isn't funny and it isn't true. I love my teenager, and, as proud and happy for her as I am, I hate to see her go.

Good luck and God bless you all.

After the ceremony, Dad and Erica took me, Diego, my mom, and a few close family friends to lunch at the Regent Beverly Wilshire. We toasted graceful endings and new beginnings and all breathed a collective sigh of relief that we'd emerged, intact, on the other side of some very tough years.

MULTIPLICITY
(1996)

Written by CHRIS MILLER, MARY HALE,
LOWELL GANZ, and BABALOO MANDEL
Directed by HAROLD RAMIS

There just isn't enough time in the day for overworked and over-whelmed Doug Kinney (Michael Keaton), a busy husband and father who is struggling to make it all work. When a scientist offers a quick fix to his problems through cloning, Doug finds himself finally getting the free time he wants, but in danger of losing the things that are most important to him.

>   DOUG
> I feel guilty for not spending
> enough time with my family. Then I
> get resentful because I don't have
> enough time for myself. Work is
> first, my family is a close second
> and I'm a distant third.

More Kafkaesque than comedic, more fascinating
to watch than out-and-out funny.
—KENNETH TURAN, *LOS ANGELES TIMES*

Director Harold Ramis had more serious ambitions.
"Multiplicity" should have been another "Groundhog Day,"
which Ramis also directed, but he comes up short.
—MICK LASALLE, *SAN FRANCISCO CHRONICLE*

"Multiplicity" took a one-joke premise—Michael Keaton
clones himself and wackiness ensues—and made it into
a winning story that deftly juggles humor, elaborate
special effects and a surprisingly thoughtful look at
the challenges of balancing work and family.
—PETER SOBCZYNSKI, ROGEREBERT.COM

As my dad settled into his fifties, he got deeper into his study of psychology and the exploration of what it meant to be a (straight, white, moneyed) man. On the surface, he appeared to fulfill the roles of his own hyphenated life with relative ease, cheerfully and seamlessly switching back and forth between his roles as actor, writer, director, husband, father, and son. Internally, he was feeling the pressure of balancing personal, professional, and societal expectations. "Real men are supposed to be Casanovas and seduce as many women as they can, but at the same time, a real man is faithful to his wife and family. We're supposed to be strong, aggressive and competitive, but also caring, understanding and emotional. We need to work hard at our jobs, but then have time to take the family skiing and drive the kids to ballet and karate lessons and the orthodontist, keep the car clean, read a book and even think a thought," he told the *Daily News* in 1996. Whereas much of his pre–*Groundhog Day* work focused outward, on society and institutions, *Multiplicity* continued his cinematic exploration of psychology and his own internal growth.

When his friend and *Animal House* collaborator Chris Miller sent over a short story he'd written about an advertising exec who gets cloned after feeling torn between his family and career, my dad jumped on board right away. In the original story, the man gets two clones and keeps them in the attic. Eventually, he tries to reclaim his work and family, but the clones refuse to let him back into his own life. My dad loved the premise but felt the message of the ending was too cynical. "I thought it was a wonderful setup because it is common to everybody. We all wish we could be in more than one place at the same time. [Working] people with families probably feel guilty all the time—if we spend too much time with our family, we feel we're not working hard enough . . . Then I realized it wasn't just about being busy, it was really about the divided self and that we are all several different people. There are different aspects of our nature that are competing. I realized that what the story really was about was how this guy fragments into his different component selves and finally gets reintegrated. That's the happy ending," he said in an interview with *Psychology Today* in 1996. My dad worked with Chris and his wife, Mary Hale, to incorporate the "mythopoetic" male archetypes into the characters (king, lover, warrior, magician, fool) and to ask probing questions about the psychology of man. They then passed the script on to Lowell Ganz and Babaloo Mandel for a final rewrite and polish. My dad was a huge fan of theirs from *Splash*, *Parenthood*, and *City Slickers* and felt that their contributions to *Multiplicity* really elevated the material. My dad's producing partner Trevor Albert described it as "a joyous development process," but the actual production proved to be somewhat less so.

There was some back-and-forth in terms of the casting, but my dad was a fan of Michael Keaton and felt that his energy and versatility could really bring the Doug Kinney and clone characters to life. Andie MacDowell had been great in *Groundhog Day* and, for my dad, seemed to epitomize a kind of lovely and nonthreatening womanhood. The rest of the cast was filled out with a group of tried-and-true comedic actors and friends—Eugene Levy; Steven Kampmann and his wife, Judith Kahan; Harris Yulin; and Brian Doyle-Murray, among others. Because the movie called for meticulous and innovative special effects to make four Michael Keatons believable on-screen, my dad returned to Richard Edlund and László Kovács, whom he had worked with on *Ghostbusters*. The shooting was difficult, not only because the special effects required extensive coverage and precision for each shot with the clones, but because Michael Keaton was going through changes in his personal life (Courteney Cox, cough cough) and seemed to chafe under the pressure of carrying the whole movie on his shoulders. In an interview with Uproxx in 2015, Michael Keaton said that he thought the movie wasn't successful because my dad's Buddhism prevented him from pushing the studio to promote it as strongly as they could have. I call bullshit on that theory—you can't blame the Buddha!—but at this point, it's neither here nor there. *Multiplicity* tested well with audiences but the studio chose not to market the film aggressively and it ended up making back only half of its $45 million budget.

As he had been with *Club Paradise* and *Stuart*, my dad was sanguine about the lack of enthusiasm for *Multiplicity*. Because he had decided to only make movies that meant something to him, the returns mattered less than whether or not he believed in the message and quality of the project, and he stood behind both. I, however, am not so sure about this one. While there are some funny moments in the movie and I appreciate my dad's authentic fascination with the subject of male identity, to me *Multiplicity* just never went far enough out of its own bubble to be truly compelling. Sorry, Dad.

Work–life balance:
Julian and Dad on set

GO, SLUGS!

When it was time for me to go to college, my dad insisted that the most important thing was that I had to leave home. His own college experience was such a transformative time in his life that he wanted to make sure that I didn't miss out on an important growth opportunity. At the time, I was living with Diego at my mom's house and was loath to be separated from him. While my dad accepted Diego warmly as part of the family, he worried that I was sacrificing my own growth and development for the stability and comfort of the relationship. He wanted me to get out and experience the world; I wanted to stay home and be a good girlfriend while Diego made music. As a compromise, I applied to all of the University of California schools and USC. Dad helped me write my admission essay, and the only thing I remember is the opening line: "I got the right side of my brain from my mom, and the left side from my dad, and I've spent the last eighteen years figuring out how to balance the two." I wanted to write about the differences between my "two worlds" but it was his idea to lead with a joke.

"Listen, do you know how many essays these admissions people have to read? And do you know how many of them are actually interesting? Not that many. So, if you can make them laugh, even a little bit, trust me, they'll appreciate it."

"You just think comedy is the answer to everything, Daddy."

"Well, duh!" We laughed. "Look, I'm not saying that opening with a joke will get you into college, but it can't hurt, right?"

I guess he was right. I was accepted at the University of California at Santa Cruz and decided to attend it because it was far away enough to be "on my own" without going so far as to be really alone. My dad and I agreed that I would live in the dorm for the first trimester and then look for an apartment or house share after that. Diego would stay with my mom but visit every other weekend and move in once I got established.

At the time, UCSC was one of the smaller UC schools with about nine thousand undergraduate students. The university's mascot was the Banana Slug, which should give you a pretty good indication of how anti–*Animal House* my college experience was. Nestled in the redwood forests above the city of Santa Cruz, the school was divided into eight different "colleges," each with its own distinct character and academic concentration, and you picked the one where you wanted to live and take your "freshperson" core class. I picked Porter because it was known as the artsy college and was slightly less hippie-ish than some of the others. My roommate, Jen,* apparently hadn't gotten this memo and was a true-blue tie-dyed Deadhead from Kansas. She put up a huge batik peace-sign tapestry, got her lip pierced in the bathroom, and ran naked

_____

* Not her real name.

through the quad the first time it rained, as per Porter tradition. I mostly stayed in our room smoking weed and playing Tetris on my laptop.

I was so crazy homesick for the first few days after moving into my dorm that I wasn't sure I was going to be able to stick it out. Hearing this, Dad came up for the weekend to tide me over and give me some TLC. We walked around downtown Santa Cruz, took my roommate out for sushi, and bought shower shoes at Longs Drugs—nothing special, but his presence there helped so much. Like always, he was able to put things in perspective and reassure me in a way that no one else could.

"It's going to be great," he told me. "Maybe not next week, or even next month, but if you give it a chance, I know you'll love it."

"But the hippies . . ."

"Oh, the hippies," he laughed. "For me, it was the squares. Listen, it takes time to find your people, but you will. Is there a Black Panther chapter you could join?"

"Ha fucking ha." I rolled my eyes. "I don't need Black Panthers, but it would be nice to find someone who smells good and doesn't listen to Neil Young all the time."

"What about Van Morrison? Are you okay with him? Just hang in there, my baby. You can make some temporary friends while you figure it all out. It doesn't need to be a perfect match. Give it time. Trust me."

He was right, of course. After the first trimester, I left the dorm, Diego came up, and we moved into a shared house near West Cliff with another couple from LA, a punk/rockabilly girl, a Siamese cat, and an iguana. Diego went to Cabrillo College in Aptos, the next town over, to study music, and I ended up making great friends, learning from some incredible professors, and finding my little niche after all. Dad visited us in Santa Cruz semi-regularly, often in conjunction with a guest lecture for the Film Studies Department or a trip to San Francisco to visit his old college friends. He was interested in the things I was reading and learning as an American studies major and, amazingly, read Hannah Arendt's *The Origins of Totalitarianism* on my recommendation. Impressive, right? I decided to minor in education and was a classroom assistant in a bilingual first/second-grade class in San Jose for a year. I loved working with kids and was happy that my dad supported my interest in teaching as a possible career.

At some point toward the end of my freshman year, Dad and Erica decided to move to Chicago. He had been thinking about it for a while and used to joke, "Nobody cares about me in LA. There's always someone better two tables over. Also, I'm tired of sucking in my stomach all the time." I think that was partly true but really, he wanted to be closer to my grandparents and give my brothers a life more similar to the one he had as a kid. "I realized, my parents have probably only seen you like twenty-five times, in your life. That's so sad. I grew up with my grandparents and all my cousins around all the time and it was great. I want more of that for the boys," he told me. Erica had grown up in LA, and all of her family and friends were there, but she hated the earthquakes, had been shaken by the robbery, and agreed that a simpler life for Julian and Daniel would be better. So they sold their house in Brentwood, packed up their life, and transported it to Glencoe, Illinois. I was busy with my own life in Santa Cruz and knew my dad would still be in LA regularly for work. Although he worried about my feeling abandoned, I reassured him that I was happy to visit the whole family in the Midwest during school breaks, and it would all be okay. I think it says a lot that I was so secure in my dad's availability and love for me that he could have moved halfway around the world and I'd have known he'd be there for me whenever I needed him.

Even though my dad had grown up in Chicago, the move was still an adjustment for him, and a bit of a culture shock for Erica. Although the majority of their LA circle of friends had not been celebrities or people "in the biz," they had a diverse social world with many creative and intellectual people who were interested in arts, culture, politics, and travel. Erica was surprised to find that many of the other parents in the boys' school community had grown up in Glencoe and never left.

"It's not that they're not nice," Erica explained to me over the phone soon after the move. "They're very nice. It's just different. I started talking about Buddhism and meditation at a school function and the other moms looked at me like I had two heads. I don't mean to sound like a snob, but there's just not the same . . . sophistication that I'm used to. I mean, it's not Podunk, but it's definitely not LA. Maybe I need to join a book club."

"Maybe you could start your own!" I laughed. "You could call it People Who Like to Think and Talk About Things."

Part of my dad and Erica's agreement around the move was that he would try to work in Chicago and, at the very least, would not do any location work for one year. They got my brothers adjusted to their new schools, saw my grandparents three times a week, and slowly started to make some new friends. Though my dad had pictured spending weekends with all of his cousins and having the boys grow up in a tight-knit extended family, it didn't really work out that way. "I thought everyone was always getting together and having barbecues without us, but it turns out, they weren't. Everyone has their own lives and we see them a few times a year, just like when I lived in LA. Oh well . . . Family: they just don't make 'em like they used to." After the initial settling-in period, my dad really embraced his Midwestern homecoming. He took the role of hometown hero seriously and was active in several civic projects through Mayor Daley's office—Principal for a Day, the Chicago Humanities Festival, Gallery 37, and more. He coached the boys' basketball teams, set up an Ocean Pictures office in Highland Park, and enjoyed the regularness of day-to-day life. He knew the owners of all the diners and mom-and-pop shops he frequented, liked being recognized by the suburban moms, and seemed to relax into this slower, friendlier world. In 1999, he mused about the move in *Northshore* magazine, saying, "In a normal life, you would know as many people as know you. But for me, more people know me than I know. It's a nice, comfortable, safe feeling." For him, living in the North Shore was a lot like Mayberry, but with Starbucks and Nordstrom Rack. For me, our relationship stayed strong, and I was happy that he felt embraced by his new (old) home.

WHAT NOW?

My senior year of college ('98–'99), I was on my own for the first time in my life. Diego had been accepted to Berklee College of Music in Boston and I had originally planned to join him there after graduation to pursue a master's in education. It was a good plan, and he was and is a great guy, but it didn't work out. Things got messy pretty quickly when I went to Mexico City in September with my friend Cynara and met a guy. He was Cynara's cousin's best friend and we rode motorcycles all around the huge city, went to the pyramids, and drank beer on the painted boats of Xochimilco. It was pretty romantic, even when he couldn't stop looking at me in the side-view mirror and crashed our motorcycle into the highway median, dragging us both across fifteen feet of asphalt. My right leg looked like hamburger meat but I didn't care. I called my dad, crying: "I met a boy and we kissed and then we got into a motorcycle accident and now I don't know what to do!"

"Thank God you're okay!" he said. "I could kill you for getting on a motorcycle at all. Please don't ever do that again. Now go figure out how to deal with this mess. I love you, my baby. Everything will be okay. Tell Diego we love him and will always be here for him, no matter what."

Looking back, I recognize that I created a dramatic situation to allow me to exit my relationship with Diego. He was such a good guy, and we were so comfortable together, but my heart just wasn't in it anymore. I ended up letting the guy from Mexico stay with me in Santa Cruz for three drama-filled months. He spoke in Spanish and I spoke in English and I think we each understood about 75 percent of what the other person was saying. The sex was amazing, though. Ultimately, we got in one too many fights and when he tried to make out with my friend, I sent him packing. That whole period was another major re-awakening for me. Who could I be on my own? What did I want? Thankfully, I had a group of wonderful girlfriends who supported me through it all.

During my senior year, Dad came to visit during a break in post-production for *Analyze This*. We sat drinking coffee at Caffe Pergolesi, musing on how much things had changed since the first time he visited. "Feels good, right? You made a really nice life for yourself up here. You learned a lot, you have great friends . . . Well, get ready to leave it all behind. I mean, I'm joking, but not really. It's time to start figuring out what you might want to do after graduation."

The truth was, I had no idea what I wanted to do after graduation. Two of my close friends were going backpacking through Israel and Egypt and invited me to go with them. I considered it but wasn't sure I could handle the way they intended to travel.

"I'm too much of a control freak," I told my dad over the phone. "Plus, I'm not so sure about Israel. I mean, the politics . . ."

"Knowing you, you'd end up marrying a Palestinian . . . or finding the one Mexican guy in Israel. If you want to go, of course I'll help you, but . . . what about New York?"

"What about it? I mean, you know I love it there but it's so expensive and I'd have to have a really good job and—"

"We can help you with all that. Think about it. If not now, when? It would be a real adventure."

I considered his proposal but was still unsure about what to do. Wasn't I supposed to be establishing myself as an adult now—getting a real job and settling down? How could I do that if I opted to stay "on the dole"? What kind of job could I actually get with all my big ideas but very few practical skills? Busy completing my coursework and writing my final thesis (on immigration, domestic labor, and education), I put off answering these questions for as long as possible.

As graduation approached, my dad was asked to speak at the commencement. He absolutely nailed it (again) and ended up using the same speech a few more times after this, but it was worthy of the repetition, and it's worthy of reprinting here.

UC SANTA CRUZ COMMENCEMENT
JUNE 12, 1999

Thank you _____, graduates, faculty, families, and friends. When I was asked to speak at this commencement ceremony, I was honored, of course, but more than a little worried about the great responsibility of addressing you on such an important occasion as this. Then I thought back to my own graduation from Washington University in 1966 and realized that I had absolutely no memory of who spoke or a single thing that was said. So years from now, if anyone asks you about this speech, all you have to remember is that it was really great and it totally changed your life.

In fact, you might wonder what you will remember from your college years. I remember that ontogeny recapitulates phylogeny, but I don't remember what it means. I remember synclines and anticlines, I remember supply and demand, the Council of Trent, the Diet of Worms, and, my personal favorite, the Defenestration of Prague, in which someone was apparently thrown out a window, in Prague apparently, for a reason I cannot recall. I do remember that I could write a pretty good answer on an essay test using the acronym PERSIA—Political, Economic, Religious, Scientific, Intellectual and Artistic—but I don't remember any of the questions. In one course I read eleven 19th-century English novels but all I remember is a character named Diggory Venn the Reddleman. Reddleman is not a job category you hear much about these days.

I guess the centerpiece of any good commencement speech should be some kind of advice to the graduates. As you may know, my own daughter Violet is graduating with you today and in thinking about what advice I'd want to give her, I thought about my own father and I realized that in my whole life the best advice my father ever gave me, the only advice he ever gave me, was, "Don't go into retail." Simple but deeply profound, and I pass that along to you for whatever it's worth.

Perhaps the most famous father-son advice comes in the first act of Hamlet from Polonius to his son Laertes as he's going off to college.

He says, "And these few precepts in thy memory . . . Give thy thoughts no tongue, nor any unproportioned thought his act. Be thou familiar but by no means vulgar. Those friends thou hast, and their adoption tried, Grapple them unto thy soul with hoops of steel, budda

budda budda . . ." He's basically saying keep your good friends close but don't waste time with every idiot who comes along. Let's see, "Beware of entrance to a quarrel dubba dubba dup . . . Give every man thine ear, but few thy voice. Take each man's censure, but reserve thy judgment. Neither a borrower or a lender be, blah, blah, blah . . . This above all, to thine own self be true, and it must follow as the night the day, Thou canst not then be false to any man."

The one thing he forgets to tell him is, "Don't get into a sword fight with Hamlet. He's nuts. He'll kill you." Which is exactly what happens in Act Five. Then it's all "Good night, sweet prince" and everybody's lying there dead. Point being, all the good advice in the world won't help you if you just go off and do something stupid.

I'm not going to say that you're the hope of the future or that it's up to you to save the world. That's up to all of us. But I think you have to do good wherever and whenever you can. There's a lovely Buddhist belief that says, "We owe infinite gratitude to the past, infinite service to the present, and infinite responsibility to the future."

And of course, obligatory in any commencement speech, follow your dreams. When I was leaving college, my best friend Michael Shamberg and I made a pact: that we would never take a job we had to dress up for, and that we would only do things we enjoyed. Michael is now a successful movie producer, so we are living proof that one can make a career in the arts. I've since modified my rules—in some jobs you just have to wear a tie—but I do believe that the real challenge, no matter what field you're in, is to do what you like and like what you do.

So go for the gold, just do it, be all that you can be, but remember, as the Zen poet Thich Nhat Hanh said, "The miracle is not to walk on the water. The miracle is to walk on the green earth, dwelling deeply in the present moment feeling truly alive."

So let me close now by wishing you all the political, economic, religious, scientific, intellectual and artistic success one could hope for. Good luck and may God, whatever you understand that to mean, bless you.

Oh, yeah. Everybody's always asking me, "Harold, Harold! What's the meaning of life?" Well, it's pretty naive to think that life has one intrinsic and universal meaning that applies to each and every one of us. The fact is, it's up to you to discover the meaning in each and every moment of your lives. Viktor Frankl the psychologist said a great thing. He said, "Act as if you're living your life for the second time and you're not going to make the same mistakes again."

1995

1999

ANALYZE THIS (1999)

Written by KENNETH LONERGAN,

PETER TOLAN, and HAROLD RAMIS

Directed by HAROLD RAMIS

Even gangsters get the blues. When mob boss Paul Vitti (Robert De Niro) starts having panic attacks, he strong-arms therapist Ben Sobel (Billy Crystal) into treating him. As the boundaries between doctor and patient begin to blur, both men struggle hilariously to regain control over their lives.

```
          DR. BEN SOBEL
When I got into family therapy,
this was not the "family" I had
in mind.
```

Funny partly because De Niro and Crystal
do what we expect them to do, and
partly because they don't.
—ROGER EBERT, *CHICAGO SUN-TIMES*

Director Harold Ramis keeps the gangsters
real and funny at the same time.
—BOB FENSTER, *ARIZONA REPUBLIC*

Ramis has made a fleet, unself-conscious, eminently enjoyable
picture, where one-liners carom merrily like stray bullets, and
where there's casual ease, like the drape of a sharpster's
trousers, in the rapport between its two stars.
—STEPHANIE ZACHAREK, SALON.COM

My dad was approached to direct *Analyze This* right around the time he was relocating to Glencoe but declined the project when they insisted on filming in New York. When the producers came back a second time, after Dad's self-imposed yearlong hiatus was up, he agreed to direct the film. The premise was appealing, the script was solid, and the opportunity to work with Robert De Niro and Billy Crystal was too good to pass up. In his rewrites, Dad focused on the psychology of De Niro's character, the therapy sessions, and the jokes. "I used something from every psychiatrist I know," he told Mark Caro for the *Chicago Tribune*. "I know so many shrinks, and I've done therapy usually on a crisis basis, when someone in my family was having a problem or I was." He isolated two basic questions that he felt were at the heart of psychoanalysis to guide his writing and the characters' motivation: What do you really feel? And what do you really want?

Describing the casting process to me once, my dad talked about meeting lots of very nice "wiseguys." "Sometimes it's hard to tell how much they're really acting," he said. Joe Viterelli's audition for Jelly stood out. "Real nice guy, Joe. Very sweet, you know, but you wouldn't guess that by looking at him. So after he reads, and he did great, he throws his arm around my neck, pulls me close, and says, 'Give me the part or I'll throw you out the fuckin' window.' I paused for a second but Joe had this twinkle in his eye and we both laughed, shook hands, and of course, he got the part."

Dad invited me to visit New York while he was there filming *Analyze This*. "I miss you," he said on the phone, "and Erica and the boys would love to see you, too. Plus, you can meet Bob [De Niro]!" So, off I went to New York, where Dad, Erica, and the kids were living in an amazing suite at the Waldorf Astoria having the time of their lives. It was a great trip. We went to Broadway shows, I watched some of the filming, and yes, I got to meet Robert De Niro, which was very exciting even though he barely spoke or looked at me.

While there was some concern that the popularity of *The Sopranos* would take the wind out of the film's sails (and sales), *Analyze This* was a big commercial success. Audiences really enjoyed seeing Robert De Niro in his first comedic role, and Billy Crystal was in his neurotic Jewy element. My dad delighted in his new Cosa Nostra connections and, after giving his local Italian restaurant guy a bit part in the movie, got great tables and free garlic bread for the rest of his life. The studio and all involved parties were very happy with the outcome and aggressively pushed for a sequel. After *Ghostbusters II*, my dad had said he wouldn't do another sequel, but he eventually succumbed to pressure from the studio and to the lure of the paycheck they were offering.

Analyze That, the sequel to *Analyze This*, came out in 2002. Due to scheduling issues with Billy and Bob, the entire production was very rushed, and there were days my dad would be writing at the midtown production office while the rest of the production crew went out scouting locations. One of the assistant directors frequently asked my dad's assistant, Laurel, to go into the office and read over his shoulder to see if the scene said "Interior—Restaurant" or "Exterior—Restaurant" so they'd know what kind of location to look for that day. While my dad was always a collaborative writer, *Analyze That* took it to another level. I've been told that Bobby the prop guy actually came up with the idea for the heist scene, and because my dad was so far behind on the script, he asked Bobby to just type it up so he could paste it into the scene (after punching it up and adding dialogue, of course). Suffice it to say, the production moved at a frantic pace that my dad was never comfortable with and I think the movie, and his peace of mind, suffered for it.

UN BON VOYAGE (ET VÉRITÉ)

In June of 1999, my dad told me to pick any place in the world, and he would take me there for a father-daughter postgrad travel adventure. I suggested Portugal or Tokyo and he said, "Well, yeahhhhh. That would be cool. How about northern France?" A road trip through the picturesque French countryside wasn't exactly what I had in mind, but I knew that we would have a great time wherever we went. So we spent a few days in Paris, drinking café au lait and eating pâté and croissants, and then rented a car and took off for Normandy. Dad drove and I tried to navigate as we passed through Vernon, Rouen, Deauville, Etretat, and Saint-Lô. Dad's accent was so good that when we asked people for directions, they would respond in such rapid-fire French that we were left more confused than when we started. Meanwhile, he laughed at my complete lack of French comprehension when I noticed yet another street sign for Hôtel de Ville, and said, "What is that? Like a Best Western or something?" We visited Mont Saint-Michel, stayed in a sixteenth-century castle for a night, drank calvados at every opportunity, and laughed and laughed and laughed. We spent an afternoon looking at the Bayeux Tapestry and Dad bought a kit to embroider a throw pillow with the image of Harold, Earl of Wessex, who later became the king of England. We ate the most amazing meal at the Ferme Saint Siméon in Honfleur, and then went back the next night and ate the exact same thing again (lobster salad with avocado and citrus dressing, and a steak with morel mushrooms and fois gras, if you must know). We also ate really bad ham steaks in Caen at what seemed like a French Denny's.

Cafe Harold, Rouen, 1999

During that trip, while driving to yet another crumbling abbey, my dad said he had something important to tell me.

"I know this sounds crazy . . . but you have a sister." He looked over quickly to gauge my reaction.

"Amy Heckerling's kid?" I asked. He nodded, looking confused. "I know. I've known forever."

"But—wha? How?" he sputtered.

"Well," I said slowly, "I knew that you and Mom had an . . . understanding. Then, when I was a kid, you took me to the hospital to meet this random woman and her baby."

"You remember that?"

"Um, yeah! It didn't seem like a happy visit, even to a seven-year-old. What were you thinking? Why did you bring me there? Was I like your human shield?"

"Something like that." He laughed.

"I think I also overheard you and Erica talking about it once," I lied, not wanting to tell him that I'd read her journal. "And then, when I was about twelve, Mom and I saw the girl and Amy at a performance art thing and Mom was like, 'Ooh, she looks just like Harold,' so I pretty much figured it out. You dirty dawg!"

"I'm so sorry, my baby."

"It had to be a girl," I teased. "Brothers I'm okay with, but a sister? Come on. I'm supposed to be the only Daddy's girl."

"I don't think that will be a problem. She doesn't even know."

"How is that possible?"

"Oh boy." He took a deep breath. "Well, Amy and I were having an affair and she got pregnant. She was married at the time but had had a few miscarriages and really wanted a child so she said she was going to have it even though she wasn't sure who the father was. I think she was hoping that I'd leave Anne to be with her, but I knew it wouldn't work out between us. I was just getting involved with Erica . . . it was a mess.

She had the baby and she never told her husband that there was any question of paternity."

"Ouch." I cringed.

"Yeah, ouch. Eventually they got divorced. I suppose he was always suspicious, because he did a DNA test and found out that Mollie wasn't his biological child. He made Amy swear never to tell Mollie but he called me, pretty pissed off, and told me. I feel like such a jerk."

"You're not a jerk, Daddy."

"Well, I'm sure Amy thinks I am. Have you ever seen *Look Who's Talking*?"

"Yeah."

"Well, you know that married asshole that gets Kirstie Alley's character pregnant and then won't leave his wife?"

"Yeah?"

"That's me."

Le sigh.

Looking back, I wasn't particularly freaked out by our conversation. I was in a great place in my life, so the discomfort I felt when I saw Mollie at the art show was long gone. If anything, I felt happy that my dad had trusted me enough to talk to me and I figured that as long as I was number one, maybe it didn't matter if I wasn't the only one.

As the trip came to an end, we spent one last night in Paris before flying out. We had dinner at Brasserie Lipp and talked about what the upcoming year might have in store for both of us. As we walked back to the hotel, a light rain fell and I held on tight to him under the doorman-size umbrella he always seemed to have handy.

"Thank you for a great trip, Daddy," I said, suddenly fighting back tears.

"You are so welcome, Daughtie. Don't cry. I loved every minute of it, too."

In a way, our trip to France felt like a reward for surviving the turmoil of the previous fifteen years. We'd made it through the divorce, his remarriage, and my rebellion intact; I'd graduated from college with honors, and he was coming off the success of *Analyze This*, so it was a perfect celebration of our individual successes, along with the strength and resiliency of our relationship. The next morning, we flew back to Los Angeles and our separate lives. I prepared for my next move and he started pre-production for his next project, *Bedazzled*. To this day, that trip remains one of my most cherished memories of time spent with my dad.

BEDAZZLED
(2000)

———

Written by PETER COOK, DUDLEY MOORE, LARRY GELBART,
HAROLD RAMIS, and PETER TOLAN
Directed by HAROLD RAMIS

In this modern take on the classic Faustian bargain, Elliot (Brendan Fraser) makes a deal with the Devil (Elizabeth Hurley) to win over his workplace crush, Alison (Frances O'Connor). As he uses his seven wishes to become the person he thinks Alison wants him to be, Elliot soon discovers that the Devil has a wicked sense of humor.

```
              ELLIOT
     Why does the existential dilemma
     have to be so damn bleak? Yes,
     we're alone in the universe. Yes,
     life is meaningless, death is
     inevitable, but is that necessarily
     so depressing?
```

The new movie has been directed by Harold Ramis from a
screenplay that uses the 1967 film more as inspiration than

source. It is lacking in wickedness. It doesn't smack its lips
when it's naughty. When its hero sells his soul to the devil,
what results isn't diabolical effrontery, but a series of
contract negotiations and consumer complaints.
—ROGER EBERT, *CHICAGO SUN-TIMES*

Co-writer and director Harold Ramis ("Analyze This"), working
with scripters Larry Gelbart and Peter Tolan, clearly had
departure in mind. Fans of the original might cry foul, but the
new, retooled "Bedazzled" is loaded with brilliant, witty
moments that will have audiences laughing loudly, and
without the need to indulge in comparative cinema exercises.
—PETER STACK, SFGATE.COM

My dad was a huge fan of the 1967 Peter Cook and Dudley Moore film *Bedazzled*. He loved the Faustian premise of selling your soul to the devil in exchange for the things you think will make you happy and felt that its themes spoke to a particular paradox of modern life for many people. In an interview for the *Bedazzled* DVD he elaborated, "Most people spend their lives in eternal longing, wishing they had something they're not gonna get, and even when they get what they want, they find it's really fleeting and not as satisfying as they hoped. We're not happy in ourselves, with ourselves, with our situation. Whatever we have, we're looking beyond to something that could be better." After the shooting at Columbine High School in 1999, my dad felt that this cultural tendency to live in a perpetual "wish state" really needed to be explored and decided that *Bedazzled* could provide a rich creative landscape in which to do so.

As the script came together, Dad and the producers began to discuss casting for the film. It was Erica who suggested that the Devil be played by a woman. Several well-known female stars were interested in the role but it was Elizabeth Hurley who embodied the powerful, sexy, playful devil they were looking for. My dad appreciated her confidence and sophistication as a person, and he counted on her willingness as an actor to jump into camp and fantasy as she took on the Devil's many incarnations.

In casting the male lead, agents and studio executives pushed hard for a big-name comedy actor to play the part of Elliot, but my dad had something else in mind. He wanted someone with tremendously broad range and flexibility as an actor who could really lose himself in the extremes of the wishes depicted in the film. In an interview with Charlie Rose, my dad said, "When we looked at Brendan Fraser's work, he seemed to have it all. In each movie he was completely different. He's one of those very well-trained classical actors who can really transform himself." My dad and Brendan clicked right away and bonded over a shared drive to create thoughtful, meaningful work.

I wasn't around much during the filming of *Bedazzled*, but I did visit the set for a few days while they were filming on a gigantic soundstage at 20th Century Fox. My dad, once again, was in his element as a director. *Bedazzled* was a big-budget movie with a top-notch crew, great catering, and the most amazing production design I had ever seen up close. When I met Elizabeth Hurley, she was gracious and charming, with the kind of beauty that's almost hard to look at directly. Brendan was warm and down-to-earth, and seemed to enjoy working with my dad so much that his eyes would light up in between takes as Dad gave him feedback on the scene.

Julian and Daniel were nine and five during the filming of *Bedaz-zled* and it was very "circle of life" to see them sitting on my dad's lap as he called action or hanging out with the electricians and prop guys the same way I used to when I was young. At twenty-three, I was more interested in making out with the grips than learning the tools of their trade, but it was sweet the way they let my brothers climb around the trucks and gave them tool belts and little jobs to do.

Julian holding a tripod

My dad seemed totally delighted with how the production was going and was cautiously optimistic about *Bedazzled*'s anticipated success. Things changed after the first few test screenings, when audiences expressed their strong dislike for one of the wish segments—a dark, *Sid and Nancy*–esque scene where Elliot and Alison are a rock-and-roll couple, finally in love with each other but so miserably drunk, drugged out, and disgusting that after a lot of sloppy kissing, a near overdose,

Ramis family *(left to right)*: Steven, Ruth, Harold, and Nate in 1956 or 1957

◄ Dad on the
  stepladder, 1968

❯ Mom reading
  Dance Magazine,
  1968

▲ Coolest work ID ever?

▼ Anne and Harold, 1970s

Baby me with Mom and Dad in Hydra, Greece, 1977

◄ "I'll just hang out here for a while." 1977

▲ *(Clockwise from front left)*: Bill, Dad, Brian, our babysitter Laurie, Chevy, and me (very focused on my Tater Tots)

▼ Dad, me, and Mom on the beach in Fort Lauderdale, 1980

On set with Dad and Chevy. Bill and Rodney are in the background. ▲

▲ Face-to-face with Dr. Spengler

▼ Dad showing me the ropes

▲ Aw, Dad, can we keep him?

▲ Jimmy Cliff and Dad (nice socks), Port Antonio, Jamaica, 1985

▼ Erica, me, and the Santa Monica sunset, 1986

▲ Bride and groom, 1989

▼ Father-daughter dance at the wedding. All the feelings . . .

◄ Dad and
teen V with
Manic Panic
hair. He still
loved me,
though.

⌄ Mi vida loca,
tenth grade

CONCORD
HIGH SCHOOL

1992–1993

▲ Laughing on the set of *Stuart Saves His Family*

▼ *(Left to right):* Ayda, Julian, Dad, Erica, Daniel, and me, 2012

Headed to the Bedazzled *wrap party, 2000*

and vomiting on his drummer, Elliot realizes that the bad boy lifestyle is not for him. By the time my dad was forced to admit that this scene had to go, Brendan was already shooting the *Mummy* sequel in England, so they took the show on the road and filmed an entirely new wish involving Abraham Lincoln at the Richmond Theatre outside of London. Although Dad initially resisted cutting the rock-and-roll scene, and Brendan reportedly cried because he thought it was some of his best work, in the end, my dad trusted the audience and made the substitution.

Ultimately, this change did not save *Bedazzled* from the lackluster response it garnered from critics and theatergoers. In this case, my dad could not have cared less. He believed so strongly in the message of the movie and in the performances by the actors that he was honestly impervious to the critique and general indifference *Bedazzled* received. I really enjoyed the movie but thought it could have been more interesting if it were a little edgier and less on-the-nose. Watching the movie again recently, I was touched by Brendan's portrayal of Elliot's longing and snickered at the misfires of his wishes, but still felt that something about the slickness of the production and the unrelenting sincerity of the characters ended up detracting from the power of the film's important message.

IF I CAN MAKE IT THERE . . .

Like many recent college graduates, when I finished at UC Santa Cruz, I was full of ideals and was all fired up, ready to get out there and make a difference. The wonderful comedian Lotus Weinstock, a dear friend of my mom's, once said, "I used to want to save the world, now I just want to leave the room with some dignity." I toyed with the idea of making political documentaries, but my aversion to the entertainment business made this a difficult leap. The Hollywood life I had been exposed to seemed way too superficial for me. I grew up seeing the type of people that were successful in the film industry and they mostly seemed like people I didn't want to be around. Since I wasn't pretty enough to be in front of the camera or ambitious enough to be behind it, I knew I had to find my own niche. Just after graduation, Dani,* a woman I had befriended at UCSC, told me she was going to graduate school at NYU and asked if I was interested in sharing an

---

* Not her real name.

apartment in Brooklyn. Already leaning toward New York based on my dad's encouragement, I jumped at the opportunity. Even though I didn't know exactly what I wanted to do when I got there, since my dad was willing to help fund the transition, I figured I could just find any old job and work for a while until I figured out my next steps. Privilege—check! The apartment share ended up falling through, though, and my dad and Erica were so terrified that I would end up in Alphabet City* (God forbid!) that they bought me an apartment in a small co-op on the Upper West Side.

I made the move in September of 1999 and immediately felt at home in New York. I basked in the energy and excitement of the city and was grateful to reconnect with old friends. Ethan and some other people I knew from LA were living in the East Village, and we had fun roaming around the city, smoking, talking, and laughing, just like old times—only better because we were adults now and could go to bars. We played pool at Blue & Gold, danced salsa in the back room of the Parkside Lounge, and took in the sights at Milk Bar before stumbling to Veselka for French fries at four in the morning to fortify me for the cab ride back uptown. As cool as the downtown bar scene seemed at the time, I loved the quiet of my tree-lined block and the beauty of Central Park. My friends and I used to say it was our version of "upstate."

Soon after settling in, I ended up landing work in the nonprofit sector. I stayed in this field for about a year doing program support (mostly clerical work) and event planning (begging people for donations) for a

---

* At the time, Alphabet City—the east side of the East Village—was still considered "scary" by some, even though the gentrification process had already begun. Now all of the burned-out buildings and most of the drug dealers are gone, and the entire neighborhood is owned by NYU and is pretty much unrecognizable.

few different companies. Some of my bosses were clowns and some of the causes were hopeless, but some of the organizations were doing truly amazing work and it was a great learning experience for a New York newbie. I basically worked for free, but my dad was supportive of my choices, emotionally and financially. "Do what makes you happy, baby," he'd say. "What is all this money for if not to make all of our lives more comfortable?" After a year, I wanted to get back to working with kids and was again considering getting a master's in education, so I got a job as an assistant preschool teacher at the Children's Aid Society in the West Village.

September 11, 2001, was the first day of school and my first day on the job. Dad and Erica had been visiting me and were on their way to the airport to fly back to Chicago. I was getting the classroom ready to welcome the kids and parents when the head teacher and I heard the sound of a plane engine that seemed much too loud. We ran to the window but couldn't see anything. Then the teachers in the corner classroom screamed. We raced over and saw what looked like a small hole in the World Trade Center. As word of what was going on spread, other staff members arrived to take in the view and try to figure out what the hell had just happened.

By the time we finished the morning session with the students, around eleven a.m., the second plane had hit, both towers had collapsed, and clearly, none of it was an accident. I started to panic, worried that one of the planes had been my dad's, and I was unable to reach him via cell since all lines were busy. I used the phone at the school to call the house in Chicago and they told me he had just called and was fine. I was both hysterical and numb at the same time. I didn't know anyone who worked in the World Trade Center, so once I knew my family was okay, it wasn't personal. And yet, it was. Here I was in the city I had fallen in love with, taking care of twelve toddlers, trying to help them feel comfortable and safe as they separated from their parents, and the world was showing me, and everyone else, just how much of an illusion all of that really was.

On their way to LaGuardia, Dad and Erica saw the second plane hit from the Queensboro Bridge, and by the time they got to the airport, all air travel had been suspended indefinitely. The airport was pandemonium, and since they had no idea when they might be able to fly out, they commandeered a complete stranger's town car and driver and the four of them drove to Carroll Gardens to eat Chinese food and watch the news at my college friend Dani's house. Anxious to get home to the boys, my dad and Erica rode with this woman back to her mansion in Greenwich, Connecticut, gave the driver $1,000, and then rented a car and drove eighteen hours straight to Chicago.

The day was an entirely surreal experience. I got a hysterical message from Ethan telling me he had been doing rooftop landscape work in Tribeca and saw people jumping from the building. I wandered around the West Village, not knowing what to do. I remember seeing people walking around like zombies, covered in asbestos dust from the buildings. Sirens wailed from all directions and doctors and nurses waited outside the ER at St. Vincent's for a rush of patients that never came. The smell in the air is something I'll never forget. It lingered for weeks. Eventually, I walked across the Brooklyn Bridge to Dani's and, not wanting to be alone, stayed there for a few days. On Friday, I went home to my half-renovated apartment "upstate" on West Eighty-Seventh Street, where the air was clear and, bizarrely, life seemed to go on much as it had before.

At the risk of sounding narcissistic in the face of mass tragedy, I felt pretty raw and lost after 9/11. I shared none of the moral outrage or patriotic pride that seemed to be the only two acceptable responses in the country at that time. I just felt small and vulnerable and anxious about the fate of the world, or my world, at least. I would make eye contact with strangers on the subway and start crying, thinking about the fragility of life. A few weeks later, Dani and I took mushrooms in my apartment and spent about an hour sobbing before coming up with a beehive analogy for NYC that made us feel better because "hey, we are all connected after all! We may not know what's going on in other parts of the hive but there are bees/people everywhere, going about their business, finding flowers, making honey, and it's all going to be okay. We're not alone." Yay for drugs! (Just kidding, kids.)

In the same way that my father's generation reeled from the assassinations of JFK and then MLK, the effects of 9/11 rippled out from personal loss and grief to national trauma. It may not have made me feel more American, but being so close to the event and living through that day definitely solidified my identity as a New Yorker.

BABY ON BOARD

A few months later, I got pregnant with my first child. I was twenty-four and had only known the father, Keet, for about a month. We met through a series of random events that are actually not random at all if you read *The Celestine Prophecy* in high school like I did. To make a long story short, in the summer of 2001, I was in LA visiting my mom and went to a party at an old friend's house. I took MDMA and met a woman I really liked (little did I know at the time that she and her husband were trying to pick me up). She and I kept in touch, and I told her she could stay with me any time she visited New York. That November, she took me up on my offer and, a few days into her visit, introduced me to a group of guys she had met ten years prior, at a club, when she was in town for one night on her way to London. Are you feeling the cosmic chills yet? Keet walked into my apartment with three of his friends, a Solo cup of Johnnie Walker, a cocky attitude, and a beautiful smile, so of course, I liked him right away. After drinking and listening to music at my apartment, twelve of us piled into two cars and went to Sue's Rendezvous, a strip club in Mount Vernon with the laziest strippers I have ever seen. Keet and I ended up talking the whole night, and I ended up sleeping with him (of course). But he surprisingly came back the next day, and the next, and maybe even the next after that. I liked him but didn't expect it to turn into anything serious. I had recently gotten out of an intense relationship and just wanted someone to hang out with, maybe go to a movie with—simple things. Keet fit the bill perfectly.

Keet was a born-and-bred New Yorker from Washington Heights (half black and half Italian but always mistaken for Dominican), raised with his sister by an eccentric single mom. He worked in food service at a nursing home (where he has been for the past twenty years and counting), drove a limo on his days off, and had dreams of being an actor. I immediately fell for his goofy sense of humor and sweetness, which seemed incongruous with his love of Mobb Deep and motorcycles. He wasn't "book smart"—he'd dropped out of college after one year to help his mom financially—but was practical, organized, and a self-proclaimed "king of common sense." We were different in so many ways but had a strong physical attraction and enjoyed each other's company.

After my teenage abortion experience, I decided that, while that had been the right decision for me at that time, I had used my "Get Out of Jail Free" card once and would not do it again. I gave a little speech to anyone I had questionably protected sex with:* "We are adults and we should use protection. That being said, if we're not being super-careful, we both know what could happen. If I get pregnant, I will not have an

---

* Basically, using a condom, but not consistently, or not for the whole time.

abortion, so be warned." When I told Keet this, he said that he totally understood and felt the same way. "So, let's have babies," he said. I laughed and blew a smoke ring in his face. When I took a pregnancy test around Christmas and it came back positive, I had stopped laughing. Was I crazy? In spite of the conviction of my little speech, and my lifelong desire to have kids, I was terrified and unsure if I was really doing the right thing.

I called my mom first and she got on board right away, bless her heart. She said, "We have two choices in life, Violet. We can choose fear, or we can choose love. Everything comes down to that. I happen to know that you were born to be a mother and I think it's wonderful that you want to do this." My dad wasn't initially supportive and it was very hard for me. He said I was too young, that I was foolish to embark on the most intense journey of life—parenting—with someone I barely knew. He said I was being unrealistic about how hard it would be to support a family in New York without his help. I was crushed—hurt, angry, betrayed, abandoned. I had hoped that everyone would rally around to support me and my new little family. I was ready to say "fuck it" and get a side job at McDonald's when my dad started to come around. I remember talking to Erica on the phone, with her serving as the emotional interpreter between me and my dad.

"Oh, Violetti, we just want the best for you."

"I know, and I appreciate that, but why is your best better than my best? What if this is the best thing for me?"

"You know your daddy loves you."

"I know."

"And he's always been there for you."

"I know."

"Just *ask* him for help. Tell him you know this is hard and you understand how he's feeling and you really want his blessing and his help."

"You think?"

"Yes, I do. I know. I love you so much."

"I love you too. Thank you."

So on Erica's advice, I swallowed my pride and decided to ask for help. I invited my dad to come to New York so we could have a few therapy sessions together to figure out where we stood. My dad and I sat on the sad leather couch in the therapist's apartment/office and I took a deep breath and said, "I know this isn't what you wanted for me, but this is what's happening. Your love and support have always been everything to me and I really hope that you can find a way to be happy for me. If I have to do it on my own, I will, but I don't want to. Will you please help me?" He cried and said he needed a little more time to think about it but told me how much he loved me and that nothing would ever change that. This "breakthrough" was followed a couple of days later by a very awkward dinner on my twenty-fifth birthday with me, my dad, and Keet at Ruth's Chris Steak House in midtown.

Keet was understandably very nervous on the way to dinner. He knew how close my dad and I were and was worried about the pregnancy's disrupting that. He also knew who my dad was and, as a "regular, blue-collar guy," felt intimidated by my dad's "status." I tried to reassure him that my family wasn't like that and wouldn't judge him. As long as he was a kind, caring, and responsible person, that was all that mattered to them.

My dad walked in, hugged me, and shook Keet's hand. By the way he cleared his throat and kept touching his ear, I could tell he was nervous, too. When we sat down, I told them both to have a drink and did my best to keep the conversation easy-breezy. Keet talked about his childhood, his family, his work, and his aspirations. My dad talked about his early jobs and his current pre-production work on *Analyze That*. When it was time for dessert, I made a big deal about avoiding chocolate because I wanted to show my dad I was taking motherhood seriously and had been reading a horrible pregnancy book that made me scared to eat anything.

"Key lime pie?" my dad suggested. "Ice cream?"

"No," I said, pouting. "I really wanted cake but they only have chocolate and chocolate has caffeine and caffeine is bad for the baby so I just won't have anything."

"Hold on," Keet said with a Cheshire cat smile, and pulled a mini carrot cake from Carrot Top Pastries out from his backpack. I burst into tears of appreciation and excused myself to go to the bathroom. Looking back over my shoulder, I saw my dad pat Keet on the back and smile. There was no denying that Keet was a good guy, and I breathed a sigh of relief that the ice had been broken and they seemed to be getting along well.

By the time Dad was ready to head back to Chicago, he was okay with the situation and said that he and Erica would help me financially so I could stay home with the baby for a while. I was beyond grateful for their help and relieved that I wouldn't have to figure out how to make a minimum-wage job stretch to fit New York living with a baby. Keet and I adjusted to our new relationship as we rearranged the apartment, planned baby showers, and took a Lamaze class. It wasn't the typical honeymoon phase of a new romance—although he did give me amazing foot massages every day after work—but we were young and optimistic and quickly settled into a comfortable routine. When my wonderful son Keon was born in August of 2002, my dad had come full circle—requesting to be called Grand Dude and proudly telling his friends that I didn't feel the need to get married, that a baby was enough of a commitment.

My father, my son—my loves, 2002

JEW-ISH

Throughout my childhood, we had always gone to my dad's family in Chicago for the Jewish holidays but in the spring of 2002, I hosted a Passover Seder at my apartment in New York. Without my ever having gone to Hebrew school or practiced any religion at home, the cultural part of Judaism was what really resonated for me—the songs, the stories, the food, the family—and I was excited to re-create some of that old tribal magic. As a kid, I'd loved the rituals of Passover even though I didn't understand or connect with the symbolism: the horseradish representing the bitterness of slavery, charoset for the bricks made by the Hebrew slaves, the little bowls of salt water standing in for the sweat and tears of the Jewish slaves, the Four Questions. Although I followed no religious conventions in my daily life, it was obvious that night that there was something special, if not sacred, about carrying on these traditions, as my ancestors had done for thousands of years.

That Passover, Erica, Julian, Daniel, Keet, my friend Dani, and her friend Natalie were there with me to experience the joy of my dad in full-on radical rabbi mode and were treated to the funniest and most thought-provoking "religious experience" of my life. We had Haggadahs, but we barely looked at them. My dad not only knew every biblical story from memory, he told them in a historical and geopolitical context that had us all scrambling to remember our early-civilizations education ("So-and-so likely lived in which Mesopotamian city . . . ? Anyone? Anyone? Uruk, that's right!"). I can't tell you how many times since then I've wished that we recorded that night, but there's one lesson I will always remember: babies who supposedly got floated down the river in baskets were usually just illegitimate (I'm looking at you, Moses!).

My dad was not what I would call a religious person, although culturally, he strongly identified as Jewish, and spiritually, more as a Buddhist. As an adult, he studied religion from a historical and political perspective and was able to incorporate what he learned alongside existential philosophy and psychology to form a sort of meta-belief system. He did not believe in God, per se, but was quick to say, "We live in a miraculous world, and it's driven by forces we may never understand. It's awesome, it's mysterious. But I don't give it a name. I don't pretend to understand it or accept that there's some moral code that derives from it that other people know that I don't. I have no problem with God, but making God an entity is not important to me." In *Bedazzled*, he defined it more succinctly as "that universal spirit that animates and binds all things in existence."

Dad had the foundation of the Hebrew school training he'd received as a boy, but his eternally curious mind had gone on a deep dive into the origins of theism across the spectrum. "Well," he'd say, "you have your big five—Christianity, Judaism, Islam, Hinduism, and Buddhism. They all involve some form of deity, whether it's the One God—Holy Father, Adonai, Allah; multiple gods—Brahma, Vishnu, Shiva; or the god (small g) in all of us. And even though they are all actually interconnected, each religion has its own distinct set of rules and rituals that were supposedly mandated by God but really have more to do with the social, economic, or political climate at the time." Then he would go on about how this powerful Jewish leader raised sheep and was at odds with the pig farmer down the river, which may or may not have had something to do with the designation of pigs as *trayf*, or unclean. Of course he would say this as he joyfully bit into a bacon-wrapped shrimp or some other equally verboten delicacy.

LIKE SO MUCH OF Dad's New Life, his interest in Buddhism really grew out of his relationship with Erica, who, as a young adult, had immersed herself in the study and practice of Zen meditation. In his ever-present quest for knowledge and commitment to self-examination, Dad connected deeply with the Four Noble Truths of Buddhism: all existence is suffering; the cause of suffering is desire; freedom from suffering is achieved through the elimination of desire; elimination of desire and suffering can be reached through the Eightfold Path (Right Understanding, Right Intent, Right Speech, Right Action, Right Livelihood, Right Effort, Right Mindfulness, and Right Concentration). In a conversation with Rainn Wilson for his SoulPancake series, he elaborated, "We're suffering beings. It's our nature. We suffer from the want of what we don't have. The fear of losing what we do have. We are engaged in this process for the rest of our lives. And there's no ending . . . until our last breath." He often talked about professional success as a sort of wake-up call: *Okay, I've achieved all of these great things and, guess what? It's still not enough. So there must be more to life than money, power, and fame, but what?* It was this search for something more that led him, aptly, to Viktor Frankl's book *Man's Search for Meaning*. In it, Frankl, a psychiatrist, recounts his experience in Auschwitz during World War II and uses that experience to introduce his theory of logotherapy (basically, an approach to psychoanalysis that focuses on finding and pursuing meaning in one's life). This really resonated with my dad and seemed to synthesize perfectly with the teachings of Buddhism (many paths to enlightenment, blah blah blah—and I mean that "blah blah blah" in the most respectful way possible). To help the spiritually challenged, like myself, Dad came up with "The 5 Minute Buddhist" (see below), which he had printed, laminated, and folded like a takeout menu, ready to hand out to anyone who expressed an interest.

THE 5 MINUTE BUDDHIST

❖ Man is supreme and responsible for his own thoughts, ideas, beliefs, and actions.
❖ All existence is conditioned, relative, interdependent, and based on cause and effect.
❖ The self, the soul, the ego are mental projections, false beliefs—*Anatta* (no-self, no-soul). They exist as conventional truth, but not as ultimate truth.

The Five Aggregates
"Being" is experienced as:
1. Matter
2. Sensation
3. Perception
4. Mental formation
5. Consciousness

The Four Noble Truths
1. Life is characterized by impermanence and suffering, or Dukkha (insatiable thirst).
2. The Origin of *Dukkha* (suffering) is attachment to desire.
3. The Cessation of *Dukkha* is achieved, not by belief, but by the contemplation, understanding, and elimination of desire and attachment.
4. The Noble Eight-fold Path is the way to achieve the cessation of *Dukkha*.

The Noble Eight-fold Path
1. Right Understanding
2. Right Thought
3. Right Speech
4. Right Action
5. Right Livelihood
6. Right Effort
7. Right Mindfulness
8. Right Concentration

Resulting in:

Ethical Conduct — speech, action, livelihood
Mental Discipline — effort, mindfulness, concentration
Wisdom — understanding and thought

To create:

The Seven Factors of Enlightenment
1. Mindfulness
2. Investigation and research
3. Energy
4. Joy
5. Relaxation
6. Concentration
7. Equanimity

Which result in:

The Four Sublime States
1. Unlimited universal love and good will
2. Compassion for all suffering beings
3. Sympathetic joy for the success and well-being of others
4. Equanimity

The Five Hindrances
1. Sensual lust
2. Ill-will
3. Physical and mental languor and torpor
4. Restlessness and worry
5. Doubt and skepticism

The Five Precepts
The moral obligations of a lay Buddhist:
1. Not to destroy life
2. Not to steal
3. Not to commit adultery
4. Not to lie
5. Not to take intoxicating drink

❖ Don't know.
❖ Only go straight for 10,000 years.
❖ Save all sentient beings from suffering.

The Miracle is not to walk on water. The Miracle is to walk on the green Earth, dwelling deeply in the present moment, feeling truly alive. —Thich Nhat Hanh

As with everything else, I teased him (lovingly) about his earnest proselytizing.

"What, are you some kind of Buddhist missionary now? Are you gonna start hanging out at the airport handing out your little pamphlets?"

"Nah, I'm not trying to convert anyone. It's just my compulsive need to share knowledge running up against my aversion to explaining the same thing over and over again."

"Well, *that* I can relate to."

"Ooh, my little cynic. Look, even if one person out of a hundred finds something in here that helps them live a better life, or is moved to act out of compassion for someone else, then hey, why not, right? Paper is cheap."

"Yeah, but the laminating!"

Even though he had left education behind as a career, things like "The 5 Minute Buddhist" and the deep underlying messages in many of his later films indicate to me that he never really lost his desire to teach. He so enjoyed the process of puzzling out his beliefs—learning the history, reading the experts, engaging with other deep-thinking people in his life—that once he arrived at the idea that worked for him (in this case, a spiritual and psychological philosophy that compels the discovery/creation of meaning in one's life), he couldn't help but want to share it with as many people as possible.

Dad's Buddhist cred was cinched the first time he and Erica had the opportunity to meet the Dalai Lama, in Washington, DC, in 2005. After attending His Holiness's public speech the previous day, they were able to spend fifteen minutes with him in his suite at the Four Seasons. ("Wait, Dad. The Dalai Lama stays at the Four Seasons?" "Yep. Great room, too.") They saw him again in 2007 when Erica helped produce part of HHDL's event at Chicago's Millennium Park. My dad described both of these meetings as profound and uplifting, and felt very fortunate to have spent even a few minutes in such an amazing presence. Still, his beloved Buddhism had its limits, and my dad certainly never stopped desiring and enjoying his earthly pleasures. When he took to wearing a string of meditation beads around his wrist, he told people he was on a Buddhist diet and the beads reminded him not to eat too much—though he added, "They get in the way when I'm cutting my steak, so I take them off for meals." While it would be easy to write this off as a casual one liner, I think it actually speaks to my dad's postmodern take on the theories and principles that guided his beliefs.

Rather than blindly accept any one religion or philosophy in its entirety, he plucked the bits and pieces that resonated with him and constructed his own ideological framework. For example, in a speech he made for the Aitz Chaim Congregation on Jews and creativity (available on YouTube, if you're interested), he wove together classic biblical stories (Adam and Eve, Noah's ark, Abraham, Moses, etc.) with Confucianism, Buddhism, Rodney Dangerfield, Chagall, Cinderella, and the Jewish media mafia. His point, in this particular speech, but also in life, was that while there is something inherently creative at the heart of Judaism, creativity is not exclusive to Judaism and nothing exists in a vacuum. In the same way that his approach to comedy may have felt specifically Jewish to him, it appealed to everyone precisely because it tapped into the universal themes that cut through religious and cultural differences. His ability to see the big picture, alongside his skill in making connections between seemingly disparate viewpoints, was one of his greatest strengths as a filmmaker and a person.

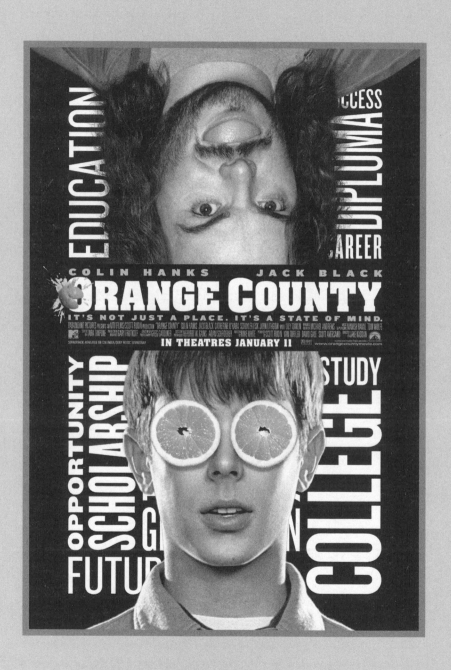

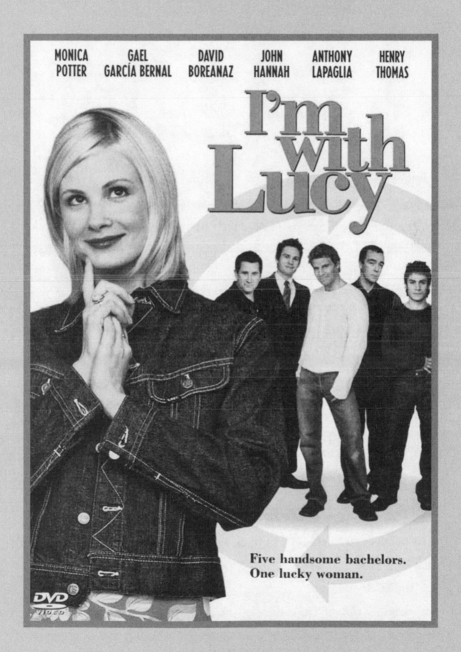

ORANGE COUNTY
(2002)

Written by MIKE WHITE
Directed by JAKE KASDAN

High school senior Shaun Brumder (Colin Hanks) has his heart set on going to Stanford. When his guidance counselor accidentally sends the wrong transcript, Shaun—with the "help" of his brother (Jack Black) and girlfriend (Schuyler Fisk)—takes matters into his own hands to set the record straight.

I'M WITH LUCY
(2002)

Written by ERIC POMERANCE
Directed by JON SHERMAN

Lucy (Monica Potter) is ready to walk down the aisle with the man of her dreams, but which one of the five blind dates she recalls—the sexy playwright (Gael García Bernal), the cocky baseball player (Anthony LaPaglia), the nerdy store owner (Henry Thomas), the handsome physical therapist (David Boreanaz), or the shy doctor (John Hannah)—will turn out to be Mr. Right?

Although my dad did some acting over the years, with big roles in *Baby Boom* and *Stealing Home* and smaller parts in *Airheads*, *Love Affair*, *As Good As It Gets*, *Walk Hard*, and *The Last Kiss*, to me, he generally did not seem as comfortable in front of the camera as he did behind it. Jake Kasdan, who directed *Orange County*, is an old family friend and knew when he got the green light for the film that he wanted my dad to be a part of it. My dad loved the *Orange County* script and was really excited to work with Jake in his role as the college admissions dean. When he described the film to me and explained that his character accidentally takes several hits of MDMA, I asked, "Soooo . . . do you want me to get you some Ecstasy for research purposes?"

"I don't think so, my baby," he laughed, "but thank you. I've heard it's like a mix of LSD and speed, and as you know, I researched both of those extensively back in my youth, so I should be okay." It was on the set of *Orange County* that my dad first met Jack Black, who would later star in *Year One*. They hit it off right away, bonding over their shared love of music and my dad's affection for Jack's band, Tenacious D.

My dad liked his creature comforts but was not a diva when it came to being part of someone else's project. Sadly, my grandmother Ruth passed away the night before my dad's last day of filming on *Orange County*, but he went ahead with the workday as planned, because he knew how difficult it would be to reschedule the day. The one request he did make of Jake was to change the scene in which his character went down on the male lead. "I didn't want to be walking down the street and have school buses of kids rolling by and shouting, 'Hey, Blow Job Guy!'" In the end, he was happy with the work he did on *Orange County* and I, as always, love how his real personality shone through his character, even in a totally ridiculous situation. We would often make each other laugh in the years to follow by repeating his line "Sean, you're the same height as me. That is neat!"

I was very pregnant with Keon in the summer of 2002 when Dad did about a week of work on *I'm with Lucy*, playing Monica Potter's father opposite Julie Christie (which he was very excited about). He liked Monica a lot and really bonded with Anthony LaPaglia, whom he later cast in *Analyze That*. It was fun to hang out on set with him in Central Park. I remember joking that he should make the most of the father-of-the-bride scene because I would probably never get married.

Even though my dad always saw acting as the weakest link in his creative chain, he seemed to revel in the novelty of the attention he got from being in front of the camera rather than behind it. The only role

I know of that he ever submitted himself for was a part in the Coen brothers' *A Serious Man*, which he didn't get. As he got older, his self-consciousness about his appearance probably prevented him from creating and seeking out more opportunities to act, but when asked, he was more than happy to oblige.

DO GOOD

A lot of my dad's advice about life, as an adult, did not seem very practical: *Go stand next to the smartest person in the room; Be in the right place at the right time; Do what makes you happy and the rest will follow; Be great at what you're doing and the right people will notice*; etc. Given the serendipitous nature of his own success, I understand that this perspective came out of his own experience, but it wasn't something that could be easily replicated. Sometimes I wish he had told me about things like what kind of jobs make good money, living within your means, how to balance realism and expectations, or tips to avoid getting stuck in a rut.

After about a year and a half of my being a full-time mom, I started to think more seriously about what I wanted to do as a career. "You're lucky," my dad said. "We've been more than happy to give you a financial safety net . . . But it's not a hammock for you to just lay around in, so it's time to get up and get out there." Even though he said this in the nicest, gentlest way, I panicked. What was I going to do? I didn't want to go back to teaching, because I worried about having enough energy and patience to deal with kids all day and then come home and still be good for my own kid. I had also been frustrated by the limits of the classroom when it came to students' emotional and behavioral issues. I hated to hand these kids off to the school counselor, or worse, just smile and nod at the parents every morning even though we both knew their child was struggling and needed help. I knew I wanted to be in a "helping" profession but wasn't sure what specialty would suit me best. I looked at a few different options (psychology, art therapy) and eventually decided that social work would offer the most flexibility in terms of jobs. I was concerned about not making enough money as a social worker to support myself in New York but my dad reassured me that this should not be the deciding factor in my choice. "Listen, I do what I do because I like it, but also because it gives us all the luxury to have the kind of lives we want. I want you to be happy and productive and engaged with the world. If that means subsidizing your income, so be it. You're doing the good karmic work for all of us." So with my dad's generous emotional and financial support, I entered the master's program for social work at Yeshiva University in 2004.

Going to Yeshiva was a bizarre experience. The graduate program is actually only 50 percent Jewish but the majority of those are Orthodox, and to them, even though I am 100 percent Ashkenazi, I might as well have been a deacon in a Southern Baptist church. I loved sitting in the lounge between classes listening to groups of wigged twenty-two-year-old girls talk about the trials of finding a good match (cue the yenta) or how wearing skirts over their sweatpants at the gym made it hard to use certain weight machines. I did not love being in classes with people who seemed to have no business going into the profession of social work, who said things like "Why should illegal aliens get government services?" or "[Insert horrible thing] never happens in *my* community!" or "I don't know why we need to take cultural competency courses. I'm not going to work with any of those people." Hearing these kinds of statements, my heart would start pounding and I would get so angry, I'd be shaking, too afraid of losing control of my emotions to say anything.

"So speak up!" my dad said when I called him one night after a particularly challenging class. "You never have a problem telling me when I'm wrong."

"Well, you're hardly ever wrong," I laughed. "Plus, I know I'm not going to change the way they think, so what's the point?"

"The point is, it's your duty as a human being to do the right thing. Jewish Orthodoxy is no different from Islamic or Christian fundamentalism and people need to hear opinions outside of their bubbles. Rabbi Kula said that fundamentalism has a way of making God very small. Does God care more about your clothing choices than he does about thousands of people starving or being tortured? Are you familiar with the phrase '*tikkun olam*'?"

"Yes, rabbi, 'repair the world,' I know," I teased. "But it seems like they're only interested in 'tikkuning' their own 'olam' and I don't know enough to make any religious arguments against their ignorance."

"'Tikkuning' their own 'olam,'" he repeated, chuckling. "You're a funny girl, did you know that?"

"I think it runs in the family."

The next day, I met with one of my professors and explained the problem. He helped me come up with a scripted response that I still use today. "I'm having a strong reaction to what you just said. Can you clarify your point so I can make sure I understand? [*Listen*] It seems like you may not be aware that what you're saying is rooted in racism/sexism/homophobia/xenophobia/etc. Are you interested in having a conversation about that? Yes? Great. No? Well then, please know that your comments come across as highly ignorant and offensive."

My fieldwork during the three-year program consisted of community organizing for a corrupt city council member in Washington Heights, running support groups for teens in an after-school program of the Harlem Children's Zone, and doing individual counseling and Medicare enrollment for seniors at a nursing home. Although these were all amazing learning experiences on many levels, none of them was exactly the type of work I wanted to do. I ended up landing the perfect job on the first interview I went on after graduation—maternity/NICU social worker at Metropolitan Hospital Center.

Over the next few years, I worked with hundreds of pregnant and postpartum women, providing assessment, counseling, and referrals to other agencies, as they dealt with a full spectrum of perinatal and life issues. Because Met was a public hospital (part of the New York City Health and Hospitals Corporation system), every patient was considered high-risk. That meant that even the least complicated cases usually involved women with extremely limited financial resources and very little social support. Apart from the most basic manifestations of poverty (crowded living conditions in poorly maintained housing, no money to buy baby supplies), many of the patients also suffered from severe depression and anxiety, particularly the large population of immigrant women, who had often left their entire families behind in their home countries to come and work in the US. And those were the "easy" cases. Issues around domestic violence, sexual abuse, drug addiction, homelessness, severe medical conditions, mental illness, and fetal demise rounded out my caseload. It was tough work but I loved it, and at the end of even the most difficult days, my dad was always just a phone call away, ready to let me vent or make me laugh as needed.

"It's just so horrible and so frustrating," I half-sobbed into the phone after a particularly tough day. "I can bend over backward doing every-thing I possibly can for these families and in the end, it doesn't make a damn bit of difference. It's a drop in the bucket."

"But you're there for them, Violet, and that's important."

"Is it? Really? This woman has the mind of a ten-year-old, had three other children taken away from her, the boyfriend is an asshole, she lives in a shelter, and now she's pregnant with a baby that has so many medical problems, it probably won't even survive. What can I possibly do for her? Almost nothing."

"God, that's sad."

"I know!"

"But look, even if you can't solve her problems, treating this woman with respect and compassion is important because she probably doesn't get much of either. When I worked at the psych ward, I spent a whole weekend on suicide watch with this woman. On Monday, the doctors cleared her to leave and she smiled at me over her shoulder as she walked out the door. I was so naïve, I thought, *Well, I really helped her.* The next day they told me she'd slit her wrists as soon as her husband went to work. I felt awful, of course, but as time wore on I realized that sometimes just being a point of light on someone's path, wherever it takes them, is all you can do. And it may not be much, but at least it's something. And I'm really proud of you, whatever that's worth."

I continued doing this type of work for the next eight years. Sometimes I was actually able to help people, and sometimes I felt like I was sending people out the door with a Band-Aid on a broken leg. Either way, my dad's words hit home and were a source of comfort to me on difficult days, even after he was gone.

NERD ALERT

My dad loved words. He did the *New York Times* crossword puzzle daily, in ink, for as long as I can remember. Monday puzzles took him about ten minutes; Saturday and Sunday, thirty minutes, tops. He obsessively played an anagram game on his handheld digital dictionary and would happily discuss the origin of this word or that, or educate you on the world's longest palindrome. He was also very creative with his swearing, coming up with profane hybrids to fit whatever frustrating situation he was in. "You shirtfuck!" he once growled at his suitcase as he packed and one shirt refused to lie flat. "Waterfucker asshole!" he'd yell at the sink when the faucet sprayed all over him. In all seriousness, though, he knew the answer to almost every question on *Jeopardy!* and had deep knowledge of a variety of subjects, ranging from antidisestablishmentarianism to the global cultural history of the zither.

When I would tell him how smart he was, he'd say, "Nah, I've just been around for a long time." But it was more than that. He had an amazing memory; he could tell you the name of every teacher he ever had and what their quirks were. He had an ear for languages and over the years had picked up enough Yiddish, German, Russian, Greek, and French to have charming and pointless conversations wherever he went. Fans and friends alike were delighted to be greeted with little gems like *"Dos hitl iz gut nor der kop iz tsu kleyn"* (The hat is fine but the head is too small) or *"Uzhasno kholodno. V takuyu pogodu tol'ko doma sidet"* (It's so cold. Better to sit at home). He devoured knowledge as if it were a rack of lamb, reading voraciously and then finding practical and fascinating ways to work any new information into his everyday conversations. The nonfiction he read—*Guns, Germs, and Steel*; *Quest for Identity*; *A History of God*; *Man's Search for Meaning*; *A Distant Mirror*; *A Brief History of Time*—sat by his bedside next to the storytellers he loved: Paul Bowles, Philip Roth, Paul Auster, Jonathan Lethem, David Sedaris. These were his bibles. He had been educated in the Chicago public school system of the 1950s, and while there may not have been a lot of critical thinking going on, he'd read all the "classics," knew US history backward and forward, had memorized the periodic table, and could diagram a sentence like nobody's business.

Because of his work, Dad had the opportunity to meet and become friends with some of the filmmakers, artists, and writers he admired so deeply and he wasn't shy about expressing his enthusiasm for their talent. In an email he sent to Richard Russo (see page 276) my dad shared how much he had enjoyed his latest novel.

More thoughtful than just your average fan letter, this correspondence illustrates both how comfortable my dad was sharing his personal connections to Russo's work and how, even when swept away by a compelling narrative, he still maintained a sharp eye toward copyediting. In fact, Dad once received a fan letter that was so poorly written, he

that old cape magic ▢ Inbox x

harold ramis   6/23/09 ☆ ↩ ▾
to Richard ▾

rick,
i got the advance copy of the book and took it with me to nantucket this weekend for the film festival. strange coincidence to be
reading it as we flew over the cape. i finished it this morning sitting in bed with erica and burst into tears at the end. i might have
said this to you before, but i don't think anyone writes about marriage, especially long marriages, with more insight, wisdom or
compassion. these issues of grief and isolation are recurring themes in my life, and judging from the kind of sitcom banter i hear
between other couples we know, i am not alone in this. i don't know to what extent your writing reflects your own experience, but
i do know that it takes courage to speak the complicated truth about love and loss in committed relationships. i recently read
philip roth's *exit ghost,* and i know he'd make the deconstructionist argument that the real facts of your own marriage have
nothing to do with the text, but i feel like you've been there and that thought somehow comforts me. as i race through my mid-
60s, life is getting steadily easier socially and professionally, and more complicated, ambiguous, and poignant on the personal
and family front. you're my hero; punched in the face, rear-ended by karma, and man enough to keep coming back.

okay, one proofreading note. on p. 192, last sentence of the middle paragraph, "heal" where it should be "heel."

congratulations,
harold

corrected the grammatical errors in a red pen and sent it back. Afterward, he felt badly about it, but he was ultimately vindicated when,
years later, the fan approached him on the street and told him that receiving the corrected letter had been humiliating, but also pushed him
to go back to school and ultimately changed the course of his life.

In my mind, there was nothing my dad didn't know. In 2004, after
watching fourteen-year-old David Tidmarsh win the National Spelling
Bee with the word "autochthonous," I bragged to my friends that even
though none of us had ever heard this word before or had any idea what
it meant, my dad *definitely* would. "No way," they said. "Call him now."
I got him on the phone and told him the word. "Nope," he said. "No
idea." "You've disgraced our family name," I joked. "Oy, sorry, my baby.
I'll do better next time." My shame, of course, was feigned, but I was
actually shocked that there was a word out there that my father didn't
know. His scope was that broad and his knowledge was just that deep.

SISTER ACT

One day in the spring of 2004, my dad called. His voice sounded slightly off, maybe a little forced, as he broke the news. "I heard from Amy Heckerling."

"Oh, really?" I made sure to keep my tone casual and calm even though my stomach lurched a little. "What did she say?"

"She said that Mollie knows everything and wants to meet me."

"Really? Wow. How do you feel about that?"

"Oy, I don't know. Nervous. Excited."

"I bet."

"She goes to NYU and they have an apartment on the Upper West Side."

"That's crazy. What if she's, like, my next-door neighbor?"

"Well, we'll find out. I'm thinking I'll meet her when we're in town next month on the way to the Vineyard."

"Yikes. Okay."

"I'm going to talk to her on the phone later this week. Are you okay with this? Does it freak you out?"

"Not really. I thought it would but . . ."

"Erica is kind of freaked out."

"Really? Why?"

"Ohhh, I think she's worried about the potential for disaster."

"What's new?" I laughed. "They don't want anything from you though, right? It's not going to be a big dramatic scene, is it? She just wants to meet?"

"I think so. That's what Amy said. We'll see. Oh my God. I hope it isn't a total disaster."

"It won't be," I reassured him. In truth, I had no idea if it would be a disaster or not, but I wasn't used to seeing my dad so out of sorts and I wanted to give him the same comfort and confidence that he'd always given me.

Phone calls happened, arrangements were made. The plan was for all of us to meet her and say hi and then Mollie and Dad would go alone to have coffee and talk while Amy, Erica, Julian (then fourteen), Daniel (then ten), toddler Keon, and I would have lunch and wait for them. If things went well, we could all go back to my apartment. If they didn't, we'd go our separate ways. Dad was so nervous—blinky and compulsively adjusting his shirt. Erica kept squeezing my arm and saying, "I can't believe this is happening." I can only imagine the excitement, worry, and anticipation they were feeling because I felt nothing, disassociated— in other words, my default mode for when other people are emotional.

Mollie and Amy walked up to us on Broadway and introductions were made. I greeted Mollie warmly and we awkwardly embraced. She was eighteen, in a flowery dress and army jacket, with long red hair and my dad's face. Amy was petite and pale and looked like a rock star who had just rolled out of bed. Dad and Mollie went off to French Roast while the rest of us went to Artie's Deli. Amy and Erica chatted and drank iced tea while the boys ate bagels and I wrangled Keon. After about an hour, Dad and Mollie walked in smiling and we all went back to my apartment to hang out. What I remember most about that first day is how Mollie seemed so similar to us and yet so different at the same time. Physically, there was an undeniable resemblance. I mean, she looked even more like my dad than I did, fiery red hair notwithstanding. In fact, seeing her made me realize how much of my looks had come from my mother. But where nature ends and nurture takes over, Mollie was like a stranger. Her vibe, cadence, and timing were so different from ours. Granted, it was an overwhelming day for her, but she seemed shy and hesitant in a way I hadn't anticipated. I could tell she was funny, and we kept trying to connect, but I felt like we were always just a beat off from really clicking. Mostly, though, I was just relieved that it seemed to be a drama-free encounter. As we wrapped up the evening, she and I exchanged phone numbers and said we'd get together soon.

Of course, after Mollie and Amy left, we grilled my dad on how their conversation had gone.

"I think it was good," he vocal-fried. "It all just feels so big."

"Okay, just give us the nutshell," I nudged.

"Well, she wanted to know the story from my perspective. I told her and she seemed okay with it. She told me how it was for her to find out. I don't know. I apologized."

"For what?"

This isn't awkward at all, right? (Left to right): *Julian, Keon, me, Daniel, and Mollie, 2004*

"For not having been there for her. It seemed like the right thing to do at the time but . . . who knows? Right for me, but maybe not for her."

"It seems like she turned out pretty well in spite of it all though, no?"

"Oh yeah, she did just fine without me. She's smart. She's funny. She writes . . . But still. It's big, my baby. Big, big, big!"

A few months later, Dad was in New York alone and asked me if I wanted to go to Mollie's birthday party with him. We went to someone's apartment downtown and smoked pot with some people on the roof. I, not knowing who knew what, mistakenly introduced myself to a young woman as Mollie's sister. She was immediately taken aback. "What? I'm her cousin. How is that possible?" Oops. Mollie was tough to read but tried to reassure me it was okay. I felt bad about possibly messing things up for Mollie with her family, but I was also confused. Now that we all knew each other, weren't things going to be out in the open? Apparently not, as there were still strong feelings and issues to be resolved in this complicated situation.*

Mollie and I didn't talk for almost two years after that. Not because we didn't want to, just because we were both lazy flakes. She and my dad spoke and emailed from time to time but didn't seem to develop a steady rhythm with each other. He always spoke about her with a kind of wistfulness that I found heartbreaking. I know he was the bad guy in their scenario; that wasn't a position he often was in, and it weighed on him.

About five years after our initial meeting, Mollie came over to my apartment. We got stoned, clicked (hallelujah!), and started to have a real relationship of our own. She was hilarious and creative and ballsy and we were amazed at all of the overlap in our personalities and up-bringings despite the differences. Now, I may be partial to oddly neurotic Jewish girls who say "fuck" a lot and aren't afraid of a good Holocaust joke, but she was like a dream come true. Actually, I had never met anyone like her, and I was kind of in love. She came over every Tuesday night for the next year and we became really close. My kids loved her because she made dirty jokes and laughed at their shenanigans. One night, as she watched me wage full-scale bedtime warfare against my two little rebels, she laughed into her beer bottle as

---

* Still ongoing, issues around the truth of Mollie's paternity led to her being cut off by some members of her family. This is, in part, why I've chosen to reveal this long-held secret and claim Mollie officially (with her consent, of course) as one of us. I know my dad would have stepped up and done the same if he were here.

I finally closed their bedroom door and tiptoed back into the living room. We'd just started talking when, out of nowhere, she flipped me the bird.

"Did you just give me the finger?" I asked mock incredulously.

"No, Keon is behind you making faces and being a little shit," she laughed.

"Oh," I said, grinning from ear to ear, "well then, that's fine."

The parallels and contrasts between Mollie and myself would make for a great psychological study, or at the very least, an interesting episode of *Separated at Birth*. We grew up in similarly unusual Hollywood families, so our frames of reference line up almost identically; however, whereas I am confident but shy, she struggles with low self-esteem but is very brave. She was the lead singer in a rock band for several years and is now writing scripts, making puppets, and doing stand-up comedy. Badass, right? Our mutual admiration for each other ("You're

Sisters

amazing!" "No, you're amazing!") allowed us to get close without it ever feeling competitive.

Ironically, in 2004, another sister joined the family when Ayda Wondemu came from Ethiopia to stay with Dad & Co. and attend Julian and Daniel's private school. Ayda, fifteen and entering her sophomore year, had researched schools and contacted the admissions department on her own, outside of any established exchange program. They, in turn, reached out to my family, who agreed to host her. Erica and Dad agreed right away. For the first year she lived with Dad and Erica, Ayda pretty much ate only meat and chocolate (separately, of course) and read romance novels obsessively. I think she clung to these familiar things because the adjustment to a totally new life was so overwhelming. Over time, she expanded her tastes—in both food and reading—and she thrived socially and academically at school. Amazingly, despite the differences in background, she fit right in with the family and all of our *mishigas*.

Ayda, Julian, and Daniel lived as siblings and were very close. Ayda and I liked each other from the start but both felt a little threatened nonetheless. She stayed in what had originally been "my" room in the Glencoe house and seemed to fulfill all of my dad's daughterly requirements—funny, sweet, intellectual, creative. Was this the other daughter I should have been worrying about instead of Mollie? Thankfully, no. As it turned out, whatever concerns I had were totally unfounded. My dad adored Ayda (and Mollie) but there was plenty of love to go around.

What was supposed to have been a one-year stay stretched into two, then three, and Ayda graduated from North Shore Country Day in 2007. She then went on to Tufts, where she double-majored in international

Me and Ayda, 2009

affairs and French literature, receiving her BA, with honors, in 2011. We remained her home base through college—Dad, Erica, and the boys in Chicago, and me and my brood in New York. Ayda did a few rotations of relief work in the Philippines and Uganda before eventually getting her master's in international affairs from Johns Hopkins. She is now working at an NGO refugee camp in South Sudan. We all talk to her regularly and are hopeful that she will be able to return to her second home and us, her second family, soon.

Far from where I started as a lonely only child, the big, jumbled mess of our family now includes five siblings connected in various ways by DNA, shared history, choice, and, most important, love. Julian, Daniel, Mollie, Ayda, and I may not all share the traditional bonds of parentage or the experience of growing up under the same roof, but we are deeply and undeniably connected, and I value the relationships I have with all of them beyond anything I could ever have imagined. Even though he's not here with us, I know that my dad, always the proud patriarch, is beaming at us—his beautiful mess of a family—from wherever he is.

THE ICE HARVEST
(2005)

―――

Written by RICHARD RUSSO and ROBERT BENTON
(based on the novel by SCOTT PHILLIPS)
Directed by HAROLD RAMIS

Mob attorney Charlie Arglist (John Cusack) plays by his own rules. When he and Vic (Billy Bob Thornton) decide to steal money from the big boss (Randy Quaid), their plan to leave town falls apart when an ice storm sweeps through the area on Christmas Eve.

CHARLIE
It's Christmas! Everyone's nice on Christmas!

VIC
Only morons are nice on Christmas.

Ramis is at his best when dealing with men facing a soul-defining crisis, and he finds plenty to work with in Russo and Benton's script, which offers Russo's trademark blend of colorful characters and slow-building dilemmas. *The Ice Harvest* finds them all operating in top form in as dark a territory as they've ever explored.

—KEITH PHIPPS, AV CLUB

There is very little fun in "The Ice Harvest," which wouldn't pose a problem if the film had some fleshed-out ideas to go along with the booze, the booty and the recycled plot points [. . .] As expected from a Harold Ramis film, there are some nice comedy bits mixed into Charlie's exchanges with friend, foe and family member. It's too bad that these bits are so few and far between.

—MANOHLA DARGIS, *THE NEW YORK TIMES*

The Ice Harvest was my dad's foray into darker, low(er)-budget waters. The script, based on a Scott Phillips novel, came to him via his agent at UTA, and he and his producing partner Laurel Ward knew right away that they wanted to make the movie. Dad had been a fan of Richard Russo and Robert Benton, and the story dealt with one of his favorite subjects: existentialism. My dad was drawn to the construct of these characters who had seemingly lost all sense of meaning and chose lives of vice and violence over the bland dissatisfaction of the American Dream. He likened it to men who stop at bars on their way home from work and then eventually just stop going home.

In one scene, Charlie (John Cusack) talks about his father and uncle, fraternal twins who lived opposite lives and died one day apart. "You do one thing, you do another . . . I mean, so what? What's the difference? Same result." This dialogue points to a much bleaker outlook than was the norm for my dad, but he connected with the material and felt the film had something important to say. Less profound, but more fun, was the fact that he spent several days auditioning exotic dancers for the various club scenes in the movie. He called me one evening from his car after a long day of watching strippers shimmy up and down a pole and said, "I saw about thirty naked and amazingly athletic women today. I don't know how they do it. Do I have the best job in the world or what?"

The book and the original script ended with the John Cusack character, Charlie, dying, but the test audiences were not happy with that. "People were really loving the movie, laughing in all the right places, but then as soon as Charlie died, it was like all the air got sucked out of the room," he told me. "I think Laurel actually threw up." Apparently, people weren't ready to embrace the ultimate existential ending—death. One of the response cards even said, "You killed Lloyd Dobler." My dad went back to the screenwriters and said, "Okay, what about if Charlie doesn't die at the end?" to which Richard Russo replied, "Well, this just really fucks Scott Phillips. I mean, God, it completely fucks him. That being said, let the fucking begin." So they rewrote and reshot the ending, but ultimately, the film, while receiving mixed reviews from critics, was not a hit.

I was proud of my dad for venturing outside of his comfort zone with *The Ice Harvest* even though I think ultimately the movie seemed more like an homage to the Coen brothers than a Harold Ramis film. He was, again, disappointed that audiences didn't show up at the theaters but pleased with the work he'd done and the performances the actors had given.

BIG HEAD, BIG HEART

My dad loved being recognized. Early on in his relationship with Erica, they were approached by some fans at a restaurant, wanting autographs. Erica, very nicely, said, "I'm sorry, but we're having dinner and would like some privacy. Thank you." My dad smiled as the fans went away, leaned in close to Erica, and said softly, "I really love you. Please don't *ever* do that again." He was confident, but like most people, especially those in the entertainment business, he thrived on validation from others. He considered things like signing autographs, talking to film enthusiasts about the production process, and donating scripts and other movie memorabilia to charities to be important parts of his job. In return, he received praise, adoration, and perks wherever he went. From throwing out the first pitch at a Cubs game, to being honored by the philanthropic organizations he was involved with, to taking my brothers to NBA All-Star weekends, to going backstage at every show he saw—he loved it all.

"It's the Golden Rule, my baby," he once said. "Treat people with respect and they will kiss your butt forever."

"Dad!"

"I'm joking!" He laughed, eyes twinkling. "But I do always try to put positive energy and actions out into the world, and it's nice when that good stuff comes back."

In the rare cases when it didn't, my dad wasn't always able to handle his disappointment in the most graceful way. In 2005, we were visiting the family in Chicago and we had all gone downtown to do some sightseeing. Hungry and tired after doing the Lincoln Park Zoo and Navy Pier, we were trying to get a table at the Cheesecake Factory. It was crowded and the host told us we'd have to wait at least an hour. My dad was *pissed*. Getting a good table at any restaurant at the drop of a hat was his version of being a hunter and bringing home an elk for dinner. There was some discussion between him and Erica as we waited awkwardly in the lobby.

"Don't they recognize me?"

"How could they not recognize you? Should you slip him some money?"

I was halfheartedly disgusted by the whole situation. I mean, it was great to get those perks when they were available, but if no one is offering, I'm of the mind-set that it's better to just wait in line like everyone else.

"Let's just wait, Dad. It's fine. It's the fucking Cheesecake Factory. Who cares?"

"I care," he snapped. "If they don't know who I am, they're idiots. If they know who I am and don't care, they're assholes."

"Okay, Mr. Down-to-Earth," I snorted.

Unwilling to wait it out, he called his assistant, Laurel, to have her call the Cheesecake Factory and say, "I'm looking for Harold Ramis. I believe he's having dinner there tonight." That sense of entitlement didn't show itself too often, but when it did . . . well, let's just say it wasn't pretty.

In line with his overall equanimity, my dad balanced out his vanity and privilege with an almost endless generosity. He felt that one of the best parts of his success was being able to pay it forward and use whatever influence he had to help the people around him. He wrote countless letters of recommendation, helped connect individuals who needed an introduction, and always gave everyone a chance. Several of the last emails he sent from the hospital, before his illness became serious, were notes like "Can you help this person?" and "My good friend's daughter is looking for a job."

He was especially loyal and helpful to those who had worked for him, often championing their rise up the ranks. Trevor Albert, who was a PA on *Caddyshack*, eventually became my dad's producing partner. Both of his longtime assistants, Suzanne Herrington and Laurel Ward, moved up over the years to producers on his films. After *Club*

Paradise, Dad hired my childhood babysitter Lin Coleman to do post-production clerical work at Ocean Pictures and invited her to observe in the editing room. When she showed an interest in the process, he helped her get an apprenticeship that eventually led to her working as an assistant editor on more than twenty films. Gene Stupnitsky and Lee Eisenberg, who wrote for *The Office* and cowrote *Year One* (among other things), started out, respectively, as a summer intern at Ocean Pictures and a waiter on Martha's Vineyard. And that is just a fraction of the beneficiaries of my dad's professional mentorship that I know about. He was not only genuinely curious about people's interests and experiences but did whatever he could to see those he cared about succeed.

OB-LA-DI, OB-LA-DA

During my second year of grad school, in early 2006, Keet and I discussed the idea of having another baby. He and I had done a lot of couples counseling, had our communication skills down pat, and were great partners in terms of practical, day-to-day life. As the only child from my parents' marriage, I thought it was important for Keon to have a sibling with the same mom and dad, so he wouldn't be alone in dealing with whatever family stuff arose down the line.

Once we agreed that we wanted another child, I went to my dad and Erica with a proposal. "Keet and I want to have another baby. If I can plan it out right, I can have it around the same time that I graduate and then I'll take some time off, whatever you feel comfortable with, and then get a job. So, really, it would only extend your support by another year, tops. If you don't want to, I understand. But it would be really great to have your blessing (and your money). So, think about it."

They were amenable to the proposal and laughed at my desire to plan everything out. When we found out I was having a girl, everyone was pretty excited. Erica went crazy buying baby clothes and my dad suggested the name Corrina after one of his favorite Bob Dylan songs.* My mom adored both Keet and Keon and was happy that we were adding to our little family. She and Erica both gave me versions of the "payback's a bitch" talk and said they looked forward to seeing how I would handle the challenges of dealing with what would undoubtedly be another feisty and strong-willed little lady in the mix.

Even without their warnings, I was already keenly aware of my own anxiety around raising a daughter. Though vastly different, my relationships with the two women in my life had been so contentious throughout my childhood and adolescence that I felt a kind of mild PTSD when I thought about the possibility of re-creating those dynamics with my own child. Even though, at four years old, Keon could wear me down with his endless questions, boundless energy, and occasional tantrums, it was standard developmental stuff that paled in comparison to the love I felt for him—my firstborn, my mama's boy. But a loving and uncomplicated mother-daughter bond? I had no frame of reference and could already feel myself building a wall between me and my unborn baby girl, certain that no matter what I did, she would be hopelessly attached to Keet and want nothing to do with me. I tried to work through these fears using tools I'd learned in my social work classes and also met weekly with a therapist. I did my best to parse the interaction of my own personality (good and bad) with my mom's and Erica's. I thought about each of their family histories, my own, and what, in an ideal world, I wanted my daughter's to be.

Throughout the pregnancy, unable to sleep, I would call my dad late

---

* We loved the name but changed the spelling.

at night. Sometimes I needed to unload whatever was on my mind and other times, I just wanted to be distracted and would ask for updates on my brothers, his work, current events—anything but the baby. He humored me with funny stories about the family or the latest Glencoe gossip but always brought it back to the heart of the matter before we hung up.

"Violet, just remember that you are not your mother and this baby is not you," he said one night as we prepared to hang up. "Why predict the worst? Don't let the pain of the past get in the way of a great future."

"Jesus, Dad. You should write for Someecards."

"What's that?"

"It's a website with, like, Hallmark cards for the emotionally damaged."

"Ooh, that's funny," he said. "Like, 'I would call more if you stopped trying to make me feel guilty all the time. Happy Mother's Day!'?"

"Exactly," I chuckled. "Go check it out. I'm going to bed. I love you."

"I love you, sweet girl. Rub that belly for me. Good night."

Although there were no slogans or magic words that could completely allay my concerns, toward the end of the third trimester, I found that I had moved past my projections of a terrible relationship with my daughter and felt genuinely excited for her arrival.

Carina Rose was born, at home, in May of 2007. The short but intense, midwife-assisted labor had gone completely smoothly and the baby was healthy, hungry, and very alert. I sat on the couch, eating toast with jam and feeling like a superhero as Keet took pictures and called my parents to give them the good news. Amazingly, Keon had slept through the night and was beyond excited to meet his new baby sister when he woke up in the morning. Erica flew to New York that day to help out over the weekend while Keet was at work, and my dad came in with my brothers the following week. My mom followed soon after to round out the welcome wagon and, like the rest of us, found herself instantly and firmly wrapped around her granddaughter's tiny little finger. Jet-lagged and still awake when I got up for the two a.m. feeding, Mom watched me intently as I gazed down at Carina. "Oh, Violet," she said, her voice full of emotion, "isn't it amazing how much you can love her, even knowing that one day, she'll slam the door in your face and tell you you're ruining her life?"

"Yes, Mama," I sighed. "It is."

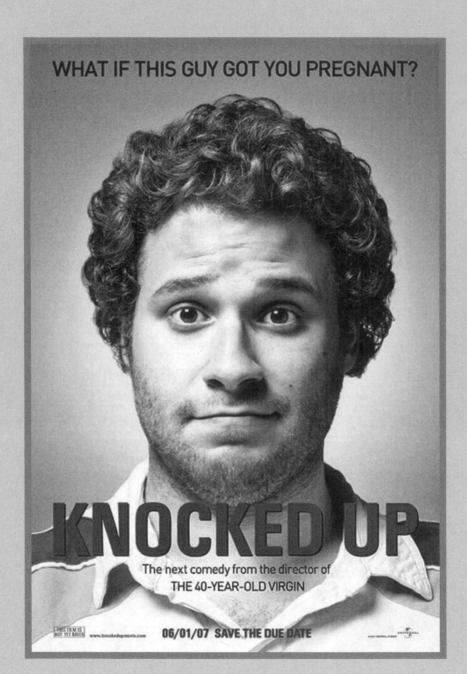

KNOCKED UP

(2007)

—

Written and directed by JUDD APATOW

Aspiring journalist Alison Scott (Katherine Heigl) finds her career path derailed when she gets pregnant from a one-night stand with stoner man-baby Ben Stone (Seth Rogen). As they stumble through the preparations to become parents, Alison and Ben have to figure out if they can (and want to) make it work as a couple.

>   DAD
>   This is not a disaster. An
>   earthquake is a disaster. Your
>   grandmother having Alzheimer's
>   so bad she doesn't even know who
>   the fuck I am anymore, that's a
>   disaster. This is good thing. This
>   is a blessing.

When Dad got the offer to play Seth Rogen's father in *Knocked Up*, it was as if he'd gotten a chance for an on-screen do-over of his initial negative response to my pregnancy with Keon. I remember his calling me and saying, "So this might hit a little close to home, but . . ." He had met Judd Apatow once in the late 1980s and then ran into him at the 2005 Deauville American Film Festival. They saw each other again later that year at the Austin Film Festival, and Judd, who credits my dad as one of his main comedy heroes, basically didn't let him out of his sight. My dad had loved *The 40-Year-Old Virgin* and was excited to be a part of this new generation of filmmakers. I think he was eager to play this role in *Knocked Up* because it gave him a chance to show off what a Cool Dad he really was.

He and Seth basically improvised their whole scene together. Watching the movie, I was amazed by how, suddenly, my dad was Everydad, or at least, the dad everyone wishes they had. His warmth, humor, and wisdom really shone through in the two minutes he was on-screen and, in my humble (and clearly biased) opinion, his "performance" provided a much needed dose of depth and dignity to the film.

Many years later and shortly after my dad's death, I found out I was pregnant with my third child. Still deep in mourning and unable to distance myself from the grief, I debated whether or not to continue the pregnancy. *I'm not ready*, I thought. *How can I bring a new life into the world when I feel so sad and hopeless all the time?* "I just want my dad," I told my husband. "He would tell me what to do."

"Violet, if Harold were alive, it wouldn't even be a question," he responded gently. The next day, I watched my dad's scene from *Knocked Up* and cried my eyes out. While I may disagree with the pro-life interpretation of his scene (and the film as a whole) from a political standpoint, there is no doubt that his message here was about choosing love and life over fear. His words were exactly what I needed to hear and my son Harold was born on June 24, 2015.

Egons in space: baby Harold and his little plush grandpa, 2015

SAME BOAT,
DIFFERENT OCEAN

I had been to Martha's Vineyard with my parents in the early 1980s when Dad, Dan, and Ivan were writing *Ghostbusters*. For some reason, my mom and I called Dan "Uncle Roy," which everyone seemed to find very amusing. Because I was so young, I remember that time almost as a series of snapshots and sense memories: the smell of ocean in the air; warm sand under my feet; the sound of laughter coming from the house as I peeked through the window to see Dad placing yet another yellow legal pad full of dialogue and stage direction onto a neat stack, ready to be typed up; Judy Belushi leading us all down a narrow path along the face of a cliff to a natural hot spring, where we covered ourselves with mineral-rich black mud and ran around the beach; Uncle Roy's big, booming voice and warm smile as he held court amid his eclectic group of friends. While Dad wrote, my mom sat outside in an enormous sun hat, filling her own blank pages with detailed landscapes in pen and ink. In the morning, I would go to the beach with my babysitter Frances and then to Edgartown for soft-serve ice cream. In the evenings, we'd have a big family-style dinner back at Uncle Roy's, and then it was party time for the adults and I was off to bed.

When Dad and Erica started renting a summer place on the Vineyard in 1997, the island itself seemed largely the same but their social circle seemed worlds away from the one I remembered. I'm sure this is a function of age and the shifts in my own emotional landscape more than anything else, but during my brief visits, the creative, funky people I remembered from my childhood had, with a few exceptions, been replaced by a cliquey group of celebrities and other wealthy people who seemed to spend a lot of time worrying about which dinner party they had or hadn't been invited to. I know they were also probably really nice, smart, and interesting people, but as an outsider, I just didn't get it. Dad often said, both publicly and privately, that no matter how successful he was, he still felt like the same "humble schmuck" he had been when he started out, but on the surface of the world he inhabited, this wasn't always apparent. Either way, there was no denying how happy he was with his family and friends on the Vineyard. He loved it, and everyone loved him. The men respected him, the women flirted with him, and he was awesome at karaoke (which is apparently what baby boomers do in their fifties and sixties instead of getting high). Of course, I would have preferred hanging out with a bunch of dope-smoking weirdos, but Dad was all in with his summer friends and told me to lighten up.

"Monday we'll have dinner at Bob Vila's. Tuesday we've been invited to go swimming at Larry David's in the afternoon and then to a karaoke party at the Ashes'. Ted [Danson] and Mary [Steenbergen] are having a barbecue on Wednesday and then Thursday, Alan Dershowitz asked us all to join him on John Henry's yacht."

"You're yachting now?"

"Well, not exactly, but why not? It'll be fun."

"Hmm, okay. I didn't know they let Jews on yachts."

"Oh come on! *Yacht* sound so Yiddish. Say it with me—yach—"

"Oy, Dad, stop."

True to her flower-child past, Erica really connected with the natural beauty of the island and became close friends with an amazing group of local women, finding a delicate balance between playing the in-crowd game and doing her own low-key thing.

In the off-season, I visited Chicago often and started to notice some interesting parallels in terms of Dad's and my respective journeys in parenting and partnering. When Carina was born, in 2007, Keon was four, and my brothers, Julian and Daniel, were seventeen and thirteen. Dad, Erica, and the boys seemed to be thriving despite the challenges of the dreaded teen years, but I know that no matter how neat their suburban life may have seemed from where I stood, it wasn't always easy. While the move to Glencoe had certainly provided my brothers with a different upbringing than they would have had in LA, the struggles of privileged adolescence—identity formation, peer pressure, social drama, drugs, alcohol, and general angst—were universal. Instead of latching on to gangs and pot like I did, they gravitated towards sports . . . and pot. The same aimless rambling that took me all over the vast expanse of Los Angeles took them from rec room to rec room across the North Shore, and the geographical difference didn't seem to change much for their parents in terms of worry and struggles around trust.

Despite the thirteen-plus years between us, my brothers and I have always been close. The age gap seemed to time out perfectly because I was old enough to help take care of them when they were small, and by the time they realized I was too old to be the "cool older sister," they were happy to have me as a sort of parental middleman who could give them tips on how to fly under the radar, get along with their parents, and still find a way to do whatever they wanted. I made them mix CDs of good hip-hop (Pharcyde, De La Soul, and A Tribe Called Quest) in an attempt to steer them away from what I saw as inferior rap (Eminem, Lil Jon, and 50 Cent). Although they'd had the "facts of life" and "no powders, no pills" conversations with Dad, I made a point of talking to them about safe sex and responsible experimentation of all kinds. Whether they had been sheltered as kids or not, it was all out on the table now and I wanted to be someone they could go to if their parents didn't feel like an option. I knew that even though, on the surface, they were firmly entrenched in the mainstream, bro-centric bubble that surrounded them, they had also grown up in a family that valued critical thinking, curiosity, diversity, and compassion, and those values, more than their understandable assimilation into their surroundings, were what defined them.

Although, like me, Julian had been prone to brattiness as a kid, as a teen, he turned out to be a very thoughtful, laid-back, and likable guy. Smart, sweet, inquisitive, and cautious, he always did well in school and somehow managed to get through his adolescence without really having to rebel. He took up the guitar and would play "Blackbird" with Dad while Erica stood by, kvelling. The one time I remember him getting into any trouble was when he and his friends snuck out the night of eighth-grade graduation and were chased by Glencoe police after being caught walking around the neighborhood at two a.m. When my dad called me the next day to tell me what had happened, he was still furious.

"He's grounded for a month."

"Oh come on, Daddy, that seems harsh. I mean, they just snuck out and walked around, right?"

"I don't care about the sneaking out. I care about him staying alive. What the fuck was he thinking, running from the police? I told him, 'If you were black, you could be dead right now. You don't even know how lucky you are to be chased by cops.'"

"Oh, well yeah, good point," I stammered, caught off guard by my dad's intensity. "I guess a month seems reasonable then."

Apart from this early and uncharacteristic misstep, as I watched him grow up during my regular visits to Chicago, I marveled at Julian's ability to get along with everyone and still pretty much do what he wanted to do. "Don't you ever get mad?" I asked him once after he was barred from attending an unsupervised party by the lake. "I mean, yeah," he said, "of course, but not about this. What's the point? You're here. I'm happy to hang out and there's always another party next week, y'know?" I could not relate at all, actually, but felt emotional seeing so much of my dad in Julian's big-picture view and ability to rise above the power struggles and conflict that had characterized so much of my youth.

Daniel, on the other hand, was intense, independent, and didn't hold back when it came to fighting for what he wanted. He was very charismatic, excelled in sports, and seemed to be the life of the party everywhere he went. He also had a great sense of humor and knew how to make our dad laugh like crazy. Daniel's comedy education started early in typical Ramis fashion—with *South Park: Bigger, Longer, and Uncut*, in kindergarten. Daniel recently wrote of his own childhood, "After you sing 'You're a cock-sucking, ass-licking uncle fucka!' at the top of your lungs with your dad at five years old, it's tough going to your playdate the next day and enjoying an episode of *Rugrats* with your buddy." Dad not only enjoyed Daniel's humor but had a real admiration and amazement when it came to his athleticism. "Look at these abs," he would say when

Daniel came in from shooting baskets in the driveway. "No one from my gene pool has ever had abs like that!" In school, Daniel did the minimum amount of work to get by and, like me, balked at the rules that Erica tried to enforce, keenly aware that while she and my dad shared the same overall goals as parents, they believed in different approaches to get there.

When it came to parenting my own small children, I felt torn between wanting total militaristic discipline and giving my kids the freedom I'd had when I was young. To be honest, I think I struggled with transitioning from a child's perspective to a parent's but here I was—a thirty-year-old mother of two—and I needed to figure my shit out ASAP. So, as Keet and I debated various parenting philosophies and practices, Dad encouraged us to prioritize the three C's—competence, confidence, and compassion—and stay focused on the values we wanted to instill in our children rather than the methods we thought we should use. Watching my brothers mature only affirmed this perspective. They were growing up very differently than I had, and yet the real variations

Dad, Erica, and Keon on the aforementioned yacht

between us had nothing to do with any of that. They were who they were in spite of their surroundings, not because of them, and what worked for one kid did not necessarily work for another. These complexities were what led my dad and me to the idea of writing a parenting book when I visited them on Martha's Vineyard in 2007.

The previous year, Dad and Erica bought a relatively modest house in Chilmark with a Zen rock garden and a beautiful swimming pool, and Keet, Keon, newborn Carina, and I went out there for ten days in June of 2007. Sitting on their big shabby-chic sofa, severely sleep-deprived and covered in drool, breast milk and God knows what else, I told my Dad, "I just have to remember that this part goes fast, and even if having a newborn is physically exhausting, it will never be this easy again."

"Who's the wise one now?" my dad teased, expertly whipping a burp cloth onto his shoulder and lifting sleeping Carina from my lap.

"Ha! I don't know shit. I just know I'd rather sit on a couch with my boobs out all day than chase a kid around the playground negotiating how much longer until we can go home."

"Well, you know what they say—little kids, little problems, big kids, big problems," he said, softly swaying and patting Carina's back so the noise from the boys in the pool wouldn't wake her.

"So it just keeps getting worse? Great."

"No, my baby. It's all hard and it's all wonderful. Well, not all of it, but most of it. You just gotta surrender and give up on the illusion of control."

"Yeah, that's never really been my strong suit." We laughed. "Plus, I'm not sure how that works as a parenting philosophy."

"Well, it seemed to work pretty well for us." He sat down next to me and took my hand into his big, warm paw.

"Really, Daddy?" I squeaked as my eyes filled up with tears.

"Yes, my baby. I couldn't love you more and I am *so* proud of you. You got your master's degree, you have two beautiful children and a great partner . . . you're amazing."

"No, you're amazing." I sniffled and rested my head against him. We sat in silence for a few minutes and then I asked, "But how do you know if you're doing it right? Parenting, I mean. Like, I think I know what's best, but who the hell knows? It could all totally backfire. You think I turned out okay, but my childhood was supposedly all screwed up, so what about the boys? You're doing things so differently this time. What's gonna happen to them?"

"It's all a mystery, Violet. You do your best, but there are no guarantees. There's no such thing as a perfect parent, or perfect child, or perfect anything for that matter."

"Ugh! You and your 'embrace the ambiguity' . . . I know it's true, but come on. Is nothing simple and straightforward?"

"Very little," he said wistfully, and a thought popped into my head.

"Maybe we should write a book," I said, "about parenting." He raised his eyebrow as I continued. "Like, how it's all a mess and you're probably doing it wrong but it can still work out okay . . . or not, but who cares because we're all gonna die eventually."

He laughed. "That's not a bad idea, actually. Existential parenting."

"Yeah, exactly! We can start with 'Birth: The Beginning of the End.'"

"Well, aren't you a funny girl?"

"I try."

"That could be pretty great, actually," he said thoughtfully as the door opened to a chorus of wet boys asking, "What's for lunch?"

"That's my cue," I said dryly, getting up and heading toward the kitchen. I looked back at my dad holding my sleeping daughter and was hit with a wave of love. "We're going to do this!" I called over my shoulder. "I love you!"

He nodded, pointed at his heart and then at me, and closed his eyes to take a nap.

He was already working on *Year One* so we agreed to keep tossing ideas back and forth until his schedule cleared. Blissfully unaware of what the future held, we figured we had all the time in the world.

Dad with lobster, Martha's Vineyard

YEAR ONE
(2009)

Written by HAROLD RAMIS, GENE STUPNITSKY,
and LEE EISENBERG
Directed by HAROLD RAMIS

In prehistoric times, a lazy and disaffected hunter-gatherer, Zed (Jack Black), is exiled by his tribe for eating the forbidden fruit and sets out on a journey with his best friend, Oh (Michael Cera). On the road, the pair encounters biblical characters such as Cain (David Cross) and Abel (Paul Rudd), Abraham (Hank Azaria) and Isaac (Christopher Mintz-Plasse). When Zed and Oh discover that their tribe has been captured and enslaved, they come up with a plan to rescue their loved ones and become the heroes they always wanted to be.

>   OH
> Do you have any idea where we're
> going?

>   ZED
> Yup, we're going to Sodom. We have
> to save Maya and Eema.

OH
[referring to Abraham]
But he said that God was gonna
smite Sodom with holy fire.

ZED
Yeah? God also told him to chop
off the tip of his dick.

Everything is indeed weird in Mr. Ramis's highbrow slapstick, in which theological questions are smuggled in between silly bits about excrement and body hair. Much as Mel Brooks and Carl Reiner did with the *2,000 Year Old Man*, Mr. Ramis, who wrote the screenplay with Gene Stupnitsky and Lee Eisenberg, is playing with history, or rather with the serious stories familiar from religious instruction and Hollywood epics.

—MANOHLA DARGIS, *THE NEW YORK TIMES*

Somehow, despite the presence of those reliable actors and the highly advanced skills of comic veterans Harold Ramis and Judd Apatow behind the scenes, "Year One" manages to be a dud.

—CHRISTY LEMIRE, ASSOCIATED PRESS

Harold Ramis is one of the nicest people I've met in the movie business, and I'm so sorry *Year One* happened to him. I'm sure he had the best intentions. In trying to explain why the movie was produced, I have a theory. Ramis is the top-billed of the film's three writers, and he is so funny that when he read some of these lines, they sounded hilarious. Pity he didn't play one of the leads in his own film.

—ROGER EBERT, *ROGER EBERT'S MOVIE YEARBOOK 2010*

Year One was born out of my dad's longtime fascination with the mythology of the biblical texts and the archetypal stories that arose from them. During post-production on *The Ice Harvest*, he started writing this script, playing with these big ideas. At this point, he had started smoking pot again but knew that Erica wouldn't approve, so when they were apart, he took every opportunity to light up. He continued writing (and secretly smoking) once he got back to Chicago in the fall and brought Gene Stupnitsky and Lee Eisenberg, two young (and unknown at the time) writers he had mentored, into the mix. His agent suggested getting Judd Apatow involved, and my dad was excited to have some new people and perspectives on board. Judd was finishing up his movie *Funny People* and wasn't around that much in the beginning but introduced my dad to Rodney Rothman, a young writer and producer who worked closely with my dad throughout the production.

Year One was filmed on location in Louisiana and New Mexico. I was busy working and taking care of the kids, so I didn't get out to visit the set, but I got a full report from Keet, who spent a week in White Sands, acting in the movie and hanging out with Dad. By all accounts, it was a fun shoot. My dad loved working with the actors and would often play guitar with Jack Black in between takes. He took his own role, as Adam (both literally and figuratively), very seriously . . . in a funny way, of course. But like the First Man, with the weight of the world and a huge budget on his shoulders, he worried. *Is this as good as I think it is? Will people understand what I'm really trying to say?* Unfortunately, it wasn't and they didn't.

Without trying to make excuses, there were several factors that contributed to this great idea's not translating into a great movie. A WGA strike cut the rewriting process short and left some major character and story issues largely unresolved. Because he had surrounded himself with young people who really admired and looked up to him, it was very hard for them to give my dad notes and easy for him to talk them out of whatever suggestions they were making. Gene Stupnitsky told me recently, "How do you argue with the smartest guy in the room? I mean, you don't. We all loved your dad so much and wanted it to be so good, and it should have been. We just didn't quite get there." Typically very Zen about success and failure, Dad was more disappointed about the generally poor response to *YO* than usual. He put up a good front, but it was hard for him. In an email to Judd Apatow, he wrote,

(no subject)   🖨

harold ramis   12/12/08 ☆   ↰

to Judd ▾

this would be hard for me to say to you so i'll do it in e-mail. i feel like i've really let you down in a big way. you invested a lot in this film and for whatever reasons it isn't paying off like most of your other ventures. i'm too old and sane to get really down on myself-- i learned long ago not to vest my self-esteem in success or failure on a professional level-- but i'm sad and i want to apologize to you for falling short on this one. whatever happens, i feel like i've learned a lot from you about commitment, initiative, perserverance, and collaboration and i'm grateful for all of it.

···

I share this because I think it speaks to the sense of responsibility my dad felt as "captain" but also to the humility that was such a hallmark of his leadership style. There was no response in my dad's email archive, but I imagine that Judd picked up the phone and called him immediately, hopefully saying something along the lines of: "Harold, you have nothing to apologize for. I may have put money on the table but you put your heart and soul into this project and *I'm* sorry it didn't turn out the way we hoped. You're a great filmmaker and great person and I feel lucky to have had this chance to crash and burn with you."

Dad, Jack Black, and Keet on set, White Sands, New Mexico

Mr. Director

BREAKING UP
IS HARD TO DO

In May of 2009, I decided to end my relationship with Keet. We were making dinner together and talking about something to do with the kids when, out of nowhere, I just started crying.

"I'm not happy," I sobbed. "I think we might need to separate."

"Where is this coming from?" he asked, concerned and completely taken by surprise. "Is it because all of your friends are getting divorced? Now you want to jump on the bandwagon?"

"No. I don't know. Maybe. I guess that got me thinking about it but honestly, I kind of always knew deep down we wouldn't last. It was just a matter of time."

"Well, that would have been good to know," he growled. "I mean, what the fuck? All this counseling and bullshit, what was that for? If you knew you didn't want to be with me, why waste the time and money?"

"It wasn't a waste. It was important. I love you and we have two kids together and we're going to be in each other's lives forever. We just might need to have different lives now."

"Yeah, whatever. You're a spoiled fucking brat. You think you're gonna be super happy all the time without me? You won't. You'll still be miserable and your life will be even harder than it is now. Good fucking luck!"

His words stung, sure, but my main feeling at that moment was relief. In truth, I felt like I was withering away within the emotional and intellectual confines of our relationship and was tired of trying to convince myself that so-so was good enough. I knew in my heart that this was the right thing to do and now it was time for everyone else to know it, too.

I called my dad the next day and told him. He and Erica went into marriage counselor mode and flew to New York that weekend to talk to us. "Are you sure you want to do this?" they asked. "Don't you think you owe it to the kids to try to work it out?" They suggested a year of intensive couples therapy before making any decisions. I know they thought they were doing the right thing, but I was 100 percent sure I was making the right choice and felt hurt and angry that they were not being supportive (sound familiar?). My dad and I talked often on the phone during that time. The conversations were strained, as both of us sought some kind of reassurance that neither could provide.

Then, in one of our daily calls, my dad told me about a fight he'd gotten into with his brother. In a rare moment of anger, he'd yelled at Steve, "Stop being a victim. You've never taken a risk in your life! You don't even have the courage to seek your own happiness."

Hearing those words come out of his mouth when he was recounting this was like being punched in the gut. It was at that moment that I realized how hurt I was that he couldn't see that the very thing he faulted his brother for not doing was exactly the thing I was trying to do. Why had it been okay for him to leave my mom in order to have the kind of relationship he wanted, but it wasn't okay for me to do the same? Why should my uncle be judged for choosing not to change his life for the possibility of something better, while I was judged for doing just that? Didn't he want me to be happy?

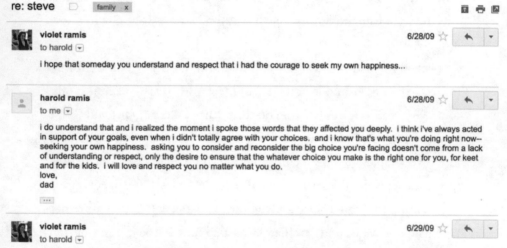

re: steve   family x

violet ramis   6/28/09
to harold

i hope that someday you understand and respect that i had the courage to seek my own happiness...

harold ramis   6/28/09
to me

i do understand that and i realized the moment i spoke those words that they affected you deeply. i think i've always acted in support of your goals, even when i didn't totally agree with your choices. and i know that's what you're doing right now-- seeking your own happiness. asking you to consider and reconsider the big choice you're facing doesn't come from a lack of understanding or respect, only the desire to ensure that the whatever choice you make is the right one for you, for keet and for the kids. i will love and respect you no matter what you do.
love,
dad

violet ramis   6/29/09
to harold

i do appreciate that you have always been supportive and i know it hasn't been easy. i don't believe that any choice i make can be "the right one" for everyone but i am working to create the best possible situation for all of us under the circumstances. i know the kids will be affected...will suffer, and i will do everything i can to help them deal with it. keet and i will hopefully continue to have some kind of real friendship and collaborative co-parenting but short of that, we're committed to maintaining a respectful and open dialogue in support of the kids and each other. there's really not much more i can say at this point. if you have questions, i'm here. i love you.

From that exchange, things between us steadily improved and we returned quickly to our mutual-admiration club.

"So, what do you think is the key to a good relationship?" I asked over the phone one day from my desk at work.

"Well, you have to be able to be entirely yourself, the full circle of who you are, and the other person has to be able to be entirely themselves, and then there has to be enough overlap between you to share and be interested in and keep you connected. And even in a great relationship, it's not easy. It takes work."

"But how much work? And how much is too much? How do you know when it's time to walk away?"

"Well, that's a question it seems you've already answered."

"But I feel so . . . awful," I said, starting to cry.

"Awful how, my baby?"

"I don't know—guilty, sad, scared. What should I do?" I sobbed into the phone.

"You're doing it. Live your life. Try to be a good person. Be honest. Be open. But it's not going to be easy. Look, guilt is not productive. It doesn't do you any good and it doesn't help the other person, so forget it. Sad is appropriate. It's an ending and even if it's one you initiated, it's still a loss. Scared will take care of itself. Either your life will get better or it will get worse but it will go on. You probably won't get all of what you want out of this, but you can get more than you were, and I know you're going to be okay no matter what."

And, yet again, he was right. The next several months involved a lot of intense and emotional negotiations between me and Keet. Whereas I had the experience of my parents' mature and amicable divorce to guide me, Keet's only frame of reference was his friends' dramatic and contentious breakups. It took time and a great deal of convincing but once he realized that he wasn't being abandoned, the kids were not being taken away from him, and my family still considered him "one of us," things began looking up. We may not have had enough between us to make a great love, but we ended up with two wonderful children and a truly great friendship. Despite the mess we went through to get there, I'm grateful for all of it.

Dad, the kids, and me at my grandfather's apartment, 2009

SO A VERY FUNNY OLD JEWISH GUY DIES AND GOES TO HEAVEN

My grandpa Nate died in November of 2009, at the ripe old age of ninety-four. He had lived completely independently up until about two weeks before he passed away, when he fell in his Northbrook Court condo. Even from the hospital, he joked, "The doctor says I have the body of a thirty-five-year-old . . . a thirty-five-year-old Chevrolet!" Ba-dump-bump. For Grandpa's obituary, my dad told the *Sun-Times*, "He was the most charming, easygoing, funniest, generous person anyone knew. He was very laid-back, never yelled or got angry, and was an avid reader. He read three novels a week and both Chicago papers every day." To me, he always seemed like a warm and loving man who enjoyed the simple pleasures in life. He played pinochle with the same group of guys for more than thirty years and loved golf, beautiful women, betting on horse races, and good comedy. He was very hard of hearing from years in the scrap metal business but refused to wear

Hipster Grandpa with bikini babes, 1970s

hearing aids, or he would wear them but not turn them on, forcing everyone around him to shout to be heard. He had bottles of Scotch stashed all over his home so he could take a nip in the bathroom, while doing the laundry, or in his La-Z-Boy chair in front of the TV, covering the smell of whiskey with Big Red chewing gum.

In my dad's talk at the Chicago Humanities Festival in 2009, he described his father as "too lazy to be any kind of role model" but also credited him with laying the foundation of his comedic sensibilities. As family lore goes, my uncle Steve and Dad would sit on either side of Nate's armchair, watching their thirteen-inch Philco television set

Dear Violet,

I have a lot of bad habits. Drinking, gambling, never calling anyone on the phone. Not even your father. I know that I should call you at least once in a while, because I really love you and your family.

One of my neighbors asked me, how do you feel Mr. Dames I said read the obituaries every day. Your grandpa is going to be 94 years old, next month, but I still love sexy films. Of course you know how proud I am of your ~~dad~~ dad

I am a very lucky man to have such a great family.

Ive always loved you.

Your grandpa

Nate

while my grandfather critiqued entertainers like Red Skelton, Steve Allen, and Sid Caesar. Grandpa steered his sons away from the Three Stooges and toward the Marx Brothers, which was a major influence on my father in terms of his own comedic identity. "In my heart, I felt I was a combination of Groucho and Harpo Marx, of Groucho using his wit as a weapon against the upper classes, and of Harpo's antic charm and the fact that he was oddly sexy," he told the *New Yorker*.

Role model or not, my grandfather was, by far, my dad's biggest fan. He clipped every movie review and article mentioning my dad and pasted them into scrapbooks that filled the bookshelves in his condo. "Son of a gun, how about that?" he would say, eyes shining with *naches*, as he pasted in a glossy magazine cover or congratulatory note from Steven Spielberg. "That's really something!" Although my dad gave Nate plenty of material for the scrapbooks, Grandpa was equally proud of my uncle Steven, who had gone into the navy after college and become a pilot. Although my uncle could have easily been resentful of the attention my dad received around his success, he wasn't.

My grandfather died on November 24, 2009, with both of his sons holding his hands, just three days after my dad's sixty-fifth birthday. Although, outwardly, my father appeared to take this loss in stride, I think it affected him more than he was aware of. In the weeks after the funeral, my dad became consumed with finishing a large and complex craft project he had initially started to offset his disappointment around *Year One*: building his own guitar. When it was finally finished, Dad shared his accomplishment proudly via email.

Once my dad admitted that he was feeling depressed, I worried about his slipping into a funk that he wouldn't be able to pull out of, but he assured me that it was all under control. We continued to keep

harold ramis 12/1/09 ☆
to Julian, me, trevor_albert, Steven, Ayda, Anne, Tom ▾

it's finished! i had a lot of help attaching the bridge and the neck and adjusting the string height, and someone else lacquered it for me, but i learned a lot getting it as far as i did. and it sounds great! my dad would have been proud. before he died he told my aunt i was making a violin.
love to all,
harold

3 Attachments

 violet ramis 12/2/09 ☆ ↰ ▾
to harold ▾

awww...it looks beautiful daddy :) great work. how are you? i love you.

⋯

 harold ramis 12/2/09 ☆ ↰ ▾
to me ▾

i'm doing okay, baby. i have a sad, empty, tired feeling but i'm sure it will pass in a few years. finishing the guitar was a real lift, though.
love you the most on toast.
dad

⋯

 violet ramis 12/2/09 ☆ ↰ ▾
to harold ▾

i'm so sorry. it will pass in time...until it comes back again. sigh. i know you have your 2nd City thing coming up but maybe after that you could start on your intro chapter draft for our book. i'm gonna try to start tonight. call me anytime if you're bored and feeling down. you're the best. xo

⋯

 harold ramis 12/2/09 ☆ ↰ ▾
to me ▾

i'll try to get going on that. i had another book offer yesterday from random house/doubleday, this one based on the 5-minute buddhist. maybe i should just write books and forget the movies.
dad

⋯

 violet ramis 12/2/09 ☆ ↰ ▾
to harold ▾

why not? movies arent going anywhere. you could take a year to write and see what happens...

in close contact and I tried to get him excited about the future—the kids, the book, his next movie project, anything to keep him busy. My dad had always said that having children and losing your parents are the two most life-changing events that people go through. He had obviously gone through many major changes over the years, but in hindsight, losing his father seemed like his biggest mortality wake-up call.

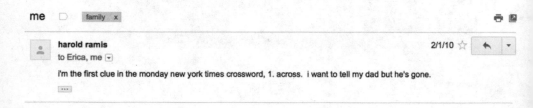

me   family   x

harold ramis   2/1/10
to Erica, me

i'm the first clue in the monday new york times crossword, 1. across. i want to tell my dad but he's gone.

OLD DOG, NEW TRICKS

In a very modern rom-com turn of events, I met Leon, my husband, in a Lamaze class at St. Luke's Hospital, when we were both having our first children, in 2002. I was there with Keet, and Leon was with his then wife, Leslie.* I remember the first time I saw him. They walked in about fifteen minutes after the class had started, and I thought, *Oh, he must be a jazz musician or something cool.* Half Chinese and half Jewish, he had shoulder-length curly hair and a scruffy beard, and wore a collared shirt, unbuttoned at the neck. Apparently he noticed me too, which I guess wasn't that strange since I had a bunch of tattoos, my boobs were enormous, and my maternity fashion generally entailed wearing as little clothing as possible. (You try being nine months pregnant in July in New York City!)

At the Lamaze reunion, when all the babies were a few months old, Leslie said she was starting a playgroup and that anyone interested in

---

* Not her real name.

joining should give her their contact info. Apparently Leon told her to make sure and get my number. I joined the playgroup and we all became friends. Messy! The four of us went out a few times as couples but Keet never really felt comfortable hanging out with them, and they didn't have much to say to him, so it was mostly me, Leon, and Leslie having playdates at the park and kid-centered outings on the weekends while Keet worked. Whereas Leslie and I primarily connected around parenting and family life, Leon and I would talk about music, movies, and philosophy. Not a jazz musician after all, Leon worked in finance but had studied fine art and technology at Carnegie Mellon University. Leslie, then a stay-at-home mom, had been an attorney specializing in securities litigation. While she was not someone that I would have been friends with if it weren't for the kids, he reminded me of the guys I'd grown up with. They had their second child in 2004 and then Leslie and I were pregnant together again two years after that. Our babies were born just two days apart in 2007 and they moved to Connecticut soon after that. Some weekends, I would take Keon and Carina out there to visit, but it wasn't the same. Lacking the commonality of city life with kids, we drifted apart.

Without going into the personal details of their marriage, Leon and Leslie were having issues and eventually separated. Leon moved back to New York City in 2009 and he and I started hanging out when he had his kids for weekend visits. All of the conversations we'd had in the park over the years picked up right where they'd left off and I couldn't get enough. Smart, funny, kind, and exceedingly attentive, Leon would send me lengthy emails on Monday morning, reflecting on the themes we'd discussed, offering links to articles and information for further consideration. I was very happy to have him in my life as a friend, especially since we were both going through the ends of our respective relationships, but over the course of the year, we both discovered we had deeper feelings for each other. I was terrified—not just of potentially screwing things up and losing this amazing friendship I had come to depend on, but also of the fallout that an intimate relationship with him would inevitably induce. In the end, I decided that life is too short to say no to love, and on New Year's Eve, Leon and I rang in 2010 with our first kiss.

We may have been head-over-heels in love but I knew it was not going to be easy. I decided to tell Keet right away because I knew he would rather deal with a problem than be kept in the dark. He, understandably, flipped out and immediately sent Leslie a Facebook message telling her what was going on. She called me right away.

"How can you do this?" She seethed, "I know I wasn't a very good wife to Leon, but I was a good friend to you."

"I know," I said. "And I'm so sorry, Leslie, but life is messy and—"

"Oh spare me!" she snapped. "Life isn't messy. You're just a mess!"

Touché. I knew that what I was doing was considered "wrong" according to the rules of conventional morality, but I had been raised to believe that those rules were arbitrary anyway. Still, the questions kept running through my head: *Does this make me a bad person? Is it wrong to choose my own happiness over other people's comfort? They'll get over it, won't they? What if this was all predestined somehow and everything that happened in my entire life was just leading me to this?*

My dad, who had met Leon and Leslie at the kids' birthday parties over the years, did not seem surprised by the latest turn of events and offered his usual big-picture perspective.

"Well, you certainly didn't pick the easiest path for yourself," he mused one day over the phone. "But I guess you never have. And, hey, it turns out you're a romantic after all!"

"Ha! I guess so, but, jeez, don't tell anyone!" He laughed and promised he wouldn't. I went on, "I don't know, Daddy. I mean, even with all the drama, it just feels so natural. Sure, there's a lot of noise around us, but between us? It's perfect. It feels like I've known him forever and this was always meant to be. Don't you believe that things happen for a reason?"

"No, baby. Some Jews believe in that kind of destiny. They call it *bashert*. Your mother believes in a different kind of destiny—past lives and soul mates and being on the planet to learn specific lessons and all that. Buddhists would probably take a karmic perspective—and not 'what goes around comes around,' but cause and effect. Our actions create reactions and those reactions affect the next set of actions we take. I just believe that things happen."

"And?"

"And it's up to us to decide what they mean or don't mean. The point is, you and Leon found each other and fell in love and made a decision to be together in spite of the obstacles. You don't need fate to validate your choice."

While this wasn't exactly the absolution I was seeking, it was enough to let me stop worrying about the judgment of others and focus on making the most of my own New Life. Even though Leon and I had been friends for almost eight years (and had five kids between us), it still felt entirely fresh, exciting, mysterious, and miraculous to be able to get to know each other in a whole new way. The children (ages seven, seven, five, three, and three, at the time) enjoyed having "mega sleep-overs" on the weekends and seemed to adjust to this latest change without too much difficulty. This is not to say that the kids haven't had their share of struggles over the years, or that they never fought, or that there were no issues for them around blending the families, but, by and large, I think we did okay. Now, at fifteen, fifteen, thirteen, ten, and ten (and two), everyone is at home and thriving (knock wood) in our sprawling family tree.

THE LAST SUPPER

In April 2010, my dad came to New York, alone, to visit me. I was still working at Metropolitan Hospital but starting to feel demoralized by the sheer number of patients, the complexity of their issues, and the systemic disregard for their needs. Leon and I were doing great, everything had mostly settled down with our respective exes, and the kids were doing fine, but after the tumult of the year, I think I was just burned out and starting to crack. Of course, my dad was the one I went to for a pep talk. I told him how close I was feeling to an emotional breaking point and he said he'd come visit ASAP, joking that if he couldn't help me, at least he'd keep me company while I fell apart.

I was up to my eyeballs in distressing cases at work and debated taking days off while he was there, but it was Keet (bless his heart) who said, "Just do it. Who knows when you'll get the chance to hang

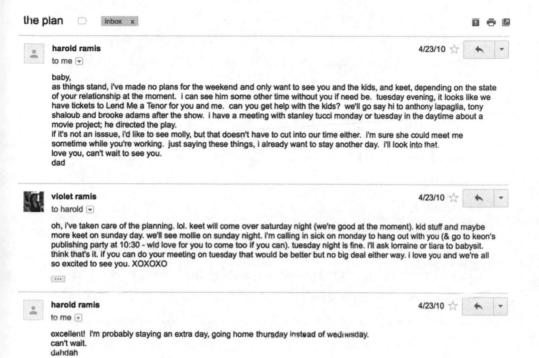

the plan ⬜ Inbox x

harold ramis   4/23/10 ☆

to me ▾

baby,
as things stand, i've made no plans for the weekend and only want to see you and the kids, and keet, depending on the state
of your relationship at the moment. i can see him some other time without you if need be. tuesday evening, it looks like we
have tickets to Lend Me a Tenor for you and me. can you get help with the kids? we'll go say hi to anthony lapaglia, tony
shaloub and brooke adams after the show. i have a meeting with stanley tucci monday or tuesday in the daytime about a
movie project; he directed the play.
if it's not an isssue, i'd like to see molly, but that doesn't have to cut into our time either. i'm sure she could meet me
sometime while you're working. just saying these things, i already want to stay another day. i'll look into that.
love you, can't wait to see you.
dad

violet ramis   4/23/10 ☆

to harold ▾

oh, i've taken care of the planning. lol. keet will come over saturday night (we're good at the moment). kid stuff and maybe
more keet on sunday day. we'll see mollie on sunday night. i'm calling in sick on monday to hang out with you (& go to keon's
publishing party at 10:30 - wld love for you to come too if you can). tuesday night is fine. i'll ask lorraine or tiara to babysit.
think that's it. if you can do your meeting on tuesday that would be better but no big deal either way. i love you and we're all
so excited to see you. XOXOXO

...

harold ramis   4/23/10 ☆

to me ▾

excellent! i'm probably staying an extra day, going home thursday instead of wednesday.
can't wait.
dahdah

out—just the two of you—again? That's what sick days are for." I am
eternally grateful to him for giving me that advice.

During that week, my dad and I wandered around the city, smoked
cigarettes, smoked pot, talked, laughed, had lunch with Leon, and dinners with Keet and the kids, and drinks with Mollie. He had his meetings and then would come with me to pick the kids up from school,
hanging out at my apartment until late, sipping B&B and musing on life
and what the future had in store. It was truly one of the best weeks of
my life.

Now, I always cried when it came time for my dad and I to part ways after spending time together. Whether it was just basic textbook separation anxiety or because we shared such a close connection, or because I am just a big baby, I could never help myself. This time, I was determined to show him how strong I was and how much better I felt after having spent the last five days with him.

As we stood on the corner below my apartment, waiting for a taxi to take him back to his hotel, I told him how much it meant to me that he had come. "I'm not going to cry, but I want you to know how hard it is to say goodbye."

"Oh, Violet, you don't have to—"

"Oh, let me," I pleaded as he smiled knowingly and motioned for me to continue. "I want to thank you for coming this week . . . really, for always coming to my rescue, even when it's been hard. It's not like you showed up and fixed everything, but you just always make me—and everyone else—feel better . . . about how horrible everything is. Just kidding! But really, thank you so, so much, Daddy." I hugged him hard and he kept one arm around my shoulders as he subtly scanned Columbus Avenue for a cab.

"You are so welcome. It was a great week. It was great to see the kids and Mollie and Keet and Leon, and you know how much I always love being with you."

"Do you have to go? Can't you just move here?"

"Maybe, my baby, maybe. If this Stanley Tucci thing happens, I'll be here a lot. But you know I'm always just a phone call away."

"I know, Daddy," I said, blinking back tears. "I'll call you in ten minutes, okay?"

"Anytime, my sweet girl, anytime."

Central Park selfie, 2009

THE LONG GOODBYE

Erica called me the Monday after Dad went back to Chicago to tell me that he'd been admitted to the hospital with a diverticulitis attack. She said that my dad was okay but had been in a lot of pain and was told by his internist to go straight to the ER. As it turned out, his colon had perforated and there was an abscess. There is no good way to distill four years of a medical and emotional roller coaster into a few short pages, but long story short, the infection in his gut went on for almost a month and triggered an autoimmune reaction that manifested as vasculitis (inflammation of the blood vessels) in his brain. We talked on the phone every day while he was home with a drain and IV antibiotics, but the next time I saw him in person, he couldn't walk or speak and no one had a fucking clue what was going on. He went from Glenbrook Hospital to Evanston Hospital to Northwestern and eventually to the Mayo Clinic in Rochester, Minnesota, where he stayed for five months. At Mayo, while being treated with anticoagulants, he suffered a brain hemorrhage, which further exacerbated his condition. He eventually regained his speech and worked his (lazy) butt off to be able to walk again, but he never really recovered.

For the next four years, my dad underwent various therapies and treatment protocols to try to stabilize his condition as much as possible. The first two years were filled with horrific uncertainty. What was happening? What parts of his brain had been affected by the illness? Would he get better? Would he be able to work again? At that point, we were still hopeful that he would be able to make a significant recovery, so in trying to protect his privacy and potential to resume his career, Erica was advised to keep his illness very quiet. While I completely understand why she chose to do that, especially in the beginning, I think that an unforeseen and unfortunate consequence of that decision was that she didn't get a lot of support and, frankly, he didn't get the outpouring of love and good wishes he deserved. Erica and Laurel Ward, his former assistant and producing partner, were his champions—at the hospital all day every day, making sure he got the proper attention from the doctors and nurses, attending to his every need, battling with the insurance company. It was endless and emotionally draining. I visited as often as I could, at least every other month and whenever there was an emergency, but Erica was the one who was present every second of every day, devoting her whole life to his care.

During his illness, my dad went through periods where he would seem very much himself. During those times, he kept his doctors laughing during regular neurological exams and charmed all the nurses. He sang along to Leonard Cohen and strummed clumsily on his guitar. On those good days, he would walk (stiffly, and with a lot of support) from his makeshift bedroom to the living room, where he would sit, watching *Kill Bill* or *No Country for Old Men*, until it was time to shuffle back to bed. Sometimes, tired of being home, his aides would take him for pancakes at Walker Brothers or for a bowl of linguine with clam sauce at the Hole in the Wall, and he tucked into those meals with the same intensity and pleasure he'd always shown for a good meal. Early on, he would even try to do the crossword puzzles he once could breeze through. I looked at them after he was done and they were mostly filled with gibberish, but he didn't seem to mind.

At one point, as part of his therapy, Dad was asked to write a letter to his children. In it, he talked about his experiences through this difficult time:

> [My therapist] asked me to write something about what it's like to be me. What existence feels like to me. What the experience of having a 'human' life feels like to me. Well, it's been great so far. I used to think I was one of the luckiest guys in the world, but now I'm not so sure. Still glad to be alive but life sucks in ways I never anticipated. I live in a world described by aches and pains and bodily inconveniences. The lessons are obvious, patience, and the knowledge that I can't take anything for granted . . . I want to be present to share in your joys and successes but my get up and go got up and went. But I'm working hard to come back. I just wish it was easier for all of us. Life is a precious gift. Don't waste it. I know I won't from now on.

As heartbreaking as that letter is, at the time, it filled me with hope that if he was able to maintain his philosophical perspective and communicate it so clearly, maybe things weren't actually as bleak as they seemed.

Those were some of the good times—when his humor and insight and spark shone through. Then there were times he would get confused and frustrated and paranoid, calling me late at night and demanding to know what was really going on. *"Why can't I use my phone? I have calls I need to make. Why are people lying to me? This isn't my house. This is a hospital that they decorated to look like my house."* At first, these calls were alarming and I would scramble to say something reassuring to calm him down. Eventually I would just listen to him, empathize with his feelings the way I did with my kids ("That sounds really frustrating!") and tell him to go to bed and I would get to the bottom of it in the morning. Generally, by morning, he had forgotten. Still, for the most part, during those first two years, he was probably 60 to 70 percent of his former self. His hearing was shot, his voice was softer, his speech was slower than it had been, and his short-term memory was shit. Because the area of his brain that had been affected by the hemorrhage controlled executive function, he lacked judgment and the ability to initiate. Still, he was essentially himself.

As I mentioned before, Dad didn't get a lot of visitors during his convalescence. Initially, I assumed this was because most people didn't know how sick he was, but honestly, even among the people who did know what was going on, most were so uncomfortable with seeing him in such a diminished state that they just stayed away. The exceptions were my great-aunt Shelly and her son, Ron, my dad's college friend David Cohn, Rabbi Jordan Bendat-Appel, Trevor Albert, Brian Doyle-Murray, and one or two other friends who came by regularly to sit with him and check in on Erica. Daniel, in high school and still living at home at the time, saw more than any child should have to see as Dad went through all the highs and lows of his illness. Ayda was back at home after graduating from Tufts and spent a lot of time with Dad—cheering him on during his various therapies, watching movies, and entertaining him with elaborate mime routines and interpretive dance. Julian was still at school in the beginning but went home as much as possible until graduation, when he moved back in. Mollie had come to the hospital early on in Dad's illness, and she and Amy flew to Chicago a few times once he was home. The visits were good but I knew that Mollie still felt like an outsider, so I did my best to keep her in the loop on his day-to-day ups and downs.

"I just feel so bad," Mollie told me when I called to let her know that Dad had asked about her. "It's like I want to be there for him, but then it seems like he has all this guilt about the past so I just end up being a reminder of something he feels shitty about."

"Mollie, you know he loves you."

"I know, and I love him . . . God, I'm sorry for even bringing it up! It's not like you don't have enough to worry about. This has got to be harder on you than anyone else."

"I think it's awful for all of us in a million different ways but honestly, I can't even imagine what you're going through—to have lived your whole life without him and then to lose him again like this? I just wish there was something I could do."

"I know," she sighed. "You're already doing it. I love you."

"Love you too."

In April 2012, Dad called to tell me that Leon had asked his permission to marry me.

"Oh, really?" I asked brightly, although Leon had already told me. "What did you say?"

"I said it sounded okay to me," he answered in his softer, breathier voice. "Why? Did you want me to tell him to go to hell?"

"Ha ha, no, Daddy. But you're not just saying it, right? You really like him? You think it's a good thing?" My voice cracked as I spoke and tears filled my eyes.

"Oh yeah, my baby, a very good thing. He told me not to worry, that it's his turn to take care of you and he wants to do it forever. He's a pretty special guy, huh?"

"Yeah," I sniffed, "but not as special as you."

"Well, yeah." We both laughed. "I couldn't love you more, Violet."

"I love you too, Daddy, so much." From that day on, his number one goal on every motivational chart and evaluation was "Get strong so I can walk Violet down the aisle." The wedding date was set for November 17, 2012.

In June of 2012, Julian graduated from Colgate University and my dad was well enough to make the trip. Leon and I drove up to Hamilton, New York, for the day to celebrate Julian and to see my dad. It was bittersweet. Dad was so proud of Julian and so happy to be there for the commencement that in some ways it felt like a great victory. But he also seemed overwhelmed and a little out of sorts to be so far from home. I couldn't help but think back to my own college graduation, cursing the fate that had my dad watching from the sidelines rather than standing behind the podium onstage, beaming his warmth and wisdom down on us all. Even though he still joked and laughed with us, when someone's grandfather sat down to talk with him, Dad signaled that he couldn't really hear and then looked to me to rescue him from the awkwardness. I felt so sad to see him this way, even at his best, so weak and vulnerable. Still, it was better than it had been and I was guardedly optimistic that he might actually achieve his goal.

After graduation, Julian moved back home to spend time with Dad and give Erica some additional support. From their reports, despite Dad's overall progress, each day seemed to present a different grueling challenge and even with a team of amazing caregivers, there were days when only Erica or Julian could coax him into cooperating with even the most basic elements of his care. Later that summer, in preparation for an elective surgery, he was taken off his immunosuppressants and soon after suffered a relapse of the vasculitis, undoing all the progress he had made and plunging him deeper into the fog that his brain had become.

That fall, as wedding plans came together and we started to think about the details of the ceremony, I really started to deal with the loss of my father. My therapist recommended the book *Ambiguous Loss*, and I read through it in two days. Written by a psychologist and intended for the families of Alzheimer's patients and others in "here but not here" situations (soldiers missing in the line of duty, empty nesters, and so on), it explores the complicated grief process of saying goodbye to someone who is still physically present, and letting go when there is no possibility of real closure. Even though he was still alive, my dad was no longer the person he used to be, and I needed to be able to mourn that person and let go of the expectation that he would return. I couldn't believe I was getting married in the first place, but it seemed even more surreal that my dad wouldn't be there. When I visited him at the end of October, he was in and out of awareness, definitely conscious but more distant. It was as if the lesions in his brain were literal holes in his personality and memory. I wasn't sure if he even remembered I was getting married but I felt I had to say something to acknowledge that this huge thing was happening and that he was going to miss it. As we were getting ready to go to the airport for our flight back to New York, I sat down by his bedside, took his hand, and said, "I'm so sorry, Daddy, but the doctors say you're not healthy enough to come to New York for the wedding next month. I'm going to miss you so much and I'll be thinking of you the whole time. I hope you're not mad at me."

"I could never be mad at you," he whispered, "don't you worry. I'll be here." Keet ended up going to Chicago to be with my dad for the week while everyone else was in New York for the wedding and Thanksgiving. I'm so glad they were able to have that time together and I think each was exactly what each other needed, at exactly the right time.

Over the next year and a half, Dad declined pretty steadily. He was back on the immunosuppressants he needed to control the vasculitis, but they made him susceptible to infection. He was having seizures and taking medication for that, but they were like tranquilizers and only increased his confusion and inertia. It was like a slowly sinking ship— we kept bailing the water out but there were just too many cracks to fill. On a good day, he might let someone get him out of bed and sit him in the living room, where he would talk a little and smile. On a bad day, he wouldn't want to eat, was silent, and stared daggers at the caregivers who showed him endless love and patience.

Still, when we visited, I would crawl into the twin-size hospital bed Erica had set up in his room and just lie there with him, trying to absorb whatever I could and offer him whatever comfort I could give. Carina, as anticipated, a hopeless daddy's girl herself, liked to dote on my dad and would rub lotion into his feet or make little circles on his temples with her tiny fingertips. Keon, understandably, didn't really know how to be with him, but would still go in every morning and kiss him, saying, "Hi, Grandpa. It's Keon. I love you!" before running off to play basketball or video games.

Just before my father died, Leon, Keon, Carina, and I spent the week in Chicago for the kids' midwinter break. Julian, Daniel, and Ayda were there too. I had negotiated with Erica to let my mom come and visit while we were there, so she also got to spend a couple days with him that I know meant a lot to her. The rest of us were pretty down about his current state. He was barely talking and slept most of the day. I would go into his room and sit for a few minutes holding his hand, but I spent the majority of that trip watching *Frozen* with Carina in the living room. My mom, in her own world, as usual, was unfazed. "He's there!" she said after spending over an hour just staring into his eyes. "There's no doubt about it. I talked to him and he squeezed my hand! The way he looked at me . . . well, I'm not saying he's fine, but he's definitely there and still understanding and connecting." I wasn't seeing what she saw but was glad that someone could still feel positive about the dismal state he was in. Erica and the boys and I had been discussing the possibility of hospice care since a particularly severe seizure had sent him to the emergency room the month before. None of us thought he should go back to the hospital to be poked and prodded when, ultimately, there was simply nothing they could do for him.

Before we left to return to New York, I sat down by his bed, kissed his face, and held his hand. He opened his eyes and smiled weakly. "I'm leaving, Daddy. I love you so much. I want you to know that you are always in my heart and on my mind. Every time I laugh, I think of you

Giving him all the love,
2010–2014

and all the times we laughed together. Every time I eat something delicious, I think of you and how much you would enjoy it. Every time I'm sad, I think of you and how you could always make me feel better. Every time I'm confused, I think about you and how smart you are and how you seem to always make everything make sense. Every time I'm happy, I think of you and how happy I am to be your daughter and how I want you to be happy too . . . so basically, all the time. You're with me, forever." He tapped my hand with his finger and closed his eyes. I walked out of the room crying, knowing it might be the last time I saw him. When we got back to New York, Erica called to say that he was refusing to eat or take his meds and she was going to call the hospice coordinator. I got on a flight back to Chicago the next day.

Erica, Julian, Daniel, Mollie, Laurel, two caregivers, two close family friends, and I sat in a semicircle around my dad's bed as he lay there, dying. His breaths were shallow and uneven, loudly rattling in his throat. Each time his breathing paused, we all froze, wondering if this was it. Then he would snort again, and we would unfreeze and exhale. Not yet. At one point Erica and I started giggling because it was so intense and we were all so in the moment and here he was, our beloved, snoring into the void. I wasn't conscious of time as we sat there. It could have been five minutes or an eternity. Finally, at 1:53 a.m. on February 24, 2014, my father stopped breathing and didn't start again.

LIFE AFTER DEATH

Dad and I used to fit our faces together like two puzzle pieces—my cheek in his eye socket or vice versa—two halves of a whole. Watching him drift away as his brain function deteriorated was heartbreaking. There was so much of him in me, I felt like I was losing myself, too. Sometimes I even thought that I was feeling his sadness from inside myself. It was devastating, not just losing him as an amazing father, brilliant mind, voice of a generation, godfather of modern comedy—but also losing the potential of what he saw in people. Who would write all those letters of recommendation now? Who would recognize something special in an intern or a waiter or in me? Who was there to make proud now? I have never felt more like an adult and more like a child at the same time.

As soon as news of my dad's death began to spread, the phone did not stop ringing and the emails and Facebook messages kept pouring in. It was emotionally overwhelming and somehow almost exhilarating at the same time. From generic but genuine condolences and cherished memories from people we knew, to heartfelt and very personal stories from complete strangers about what my dad's work had meant to them, I read and reread them all, savoring and hoarding these bits of collective sorrow like gold.

Violet, your dad was a real-life George Bailey, and there are so many people whose lives he changed who are heartbroken today— more, I'm sure, than will ever have the opportunity to tell you. I have not seen your family for so long, yet I find myself flooded with memories, and sadness, and gratitude for having known him at all. I am picturing him sitting on the couch at Ocean Pictures, strumming his gut-string guitar, singing "Blackbird." And, for comic effect, "Kumbaya."

Your dad on so many levels has made my childhood to my adult life a little more positive. I loved his writing, directing and acting. From Vacation *to* Analyze This, *he has made me laugh and smile for so many years, and of course* Ghostbusters *was a massive part of my life. Mr. Ramis was and always will be a part of my life.*

When I was a little boy I was abused and held that secret until I was thirty years old. It was films like Vacation *and* Ghostbusters *that gave me a window into happiness and escapism.*

Your dad has done more for so many than I think he realized and my life wasn't easy but he and Dan made it a little more easy.

I am so very sad to hear about the passing of Harold Ramis. Truly one of the greats. To this day, working with him was one of my fondest filmmaking experiences ever, one which I felt so lucky to have had. He was always a gentleman, always funny, and always inspired the best in everyone around him. My deepest condolences to Violet, and his family. RIP, Harold, and thank you for everything you did and left behind, you will inspire laughs and joy for lifetimes yet to come.

This may sound silly but when I heard of his passing I was upset for a few weeks and even wore black for a few days. Honestly felt like part of my own family passed away. Your father was a wonderful actor who I totally adore and still watch religiously. Really looking forward to reading your book about him. Hope you don't mind me contacting you telling you this information. All the best to you and your family xx

Hi Violet—I don't know if you remember me, but I met you at Beethoven School in the late '90s with your dad. I worked with your dad on and off for a few years on small projects because he was trying to get involved in helping the public schools. I wound up

making introductions for him to the Chicago [International]
Children['s] Film Festival, Street Level Youth Media and several
others. And then also I wrote about his work trying to bring film
production to Chicago for the Sun-Times. *We stayed connected over*
the years through various changes in life and he was always willing
to make an introduction or lend me a hand. My mother died in
1998 and I read Irvin Yalom's Existential Psychotherapy *on*
Harold's recommendation to get through that loss. When I came to
Buddhist-type spirituality in the early aughts your dad and I stayed
connected that way as well. I have been planning on writing
something about him but I am still grappling with finding the
adequate language. As you know your dad was an exceptional
person. He was politically astute—far more than I am—and saw
right through posturing and grandstanding. He always treated me
with kindness and respect, unlike the political folks who brought me
to him in the first place. (I met him right after I left Mayor Richard
M. Daley's office.) I wish he had left a book about living a good
life for all of us to enjoy afterward. Thank goodness he left us his
wonderful movies! I have many treasured memories of your dad. If
you're ever in Chicago, I'd love to meet and catch up. Blessings to
you and your family.

I moved through the days immediately following his death in an al-
tered state—making arrangements for the funeral, accepting what
seemed like an endless stream of flowers and baskets of food, and
checking in constantly with my mom, Erica, my siblings, and my kids
to make sure everyone was okay (or as okay as they could be, anyway).
The private funeral service was held at North Shore Congregation

Israel and presided over by Jordan Bendat-Appel, a young rabbi who had been very close to my father and family. The guitar my dad had made sat in a stand in front of his coffin, and Bob Dylan played softly in the background as friends and family filled the synagogue. I spoke, as did Erica, Julian, Daniel, Ayda, Trevor Albert, and my dad's best friend from college, David. At the cemetery, a bitterly cold wind whipped across the frozen ground and Chevy Chase cracked a joke along the lines of "Thanks a lot, Harold!" which made everyone laugh through their tears and chattering teeth.

As gut-wrenching as his actual death was, I had been struggling to accept losing him to his illness for so long by that point that I felt mostly numb as people hugged me, sobbing and begging me to let them know if there was anything they could do to help. We sat shiva for the next four days. Erica's three best friends (bless them) handled all of the catering, security, and communication issues as hundreds of people—friends, family, colleagues, community members, and congregants—came through the house to eat, drink, pray, and pay their respects.

In June, we had a more public memorial at the Montalban Theater in Hollywood, attended by more than six hundred people and emceed by *SCTV* alum and longtime friend Marty Short. With substantial logistical and emotional support from Second City CEO Andrew Alexander, Erica gathered an amazing group of people to speak about my dad and the impact he had on their lives and on the world of comedy: Martin Short, Joe Flaherty, Dave Thomas, Andrea Martin, Steve Carell, Eugenie Ross-Leming, Steven Kampmann, Judith Kahan, Michael Shamberg, and Billy Crystal all spoke in person, while Eugene Levy, Catherine O'Hara, Al Franken, Jack Black, Seth Rogen, and Judd

Apatow sent messages via video. In my speech, I mentioned that my dad and I had talked about writing a book together and several people approached me afterward, encouraging me to go ahead with the idea. And so, here we are.

THE STRANGE THING ABOUT losing someone as prolific as my dad is that he left so much of himself behind after his death through his work and public life. I don't have to wonder what he thought about the meaning of life or how he made sense of the world—I can watch the video of his SoulPancake conversation with Rainn Wilson (with a portrait of me that my mom painted hanging on the wall behind him like a guardian angel) and hear him say that it's up to us to find and create substantive purpose to guide and animate our lives. I can trace his creative and philosophical evolution by watching his movies and reading through the hundreds of articles and interviews pasted into my grandfather's scrapbooks. I can laugh with him through the presentation he gave at the Chicago Humanities Festival on his favorite comedies. Even though I am very grateful to still be able to access him in so many ways, it will never be enough. As wonderful as all of these artifacts are, they pale in comparison to the actual man my dad was.

For as long as I can remember, people have been telling me how much I am like my father. This is a compliment I have a hard time wrapping my head around, especially since his death. It all made sense when we were together, but without him, who am I? How can I keep his incredible qualities going without him? What if I can't? So, I write this book, in part, to remember, and so my children can remember, and to try, in whatever small way I can, to capture some of his greatness and share it with you. I loved my dad more than anything in this world and I know he loved me with everything he had. And if that ends up being the greatest accomplishment of my life—being his and making him proud—that's meaning enough for me.

Two halves of a whole, 1984

Dear Dad,

So, I wrote the book; now what?

It's been more than three years since you left us—seven, if you count the slow and torturous withdrawal of your illness—and I still feel the ache of your absence as deeply as I did on day one. How is it even possible that life has gone on and so many things have happened without you?

Sitting here, reading and rereading our story, I can't help but wonder what your big takeaway would be from all of this. To me, it kind of feels like a postmodern fairy tale: full of magic, peril, and interesting characters, but lacking in morality and the satisfaction of an uncomplicated happy ending. We ate the poisoned apples but just got a mild case of Montezuma's Revenge. We built the strongest house we could, but the wolf got in anyway. I guess even the classic heroes made a lot of mistakes, but what did we learn from ours? If there's no true measure of right and wrong/good and bad, then, in the end, what does it all mean? Barring the obvious extremes, how much does being a good person/parent really even matter? What would you have done differently if given the chance?

See, Daddy? Without your light to guide me, it's so easy to get lost in all this ambiguity. There are so many questions that no one can answer for me now. Even though I know what you would probably say—the most profound answers only come from within ourselves, there is no objective truth, the journey of seeking is more important than the destination of knowing—still, there's nothing I wouldn't give to discuss it with you over a Big Mac and some Blue Dream.

As much as I miss you every day and irrationally wish for your miraculous reappearance, the truth is, Dad, I'm okay. I'm okay because you live on in me and I carry you with me wherever I go. I can hear your voice in my head telling me how proud you are of this book, reassuring me that I'm a good enough mom, and insisting that I'm a decent person (in spite of what everyone says—haha).

So, instead of ending with heartbreak, I'll go with gratitude. Thank you for being the perfectly imperfect person you were and for making me the person I am today. Thank you for being the best father I could have ever imagined and for loving me with all your heart. Thank you, Daddy, for everything, always.

I love you.

V

ACKNOWLEDGMENTS

Writing this book was an all-consuming experience and would not have been possible without the support of many wonderful people in my life.

Most important, I'd like to thank my husband, Leon, whose devotion and good nature kept me going on the darkest days, and who has been my champion, best friend, and lover through it all.

I'd also like to thank my agent, Anthony Mattero, who was immediately enthusiastic about the project and did an amazing job of getting it into the right people's hands; the team at Blue Rider Press for believing in the book and making my dream a reality; the team at Dutton for taking over where Blue Rider left off and making a potentially difficult transition seamless; my editors, Kate Napolitano and Jill Schwartzman, for their honesty, expertise, and encouragement; my mother, Anne, for her inspiration, unconditional love, and incredible photographs; my stepmom, Erica, for having faith and always standing by me with love and humor; my siblings—Julian, Daniel, Mollie, and Ayda—for being amazing people and helping me be a better person; my children—Keon, Carina, and Harold (and stepkids)—for driving me completely crazy and being my favorite people at the same time; to Keet and Michelle Davis, Felicia Peña, and Ana de la Flor for their patience, caring, and generosity in helping me hold my life together over the past three years.

Deep appreciation for Laurel Ward, Gene Stupnitsky, Nate Garland, Trevor Albert, Michael Shamberg, Joe Grieco, Steven Ramis, Rochelle Kramer, Lin Coleman, Pam Kasper, Margaret Oberman, Jordan Bendat-Appel, and Amy Heckerling, who generously shared their letters, stories, and memories with me.

Thank you to Seth Rogen for contributing such a sweet and funny opening for the book, and to Gene (again), James Weaver, Loreli Alba Alanis, and Rodney Rothman for their part in that.

Thank you to Marya Pasciuto, Susan Schwartz, Meighan Cavanaugh, Bill Peabody, Claire Vaccaro, and Marie Finamore at Penguin Random House for their excellent work, dedication, and understanding; and to Alex Rice at Foundry Media for her tenacity and attention to detail.

Thank you to Marc Liepis, Lev Ginsburg, Marlene Adelstein, Andrew Alexander, David Kramer, Katie Zaborsky, Chris Pagnozzi, Sylvain Durand, Jim Shultz, Erica Silverman, Journey Gunderson and the National Comedy Center, Kelly Carlin, Priyanka Matoo, and Adam Frucci for their various contributions to the process of making this book and getting it out into the world.

Thank you to Verta Maloney, Ethan Eunson-Conn, Caroline Kim, Ali Jaffe, Nicole Blaine, Ilyse Mimoun, John Mattson, Katie Verbesey, Julie Holland, and everyone else I know who has encouraged me, offered to read drafts, reminded me to take a break once in a while, made me laugh, brought me coffee, or generally kept me from going crazy during the writing of this book.

And finally, thank you to all the Ghostheads and amazing Harold Ramis fans for recognizing his genius, supporting this book, and helping me keep him alive, in whatever way we can, forever!

REFERENCES

BOOKS, INTERVIEWS, AND ARTICLES

Caro, Mark. "Analyzing Harold." *Chicago Tribune*, March 14, 1999. http://articles.chica
gotribunc.com/1999-03-14/news/9903140445_1_co-writer-second-city-harold-ramis.

Evans, Bradford. "The Lost Projects of Harold Ramis." Splitsider, January 26, 2012.
http://splitsider.com/2012/01/the-lost-projects-of-harold-ramis/.

Friend, Tad. "Comedy First." *New Yorker*, April 19, 2004. http://www.newyorker.com
/magazine/2004/04/19/comedy-first.

Garfinkel, Perry. "Harold Ramis Didn't Intend 'Groundhog Day' to Be Buddhist, but
It's a Dharma Classic." *Shambhala Sun*, July 2009. https://www.lionsroar.com/
harold-ramis-profile-by-perry-garfinkel.

Heisler, Steve. "Harold Ramis Interview." AV Club, June 19, 2009. https://film.avclub
.com/harold-ramis-1798216819.

Klein, Joshua. "Harold Ramis." AV Club, May 3, 1999. http://www.avclub.com/article
/harold-ramis-13583.

Kunk, Debba. "Harold Ramis Interview." ONTV, June 1982.

Martin, Brett. "Harold Ramis Gets the Last Laugh." *GQ*, May 31, 2009. http://www
.gq.com/story/harold-ramis-director-animal-house-ghostbusters-groundhog-day.

Patinkin, Sheldon. *The Second City: Backstage at the World's Greatest Comedy Theater*.
Naperville, IL: Sourcebooks, 2000, pp. 186–87.

Psychology Today staff. "Harold Ramis: Expect the Unexpected." *Psychology Today*, July
1, 1996.

Rensin, David. "Dr. Jokes." *Playboy*, September 2000.

———. "Gross Buster." *Vanity Fair*, October 1984.

Severinsen, Kay. "Harold Ramis Returns!" *Northshore*, February 1999.

Spitznagel, Eric. "Harold Ramis." *Believer*, March 2006. http://www.believermag.com
/issues/200603/?read=interview_ramis.

UrbanDaddy staff. "Harold Ramis: On Bill Murray, Playboy and Ghost Busters 3."
UrbanDaddy, March 26, 2010. http://www.urbandaddy.com/chi/leisure/9364
/Harold_Ramis_On_Bill_Murray_Playboy_and_Ghost_Busters_3_Chicago_CHI
_Profile#ixzz3wjgM5zek.

Weingarten, Paul. "Renaissance Madman." *Chicago Tribune Magazine*, October 30,
1983.

VIDEOS

Chicago Humanities Festival. "Harold Ramis talks about his favorite movies." Recorded
November 4, 2009; posted February 25, 2014. https://www.youtube.com/watch?v=
L8V-bvaIpuY.

Levite Video. "Harold Ramis shared insights on Jewish Creativity *Rosh 5770 @ Aitz
Hayim." Posted February 24, 2014. https://www.youtube.com/watch?v=
xSl0TBCx424.

SoulPancake. "When Rainn Wilson Was in Bed with Harold Ramis." Recorded April
9, 2010; posted February 28, 2014. https://www.youtube.com/watch?v=
5PXBLpiC8Yo.

MOVIE REVIEWS

Benson, Sheila. "The Other Side of Paradise at This Particular 'Club.'" *Los Angeles
Times*, July 11, 1986. http://articles.latimes.com/1986-07-11/entertainment/ca-20153
_1_movie-review.

Berry, Joanna. "National Lampoon's Vacation." *Radio Times*, n.d. http://www.radio
times.com/film/cxccr/national-lampoons-vacation/.

Black, Louis. "Groundhog Day." *Austin Chronicle*, February 19, 1993. https://www.aus
tinchronicle.com/calendar/film/1993-02-19/139276/.

Canby, Vincent. "'Caddyshack,' 'Animal House' Spinoff." *The New York Times*, July 25,
1980. http://www.nytimes.com/movie/review?res=9E04E4D
61638F936A15754C0A966948260&mcubz=3.

———. "'Club Paradise,' a Comedy." *New York Times*, July 25, 1980. http://www.ny times.com/movie/review?res=9A0DE3DE143BF932A25754C0A960948260&mcubz=3.

Clark, Mike. "Ghostbusters II." *USA Today*, June 16, 1989. http://www.metacritic.com/ movie/ghostbusters-ii/critic-reviews.

Dargis, Manohla. "In the Beginning, God Created Yuks." *New York Times*, June 18, 2009. http://www.nytimes.com/2009/06/19/movies/19year.html?mcubz=3.

———. "On a Noir and Stormy Night Stir Losers and Hustlers." *New York Times*, November 23, 2005. http://www.nytimes.com/2005/11/23/movies/on-a-noir-and -stormy-night-stir-losers-and-hustlers.html.

Ebert, Roger. "Analyze This." *Chicago Sun Times*, March 1, 1999. http://www.roger ebert.com/reviews/analyze-this-1999.

———. "Bedazzled." *Chicago Sun-Times*, October 20, 2000. http://www.rogerebert .com/reviews/bedazzled-2000.

———. "Caddyshack." *Chicago Sun-Times*, January 1, 1980. http://www.rogerebert .com/reviews/caddyshack-1980.

———. "Ghostbusters." *Chicago Sun-Times*, June 8, 1984. http://www.rogerebert.com/ reviews/ghostbusters-1984.

———. "Groundhog Day." *Washington Post*, February 12, 1993. http://www.washington post.com/wp-srv/style/longterm/movies/videos/groundhogdaypghinson_a0a7e9.htm.

———. "National Lampoon's Animal House." *Chicago Sun-Times*, January 1, 1978. http://www.rogerebert.com/reviews/national-lampoons-animal-house-1978.

———. "Stripes." *Chicago Sun-Times*, January 1, 1981. http://www.rogerebert.com/ reviews/stripes-1981.

———. "Stuart Saves His Family." *Chicago Sun-Times*, April 12, 1995. http://www .rogerebert.com/reviews/stuart-saves-his-family-1995.

———. "Year One." *Chicago Sun-Times*, June 17, 2009. http://www.rogerebert.com/ reviews/year-one-2009.

Hinson, Hal. "Ghostbusters II." *Washington Post*, June 16, 1989. http://www.washington post.com/wp-srv/style/longterm/movies/videos/ghostbustersiipghinson_a0a945.htm.

Kehr, Dave. "Caddyshack," *Chicago Reader*, n.d. https://www.chicagoreader.com/chi cago/caddyshack/Film?oid=8574401.

———. "'Ghostbusters' Tired Sequel Is Missing the Original's Charm." *Chicago Tri- bune*, June 17, 1989. http://archives.chicagotribune.com/1989/06/17/page/12/article/ ghostbusters-tired-sequel-is-missing-originals-charm.

———. "National Lampoon's Vacation." *Chicago Reader*, n.d. https://www.chicago reader.com/chicago/national-lampoons-vacation/Film?oid=1843274.

LaSalle, Mick. "Keaton Divided, Conquered/Cloned Actor Almost Saves 'Multiplicity.'" *San Francisco Chronicle*, July 17, 1996. http://www.sfgate.com/movies/article/FILM -REVIEW-Keaton-Divided-Conquered-Cloned-2973998.php.

Lemire, Christy. "Year One Review." Associated Press, June 2009. https://www.rotten tomatoes.com/m/year_one/reviews/?page=5&sort=.

Maslin, Janet. "'Animal House': Daffy Deltas." *New York Times*, July 28, 1978. http:// www.nytimes.com/movie/review?res=9406E5D91630E632A2575B C2A9619C946990D6CF&mcubz=3.

———. "National Lampoon's Vacation." *New York Times*, July 29, 1983. http://www .nytimes.com/movie/review?res=9506E4D7123BF93AA15754C0A965948260.

———. "'Stripes' and the Biggest Wiseguy in the Army." *New York Times*, June 26, 1981. http://www.nytimes.com/movie/review?res=9402E0DA113B F935A15755C0A967948260&mcubz=3.

Phipps, Keith. "The Ice Harvest." AV Club, November 23, 2005. http://www.avclub .com/review/the-ice-harvest-4199.

Rich, Frank. "School Days." *Time*, August 14, 1978. http://content.time.com/time/ magazine/article/0,9171,946996,00.html.

Rickey, Carrie. "A Clutch of Comics Set Loose in the Caribbean." *Philadelphia Inquirer*, July 11, 1986.

Scheckel, Richard. "Exercise for Exorcists." *Time*, June 11, 1984. http://content.time .com/time/magazine/article/0,9171,926579-1,00.html.

Siskel, Gene. "Bill Murray Busts Loose with Ghosts." *Chicago Tribune*, June 8,1984. http://articles.chicagotribune.com/2014-02-24/news/chi-ghostbuster-review-gene -siskel-020140224_1_bill-murray-ghostbusters-harold-ramis.

Snyder, Eric D. "20 Years Later, the Famous S.N.L. Flop 'Stuart Saves His Family' De- serves Its Second Chance." *Vanity Fair*, April 17, 2015. http://www.vanityfair.com /hollywood/2015/04/stuart-saves-his-family-20th-anniversary.

Sobczynski, Peter. "Harold Ramis, 1944–2014." RogerEbert.com, February 24, 2014. http://www.rogerebert.com/balder-and-dash/harold-ramis-19442014.

Stack, Peter. "Bewitching 'Bedazzled' / Fraser, Hurley Shine in Fantastical Remake of Faustian Bargain." *San Francisco Chronicle*, October 20, 2000. http://www.sfgate .com/movies/article/Bewitching-Bedazzled-Fraser-Hurley-shine-in-2732813.php.

Strauss, Bob. "Harold Ramis on the Meaning of Masculinity in 1996 'Multiplicity' Interview." *Daily News*, February 24, 2014. http://www.dailynews.com/arts-and -entertainment/20140224/harold-ramis-on-the-meaning-of-masculinity-in -1996-multiplicity-interview.

REFERENCES

Turan, Kenneth. "Bill Murray's 'Groundhog Day': It's Déjà Vu All Over Again." *Los Angeles Times*, February 2, 1993. http://www.latimes.com/entertainment/movies/la-et-mn-bill-murray-groundhog-day-review-20160202-story.html.

———. "One Pod, Too Many Peas." *Los Angeles Times*, July 17, 1996. http://articles.latimes.com/1996-07-17/entertainment/ca-24845_1_doug-kinney.

Zacharek, Stephanie. "Analyze This." Salon.com. http://www.metacritic.com/movie/analyze-this/critic-reviews.

IMAGE CREDITS

ABOUT THE AUTHOR

Violet Ramis Stiel is the eldest child of beloved comedy legend Harold Ramis (*Animal House, Caddyshack, Ghostbusters, Groundhog Day*). Formerly a teacher and social worker, Violet is now a full-time writer and disgruntled homemaker. She lives in New York City with her husband and their (blended) six children.